CHALLENGES IN PSYCHOLOGY

RICHARD GROSS   PAUL HUMPHREYS   BIANCA PETKOVA

Hodder & Stoughton

A MEMBER OF THE HODDER HEADLINE GROUP

Dedication

To all those courageous enough to challenge 'the truth'.

British Library Cataloguing in Publication Data
A catalogue record for this title is available from The British Library

ISBN 0 340 65502 X

First published 1997
Impression number   10   9   8   7   6   5   4   3   2   1
Year   2002   2001   2000   1999   1998   1997

Typeset by Wearset, Boldon, Tyne and Wear.
Printed in Great Britain for Hodder & Stoughton Educational, a division of Hodder Headline Plc, 338 Euston Road, London NW1 3BH by Scotprint Ltd, Musselburgh, Scotland

Contents

Acknowledgements

The authors and publishers would like to thank the following copyright holders for their permission to reproduce material in this book:

Allyn & Bacon for Figure 2.1 (p. 31), from Carver, C. S. & Scheier, M. F., *Perspectives on Personality*, 3rd edition. Copyright © 1996 by Allyn and Bacon. Reprinted/adapted by permission; **Lupe Cunha** for Figure 2.2 (p. 34); **Mary Evans Picture Library** for Figure 3.1 (p. 38); **Debbie Humphry** for Figure 4.1 (p. 54); **Commission for Racial Equality** for Figure 4.2 (p. 59), created by Saatchi & Saatchi Advertising for the European Youth Campaign against Racism supported by the Commission for Racial Equality; **Life File/© Steve Jansen** for Figure 5.1 (p. 72, left); **Life File/© Angela Maynard** for Figure 5.1 (p. 72, right); **Ronald Grant Archive** for Figure 5.2 (p. 83) © Universal Pictures, Figure 6.1 (p. 91, right) and Figure 9.1 (p. 151); **ZEFA/Danegger** for Figure 6.1 (p. 91, left); **Press Association/Topham** for Figure 6.2 (p. 97); **Cambridge University Press** for Box 7.1 (p.116), from Bartlett, F.C. (1932), *Remembering: A Study in experimental and social psychology*; **Kobal** for Figure 8.1 © 1986, Forty Acres and a Mule Filmworks; **Jo Nesbitt/Cath Tate Cards** for Figure 9.2 (p. 157); **E.T. Archive** for Figure 10.1 (p. 167); **Telegraph Colour Library** for Figure 10.2 (p. 175).

Every effort has been made to obtain necessary permission with reference to copyright material. The publishers apologise if inadvertently any sources remain unacknowledged and will be glad to make the necessary arrangements at the earliest opportunity.

Many thanks to Tim Gregson-Williams for having faith in this project, both the original proposal and its development over a considerable period of time. While the authors may have sometimes doubted that the book would *ever* be finished, he never did! Thanks too to Liz Lowther for dealing with the detail so efficiently and good-naturedly.

Index compiled by Frank Merrett, Cheltenham, Gloucs.

Preface

Psychology is booming. There are many applied areas which provide vocations and work for many practitioners; competition for places on postgraduate and undergraduate courses is intense and over the last ten years 'pre-university' psychology courses (such as A- and AS-level, GCSE, nursing courses and GNVQ) have increased dramatically. For example, the number of students now studying A-level courses in the discipline is little less than 30,000; ten years ago the number was not even 20% of this figure. The number of psychology undergraduates has only been restrained by external restrictions placed upon the number of students universities are permitted to admit. In line with this growth 'explosion' there has been a corresponding plethora of publications in the field of psychology, and the establishment of several 'key' texts as best-selling academic titles.

In the light of all of this, why have we written a book which attempts to challenge or 'problematise' many aspects of the discipline? There are many answers to this question, several of which will be addressed in the chapters which follow, but for the moment let us consider just two. Firstly, there has **always** been criticism within psychology, as with any other academic discipline or profession. Without such 'internal' (and some external) critiquing we would not have had the paradigm shifts from introspective structuralism to behaviourism (following Watson's seminal 1913 paper) and the so-called cognitive revolution of the 1950s/1960s. However, at times other than those characterised by paradigm shifts, it could be said that much of the critiquing within psychology has been located at the fringes, rather than the heartland, of the discipline and was frequently tokenised. For example, when Methuen published their first Essential Psychology series in the mid-1970s, the one overtly 'critical' volume – *Radical Perspectives in Psychology* by Nick Heather – was seen by many, despite the implorings of the series editor, as a token gesture to self-criticism within the discipline. Another demonstration of tokenisation has been the way in which many major texts, especially revised editions, address challenges with 'boxed-up' special cases (such as those addressing so-called women's issues, cultural bias or methodological/validity concerns). Such texts can then be said to address concerns, but these concerns are 'ring-fenced' and applied only to certain, clearly demarcated areas (without impacting upon the remaining 95 per cent or so of the text!). This book has 'challenge' as its persistent, unifying theme and objective.

Our second justification for writing a book critical of much psychological practice is a simple one. We believe that self-monitoring, evaluation and commentary are essential for the health of any academic discipline or profession.

We have endeavoured to embrace as many strands of contemporary challenge as possible – for example, we address issues of gender/sexual and cultural/racial bias, concerns about the ecological validity of much psychological research, reductionist and mechanistic views of personhood, rights and responsibilities of psychologists and those with whom they work, and contentious 'misuses' of psychology. Furthermore we have elected to challenge the mainstream of psychology rather than focusing our attention upon certain specific sub-areas within the field (such as clinical or social psychologies), where much contemporary challenge is located.

Much of our challenging may be viewed as being located within the philosophy and practices of postmodern criticism (see Introduction). However, we have certainly not restricted ourselves to this, and many postmodern critics will almost certainly accuse us of having not gone far enough. A substantial number of references are given throughout the text to guide the reader who wishes to pursue particular criticisms or lines of argument further.

What this book is most definitely not, is an updating volume. Although much of the work discussed, and the critiques given of it, are highly contemporary, this was not our goal. We want to create a healthy atmosphere of critical questioning of topics which populate the general textbooks and are often put up as the 'received wisdom' of an empirical science. We hope the reader will feel less comfortable with this 'received wisdom' after reading the relevant parts of this volume.

We feel that the reader will gain most from this book by using it in parallel with the 'mainstream' texts (as a 'stand-alongside' alternative, questioning and challenging perspective). If nothing else, we hope it helps breathe new life into old topics.

While the book is the end-product of over two-and-a-half years' work by three authors, each of whom has contributed to a certain extent to every chapter, the primary crafting of the specific chapters was as follows:
Introduction: Richard Gross
Chapter 2: Paul Humphreys
Chapter 3: Bianca Petkova
Chapter 4: Richard Gross
Chapter 5: Paul Humphreys and Bianca Petkova
Chapter 6: Richard Gross
Chapter 7: Paul Humphreys

Chapter 8: Bianca Petkova
Chapter 9: Paul Humphreys
Chapter 10: Richard Gross
Each author may be regarded as having different 'challenge priorities'
within modern psychology (for example, Bianca Petkova is particularly
concerned with feminist and constructionalist critiques), but the academic
responsibility for the whole book is accepted and shared between all three.

Paul Humphreys
Richard Gross
Bianca Petkova

Introduction

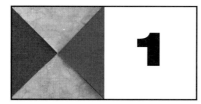

Psychology or psychologies?

Traditionally, psychology textbooks begin with an attempt to define the field, the discipline that is known as psychology. Even when a general, single-sentence definition is offered (such as 'the scientific study of behaviour and mental processes'), the author(s) invariably proceeds to point out that such a definition conceals a multitude of theoretical approaches, areas of research interest, both academic and applied, involving a range of methods. It is also pointed out that psychology currently has many important links and points of overlap with other disciplines, both scientific (natural and social) and non-scientific, and that any brief discussion of the history of psychology as a separate discipline reveals its roots in other disciplines, including philosophy, physics and biology.

In other words, psychology has many faces, both in terms of its evolution and in its present form, and it is constantly changing and evolving. This is reflected in one of its unique features as an academic discipline, namely the fact that part of the 'syllabus content' involves the attempts by psychologists to define their discipline. It is almost as if the subject matter (people, what they do, think and feel) drifts into the background, while the 'real' issues ('what is the subject matter to be?', 'how can/should it be conceptualised and investigated?') take centre stage. While those issues have remained largely unchanged throughout psychology's history, the answers have not, and this is where the discipline's evolution has largely taken place.

If there have always been different ways of 'doing psychology', or different ways of 'being a psychologist', or 'different psychologies', this is especially true of the past ten to 15 years or so. During this period of time, psychologists, influenced by both fellow psychologists and those from a variety of other disciplines (related and unrelated, academic and non-academic), have come to challenge some of the fundamental assumptions and practices of traditional, *mainstream* psychology (to be defined below). The challenges have come in many guises and are known by many different names: some of the most common – and important – include *social constructionism*, *discursive psychology*, *feminist psychology* and *cultural psychology*. Collectively, these are sometimes referred to as *the new paradigm*, sometimes, and in a more general sense, they are called *postmodern psychology* (also defined below).

What we must stress from the outset is that these challenges represent a rich diversity of theoretical and methodological approaches: critics of mainstream psychology sometimes disagree with each other almost as much as they each disagree with the 'target' of their original criticism (rather like political parties!). Moreover, it is a mistake to believe that 'all feminists' or 'all social constructionists' speak with one voice: there are many shades of opinion within each of these, and many areas of conflict. Nevertheless, just as there are certain beliefs, principles and practices that can be identified as constituting 'mainstream' psychology, so there are many fundamental beliefs shared by the various critics. One of the aims of this Introduction is to identify some of these beliefs, and one of the aims of this book is to discuss these challenges as they have been applied to topics and areas of research that will almost certainly be familiar to you from more mainstream texts.

We should also note here that certain challenges to the mainstream have come from directions that lie far outside anything that could even remotely be described as 'new paradigm' or 'postmodernist', in particular *sociobiology* and *evolutionary psychology*. Indeed, these theoretical approaches are in many ways fundamentally opposed to some of the views associated with the new paradigm (especially social constructionism and feminist psychology). Their inclusion in this book (see in particular Chapter 6) demonstrates the breadth and diversity of the challenge to the mainstream.

Defining some key terms: modernist and postmodernist

'Postmodern'/'postmodernist' implies 'modern'/'modernist', so we should begin with a definition of the latter. While *Modernity* refers to the 'age' (i.e. a particular period of the history of Western culture, dating from around 1770, often called the post-Enlightenment), *Modernism* refers to the 'spirit' of the age (or *zeitgeist*) of modernity, a commentary on it (Stainton Rogers et al., 1995) or a cultural expression of it (in art, architecture, literature, music and so on (Kvale, 1992)).

Prior to the Enlightenment (the medieval period), the Church was the sole arbiter of truth, and it was not the responsibility of the individual to discover the truth about life or to make decisions about the nature of morality (Burr, 1995). The aim of the Enlightenment was to replace irrationality with reason, superstition with empirically validated 'true knowledge', and through this to pursue 'human betterment'. Central to the achievement of this goal, and one of the crucial products of the modern age, was science, especially the human sciences:

. . . the bio-social sciences both were founded by way of Modernism and have played a significant role in making the modern world in which we live (i.e. the world which we, the writers – and most of the readers – of this book inhabit) . . .

(Stainton Rogers et al., 1995)

Science represented the antidote to dogma: the individual person, rather than God and the Church, became the focus for issues of truth and morality. It was now up to individuals to make judgements (based on objective, scientific evidence) about the nature of reality and therefore what were appropriate moral rules for humans to live by (Burr, 1995).

According to Stainton Rogers et al., the modern, post-industrialist world is permeated by ideas drawn from the bio-social sciences, including individuals-in-society, interpersonal relationships, 'selves', personality, attitudes, thinking, feeling and doing and social forces, all of which appear to be 'natural ways' of describing the world, rather than the modern *constructions* that they are. What were originally constructions have all been made so meaningful and familiar to us that they are taken to be 'essential qualities of human experience'.

According to modernist thought, science represents the end-state in a three-stage developmental theory of civilisation, starting with a primitive belief in magic, which was superseded by religious belief, which, in turn, was superseded by science. This reflects a kind of intellectual Darwinism or epistemological 'survival of the fittest', whereby, over time, less adaptive 'ways of knowing' have been replaced by ways which are more evolved and successful. As we noted above, 'Enlightenment' implies a move from the 'darkness' of myth and superstition to the 'light' of reason and scientific truth.

Postmodernity refers to an age which has lost the Enlightenment belief in emancipation and progress through more knowledge and scientific research. It involves a change from . . .

. . . a mechanical, metallurgic production to an information industry, and from production to consumption as the main focus of the economy. It is an age in which the multiple perspectives of new media tend to dissolve sharp lines between reality and fantasy, undermining belief in an objective reality.

(Kvale, 1992)

By the late 1950s/early 1960s, the assumption that Modernism inevitably represents progress came under attack, in relation to politics (e.g. CND (the Campaign for Nuclear Disarmament)), architecture, literary criticism and the social sciences. Far from offering 'solutions', Modernism was being seen as a form of intellectual imperialism, promoting the interests of the powerful by exploiting and marginalising the powerless. Moreover, science is not so much a means of human betterment but the agent responsible for the destruction of our environment, possibly of life on Earth itself (Stainton Rogers et al., 1995).

Postmodern thought does not denote a coherent theory or set of ideas but a heterogeneous collection of thinkers who focus on different aspects of a Postmodern condition. One influential contributor to the Postmodernist 'debate' is the French philosopher Foucault, who, during the 1970s, challenged many widely accepted Modernist ideas in terms of the notion of power (Kvale, 1992). 'Postmodern' implies an emphasis on *differences* and continual *changes of perspectives*, an *avoidance of dichotomies* (seeing things in 'either/or' terms) and *reification* (presenting abstract concepts as if they are 'things' with a concrete existence).

These 'principles' give rise to a further, perhaps more fundamental, principle, namely, *relativism*, i.e. the belief that there is no absolute, ultimate, objective truth (as claimed by Modernist science; see below) or universal values, only *truths* (or different versions or accounts of the truth) as judged from different perspectives and viewpoints, or *different values*, reflecting different group memberships and experiences (i.e. *pluralism*).

Part of the rejection of 'absolute truth' is denying that there is some deeper, underlying reality behind the surface features of the world. Both Piaget and Freud, for example (although in very different ways), propose the existence of underlying mental or psychic structures that account for psychological phenomena: the former can only be inferred from the latter (and not directly observed) but they are necessary if the latter are to be explained. In each case, the inferred, 'hidden' structure is seen as the deeper reality underlying surface behaviour, so that the truth about behaviour can only be revealed by analysing these structures. For these reasons, theories such as Freud's and Piaget's (but more commonly the latter) are known as 'structuralist': the (later) rejection of the notion of structure underlying forms in the real world is thus known as 'poststructuralism', with the terms 'postmodernism' and 'poststructuralism' sometimes used interchangeably (Burr, 1995).

Science, scientism and the science of psychology: defining the mainstream

As we noted earlier, contemporary academic psychology is a large, multifaceted organism, using a range of techniques to address an array of substantive questions; it is also clearly developing, as shown by the change of emphasis from behaviour to the mind, with the cognitive paradigm being predominant (Smith et al., 1995). This significant shift, based on the computer analogy, according to which the human being is seen as an information processor, is often dated from 1956; it is commonly referred to as the 'cognitive revolution' (or what Harré (1995) calls the 'first cognitive revolution'). For much of the preceding 40 years or so, academic psychology in the USA and the UK had been dominated by Behaviourism, which, as championed by Watson, rejected the study of the mind as wholly inappropriate for a scientific psychology, since mental processes are inaccessible to, and unobservable by, the investigator.

Despite this major change, certain central assumptions and practices within the discipline have remained essentially the same, and it is these that constitute *mainstream psychology*. Harré (e.g. 1989) refers to the mainstream as the 'old paradigm', which he believes was and is haunted by 'two unexamined preassumptions', namely *individualism* and *scientism*. Harré (1989) describes *individualism* like this:

> *Everything relevant to the actions of a person must, it seems, have been assumed . . . to have been found a place 'within' . . . the envelope of the individual . . . The idea of 'within' is dominated by a certain model of explanation. So instead of describing human customs and practices, psychologists have looked for (or imagined) mechanisms . . . Instead of ascribing to people the skills necessary for performing correctly, they have assigned hidden states.*

In other words, human action can be fully accounted for by reference to things taking place 'inside' individuals (such as cognitive processes, analogous to the running of a computer program) or things that individuals 'possess' (such as attitudes, motives, personality).

Van Langenhove (1995) defines *scientism* as '. . . the borrowing of methods and a characteristic vocabulary from the natural sciences in order to discover causal mechanisms that explain psychological phenomena'. It maintains that all aspects of human behaviour can and should be studied using the methods of natural science, with its claims to being the sole means of establishing 'objective truth'. This can be achieved by studying phenomena removed from any particular context ('context-stripping' exposes them in their 'pure' form) and in a value-free way (there is no bias on the part of the investigator), and the most reliable way of doing this is through the laboratory experiment, the method that provides the greatest degree of control over relevant variables. These beliefs and assumptions, as applied to the study of human behaviour and social institutions by Comte in the mid-1800s, add up to a traditional view of science known as *positivism*.

Although much research has moved beyond the confines of the laboratory experiment, the same positivist logic is still central to how psychological inquiry is conceived and conducted. Method and measurement still have a privileged status.

> *Whether concerned with mind or behaviour (and whether conducted inside or outside the laboratory), research tends to be constructed in terms of the separation (or reduction) of entities into independent and dependent variables and the measurement of hypothesised relationships between them.*

(Smith et al., 1995)

Despite the fact that since the mid-1970s the natural sciences model has become the subject of vigorous attacks . . .

> *. . . still . . . psychology is to a large extent submerged by the natural sciences model. The most prominent effect of this is the dominance of experiments.*

(Van Langenhove, 1995)

Van Langenhove sees this as having far-reaching effects on the way psychology *pictures* people as more or less passive and mechanical information-processing devices whose behaviour can be split up into variables. It also affects the way psychology *deals* with people: in experiments, people are not treated as single individuals but as interchangeable 'subjects': there is no room for individualised observations.

According to Stainton Rogers et al. (1995), mainstream psychology does not just use certain methods, it is 'methodolatrous', i.e. it idolises scientific method, according it superior status as the only self-respecting means by which 'true knowledge' can be discovered. The reason for this has more to do with the way psychologists wish to present themselves than with an open-minded evaluation of its practical utility: it offers the credentials of being 'serious' and 'scholarly', since empirical investigation can only be done by 'experts' and so confers exclusivity. 'Understanding people' is the province of the 'Academy', which Foucault (1970) defines as the locus of secret and exclusive – and thus prized – scholarly knowledge, which, even when those outside of the Academy get to know about it, cannot be fully deciphered. It is the site of 'discourse with a veil drawn over it':

> *Methodolatry thus serves the purpose of enabling psychologists to cast themselves as the sole architects of legitimate knowledge about the 'science of behaviour'.*

(Stainton Rogers et al., 1995)

Challenging the mainstream: crisis and the emergence of a new paradigm

According to Smith et al. (1995):

> *Psychology is in a state of flux. There appears to be an unprecedented degree of questioning about the nature of the subject, the boundaries of the discipline and what new ways of conducting psychological research are available . . .*

Different psychologists will react to this in different ways: turmoil is anxiety-provoking, threatening, challenging, exciting, even a cause for celebration. Smith et al. describe themselves as feeling excited, generated by a discipline engaging in healthy self-reflection: for a discipline that has traditionally taken individualism and, more importantly, scientism as its foundations, turning its attention to the theoretical basis of its work is a positive development.

Much of the early challenge was directed at scientism. For Van Langenhove (1995):

> *... the problem with experimental psychology is that, as noted by Danziger, it pretends that its experiments are in principle no different from experiments in the natural sciences. This implies that human beings are treated as if they were natural objects. Where it is clear that the physical sciences (dealing with natural objects) are causal sciences, this is not obvious for what concerns the social sciences. There is a very great difference between the working of causal mechanisms and the way people act ...*

The crucial difference is that people's behaviour has a *meaning* for the people themselves and is mainly intentional. Concern with meaning lies at the heart of *hermeneutics*, which Van Langenhove defines as the work of interpretation and the art of the technique of reading. In the context of the social sciences, people are treated as if they were texts whose meanings have to be discovered; introspection is a specific case of this approach, whereby the inner mental life is scrutinised and so treated as a text. (Ironically, introspection was first used by Wundt, one of the pioneers of 'scientific psychology' in the 1880s. Less well known is the fact that Wundt never saw the experimental method as the only possible method for gaining experimental knowledge: on the contrary, he advocated a psychology based on ethnographic studies of human culture or *Völkerpsychologie* (Van Langenhove, 1995. See below.) Hermeneutics favours *qualitative analysis* leading to knowledge of particular individuals (in contrast with the group averages of experimental research, in which individual scores are swamped).

Van Langenhove argues that, at the dawn of the emergence of the social sciences as institutionalised practices (separate disciplines), roughly between 1800 and 1830, there were available two models of studying people and society: the *model of the natural sciences* and the *model of hermeneutics*. Although, as we have seen, it is the former that has dominated (mainstream) psychology, the latter has never disappeared totally from the scene. However,

> *... if psychology should picture and treat people as persons rather than as natural objects, then speech acts should be taken as the substance of the social and psychological world. This would make the hermeneutical approach a far better model for psychology than the misplaced scientism of the natural sciences model.*
>
> (Van Langenhove, 1995)

Another prong of the challenge to the mainstream/'old paradigm'/ 'modernist psychology' came in the form of what Harré (1995) calls the 'second cognitive revolution'. This was marked by the return to the traditional, common-sense idea that psychology is the study of active people, singly or in groups, using material and symbolic tools to accomplish all sorts of projects according to local standards of correctness. A 'scientific' version of the informal psychology of everyday life is realised in *discursive psychology*, which is related to linguistics, anthropology, narratology and several other disciplines. For Harré, '. . . The second cognitive revolution is nothing other than the advent of discursive psychology'.

According to this approach, the mind is *not* a mental machine processing information; rather 'the mind' denotes certain activities, i.e. skilled uses of symbols performed both publicly and privately. Since discourse is primarily public and only secondarily private, so cognition (the use of various devices for mental tasks) is also primarily public and only secondarily private.

Discourse usually implies verbal presentation of thought or argument. More broadly, it refers to all sorts of cognitive activities which make use of devices that point beyond themselves and which are normatively constrained (i.e. subject to standards of correctness or incorrectness). Language use is just one of many discursive activities we are capable of.

Harré maintains that the first cognitive revolution, using the computer analogy, gave the impression that behind what we are doing is another set of cognitive processes – the processing of information. But there are no other *cognitive* processes:

> *There are just the neurophysiological processes running in the brain and nervous system and the discursive processes engaged in by skilled actors in the carrying out of this and that project. Neurophysiological processes are governed by the causality of physics and chemistry, discursive activities are governed by the rules and the conventions of symbol use . . .*

> (Harré, 1995)

For Harré, psychology is '. . . the study of how, why, when and where active people use signs for all kinds of purposes: thinking, planning, anticipating, judging, lying, doing calculations, forming consortia, denigrating rivals, presenting recollections of the past, and so on . . .'.

According to Potter (1996), the central idea of discursive psychology is that the main business of social life is found in interaction, stressing the practical dimension of social life. For example, how does a husband produce a particular narrative [account] of relationship breakdown to show that the problem is his wife's rather than his own? (See Chapter 5.) Or how is a rape victim presented as subtly at fault for the attack and how might she resist such a presentation? (See Chapter 6.) Through analysis of tape recordings, transcripts, videos (and other records of interaction), discursive psychologists have found that they need to rework notions such as attitudes (see below and Chapter 4), violence and aggression (see Chapter 6) and memory (see Chapter 7).

In the case of the discursive account of memory, we 'do' remembering by presenting to ourselves and others something which is taken to be a representation or description of something which happened in the past and of which we were at the time aware. We use certain devices (such as memorial brain mechanisms, keeping a diary, making marks on trees) to ground our representations of the past.

An entry in a diary is not a memory, nor is a molecular configuration in the brain. A memory is a representation. A representation is only a memory if it is an accurate or true representation of some past event . . .

(Harré, 1995)

Human memories are expressed as images, bodily realised activities or statements, they can be public or private. But how do representations that are claimed to be memories differ from those which are fantasies? In experimental psychology, this question does not arise, since the experimenter controls the past and has an indelible record of it, with which representations of the past can be compared. We do not make this distinction by reference to any quality of the image or aspect of the statement, nor do we make comparisons using the traces of the past: in our ordinary tasks of remembering ('in real life') very few of those exist ('. . . Remembering is not like a kind of home-spun domestic archaeology').

In other words, memories are created discursively. At every stage of life we publicly negotiate the authenticity of our memories, supplemented by criteria of coherence and the use of documents and other records. Studies of such negotiations have been carried out by Middleton and Edwards (1990) and are discussed in Chapter 7.

Instead of seeing 'memory' as a cognitive process taking place inside the head of an individual or as manifestations of hidden subjective phenomena, it *is* the psychological phenomenon. The discursive approach sees remembering as paradigmatically a *social activity*, making it necessary to consider the structure of the social group in which the negotiation takes place, especially the power relationships between the members, both as individuals and as representatives of memorially relevant categories of persons (such as gender) (Harré, 1995).

The difference between the mind or personality as seen in this way and the traditional view is that we see it as dynamic and essentially embedded in historical, political, cultural, social and interpersonal contexts.

(Harré (1994) in Stainton Rogers et al. 1995).

Other areas of research that have been 'colonised' by discursive psychology in recent years (Harré, 1995) include attribution of responsibility (Edwards and Potter, 1992) and, as we noted above, attitudes (Billig, 1987). Both of these, by tradition, have formed part of social psychology.

Social psychology, attitude research and discursive psychology

Much of the focus for the 'crisis talk' in psychology has been social psychology, which, according to Stainton Rogers et al. (1995), is in permanent crisis, '. . . or rather, it may be more accurate to say it is racked by a number of intersecting crises'. For many, these crises may be inevitable in a discipline trying to be both descriptive (objective and scientific) and prescriptive (concerned with 'human betterment' by intervening in human problems and issues).

Stainton Rogers et al. (1995) date the first wave of critical social psychology at around 1970. Prior to this (during the 1960s), the so-called attitude-behaviour problem threatened to undermine the entire study of attitudes, a cornerstone of social psychology in general, and social cognition in particular, for much of their history. The 'problem' lay in the failure of research to find a reliable relationship between attitudes and behaviour, such that knowing someone's attitude on a particular issue was shown to be a very poor indicator of how the person would act in relation to that issue.

From a discursive perspective, there is no reason to expect such a correlation, i.e. inconsistency between attitudes and behaviour is what we would expect to find. Why? Because traditional, mainstream, old-paradigm attitude research is based on the fallacy of individualism, which, as we saw earlier, sees attitudes as 'belonging' to individuals (implying something fairly constant and which is expressed and reflected in behaviour), while from a discursive perspective, attitudes are versions of the world that are *constructed* by people in the course of their practical interactions.

Furthermore, discursive psychology is concerned with *action*, as distinct from cognition. In saying or writing things, people are performing actions, whose nature can be revealed through a detailed study of the discourse (e.g. recordings of everyday conversations, newspaper articles, TV programmes). Social psychologists have underestimated the centrality of *conflict* in social life and the importance people attach to issues of stake and interest: an analysis of *rhetoric* highlights the point that people's versions of events, features of the world, and their own mental life are usually designed to counter real and potential alternatives and are part of ongoing arguments, debates and dialogues (Billig, 1987, 1992; in Potter, 1996).

The process of establishing a version of events as correct involves both constructing and defending a believable version of the world and of the self (the 'outer stuff' of actions and the 'inner stuff' of motives and attitudes respectively). Instead of making the traditional distinction between events and psychological processes, discursive psychology treats the nature of *both* as emergent in discourse. This can often be seen in relation to 'sensitive' issues such as 'race relations' and racism (see Chapter 4). Compared with traditional attitude research, discursive psychology tries to shift the focus away from the person towards interactions, towards a more *relational* or *distributed* focus for social psychology (Potter, 1996).

What is social constructionism?

As we have just seen, discursive psychology challenges the mainstream principle of individualism by adopting a social constructionist approach. However, this is not the only such challenge (see below), and given the central role of 'social constructionism' in the various challenges that have been made to mainstream psychology, it would be useful to take a closer look at just what it means.

According to Burr (1995), social constructionism can be thought of as a theoretical orientation which, to a greater or lesser degree, underpins a large number of approaches (including discursive psychology, 'critical psychology', 'deconstruction' and 'poststructuralism') which currently offer radical and critical alternatives to mainstream psychology (both general and social).

The emergence of social constructionism is usually dated from Kenneth Gergen's (1973) paper 'Social psychology as history', in which he argued that all knowledge, including psychological knowledge, is historically and culturally specific, and that we therefore must extend our enquiries beyond the individual into social, political and economic realms for a proper understanding of the evolution of present-day psychology and social life. Moreover, there is no point in looking for once-and-for-all descriptions of people or society, since the only constant feature of social life is that it is continually changing. Social psychology thus becomes a form of historical undertaking, since all we can ever do is try to understand and account for how the world appears to be at the present time.

The paper was written at the time of 'the crisis in social psychology' (see above). As a discipline, social psychology was at least partly rooted in the attempts by psychologists to provide the US and British governments during the Second World War with knowledge that could be used for propaganda and the manipulation of people. The research was almost exclusively laboratory based, reflecting the influence of the parent discipline of 'general' ('experimental') psychology, and so social psychology emerged as an empiricist science that served, and was paid for by, those in positions of power, both in government and industry (Burr, 1995).

Starting in the late 1960s and early 1970s, some social psychologists were becoming increasingly concerned about these issues: the 'voice' of ordinary people was seen as absent from its research practices, which, by concentrating on decontextualised laboratory behaviour, ignored the real-world contexts which give human action its meaning. Several books were published, each proposing, in its own way, alternatives to positivist science by focusing on the accounts of ordinary people (e.g. Harré and Secord, 1972) and by challenging the oppressive and ideological use of psychology (e.g. Brown, 1973; Armistead, 1974; both cited in Burr, 1995). These concerns are clearly seen today in the work of social psychologists in social constructionism. (Note that the terms *social constructionism* and *social constructivism* are sometimes used interchangeably, but Gergen (1985) recommends the use of the former, since the latter is sometimes used to refer to Piaget's theory of cognitive development as well as to a particular kind of theory of perception.)

While there is no single definition of social constructionism that would be accepted by all those who might be described in this way, different social constructionists are linked by a kind of 'family resemblance' (what Rosch (1973) meant by 'prototypes' or 'fuzzy sets'), i.e. we could loosely categorise as social constructionist any approach which is based on one or more of the following key assumptions (as proposed by Gergen, 1985), which Burr (1995) suggests we might think of as 'things you would absolutely have to believe in order to be a social constructionist':

1   A critical stance towards taken-for-granted knowledge   Our observations of the world do not unproblematically reveal the true nature of the world and conventional knowledge is not based on objective, unbiased 'sampling' of the world (see above). The categories with which we understand the world do not necessarily correspond to natural or 'real' categories or distinctions. Belief in such natural categories is called *essentialism*, so social constructionists are *anti-essentialism*.

2   Historical and cultural specificity   How we commonly understand the world, and the categories and concepts we use, are historically and culturally specific. Turning this around, all ways of understanding are historically and culturally relative. Not only are they specific to particular cultures and historical periods, they are seen as products of that culture and history. The particular forms of knowledge available in any culture are, therefore, artefacts (products) of it, and this must include the knowledge generated by the social sciences: the theories and explanations of psychology thus become time- and culture-bound and cannot be taken as once-and-for-all descriptions of human nature:

> *The disciplines of psychology and social psychology can therefore no longer be aimed at discovering the 'true' nature of people and social life. They must instead turn their attention to a historical study of the emergence of current forms of psychological and social life, and to the social practices by which they are created . . .*

> (Burr, 1995)

It also follows from the view of knowledge as culturally created that we should not assume that *our* ways of understanding are necessarily any better (i.e. closer to 'the truth') than other ways. Yet this is precisely what mainstream (social) psychology has done. According to Much (1995), a new *(trans)cultural psychology* has emerged in North America (e.g. Bruner, 1990; Cole, 1990; Shweder, 1990) as an attempt to overcome biases of ethnocentrism and disciplinary parochialism that have too often limited the scope of understanding in the social sciences.

Shweder (1990) makes the crucial distinction between cultural psychology and 'cross-cultural psychology', which is a branch of experimental social, cognitive and personality psychology. Most of what has been known as 'cross-cultural' psychology has presupposed the categories and models that have been based on (mostly experimental) research with (limited samples of) Euro-American populations. It has mostly either 'tested the hypothesis' or 'validated the instrument' in other cultures or 'measured' the social and psychological characteristics of members of other cultures with the methods and standards of Western populations, usually assumed as a valid universal norm.

According to Much (1995), the new 'cultural psychology' rejects this universalist model, implying that:

> ... an 'intrinsic psychic unity' of humankind should not be presupposed or assumed. It suggests that the processes decisive for psychological functioning (including those processes promoting within-group or within-family variation and the replication of diversity) may be local to the systems of representation and social organisation in which they are embedded and upon which they depend.
>
> (Stigler et al. 1990, quoted in Much, 1995)

As we noted earlier, mainstream psychology has had a history of ethnocentric bias in its assumptions and approach. It has become almost a 'standing joke' that experimental (social) psychology is really the psychology of the American undergraduate psychology major:

> By the standards of experimental psychology's own espoused principles of positivist science, the practice of limiting one's observational field would necessarily be an erroneous and misleading one. The population upon which American psychology is founded can hardly be considered a representative sample of humankind. It is not even a representative sample of the contemporary North American population ...
>
> (Much, 1995)

Apart from their accessibility, the argument commonly assumed to justify the practice of studying mostly student behaviour is based upon a sweeping and gratuitous universalist assumption: since we are all human, we are all fundamentally alike in significant psychological functions, and cultural or social contexts of diversity do not affect the important 'deep' or 'hard-wired' structures of the mind. The corollary of this assumption is that the categories and standards developed on Western European/North American populations are suitable for 'measuring', understanding and evaluating the characteristics of other populations.

By contrast, a genuinely transcultural psychology ('the interplay between the individual and society and [symbolic] culture'; Kakar (1982) quoted in Much (1995)) would base its categories, discriminations and generalisations upon empirical knowledge of the fullest possible range of existing human forms of life, without privileging one form as the norm or standard for evaluation.

3 Knowledge is sustained by social processes Our current accepted ways of understanding the world ('truth') do not reflect the world as it really is (objective reality), but are constructed by people through their everyday interactions. Social interaction of all kinds, and particularly language, is of central importance for social constructionists: it is other people, both past and present, who are the sources of knowledge.

> *We are born into a world where the conceptual frameworks and categories used by the people on our culture already exist. These concepts and categories are acquired by all people as they develop the use of language and are thus reproduced every day by everyone who shares a culture and language . . . the way people think, the very categories and concepts that provide a framework of meaning for them, are provided by the language that they use. Language therefore is a necessary pre-condition for thought as we know it . . .*
>
> (Burr, 1995)

By giving a central role to social interactions and seeing these as actively producing taken-for-granted knowledge of the world, it follows that language itself is more than simply a way of expressing our thoughts and feelings (as typically assumed by mainstream psychology): when people talk to each other, they (help to) construct the world, such that language use is a form of action, i.e. it has a 'performative' role.

4 Knowledge and social action go together   These 'negotiated' understandings could take a wide variety of forms, i.e. there are many possible 'social constructions' of the world. But each different construction also brings with it, or invites, a different kind of action: how we account for a particular behaviour (what caused it) will dictate how we react to and treat the person whose behaviour it is.

Related to this is another sense in which knowledge and social action go together: mainstream psychology looks for explanations of social phenomena inside the person, by, for example, hypothesising the existence of attitudes, motives, cognitions, etc. (what we earlier called *individualism*). Social constructionists reject this view and regard the social practices and interactions that people engage in as the appropriate focus of enquiry: explanations are to be found neither inside the individual psyche, nor in social structures or institutions (as advocated by sociologists), but in the interactive processes that take place routinely between people.

Moreover, the emphasis is placed on the *dynamics* of social interaction, in contrast with static entities (be they personality traits, 'the economy' or whatever): the focus is more on *processes* than structures.

> *Knowledge is therefore seen not as something that a person* has *(or does not have), but as something that people* do *together . . .*
>
> (Burr, 1995)

Social constructionism and social representation theory

According to social representation theory (SRT), people come to understand their social world by way of images and social representations (SRs) shared by members of a social group. These representations act like a map which makes a baffling or novel terrain familiar and passable, thereby providing evaluations of good and bad areas. Attitudes are secondary phenomena, underpinned by SRs. SRT tries to specify precisely what is collective about groups and to provide a historical account of people's understanding of the world (Potter, 1996).

According to SRT, common sense is a sediment from past theorising about psychology and the self. During the 1950s, the French psychologist, Moscovici, conducted what is still one of the classic pieces of research on SRs. He was interested in how the ideas and concepts of psychoanalysis could be absorbed within a culture (post-Second-World-War France), based on women's magazines, church publications and interviews. He concluded that psychoanalysis had trickled down from the analytic couch and learned journals into both 'high' culture and popular common sense: people 'think' with psychoanalytic concepts, without it seeming as if they are doing anything theoretical at all. But rather than the general population of Paris being conversant with psychoanalytic theory in all its complexities, they were working with a simplified image of it, with some concepts having a wide currency (such as repression) and others not (such as libido) (Potter, 1996).

As we have said, SRT is a constructionist theory: instead of portraying people as simply perceiving (or misperceiving) their social worlds, it regards these worlds as constructed, and a SR is a device for doing this construction. It allows someone to make sense of something potentially unfamiliar and to evaluate it. For Moscovici, all thought and understanding is based on the working of SRs, each of which consists of a mixture of concepts, ideas and images; these are both in people's minds and circulating in society. According to Potter (1996), SRs are truly social because:

a they *are generated in communication*. When people interact through gossip, argue with one another or discuss political scandals, they are building up shared pictures of the world: 'social representations are the outcome of an increasing babble and a permanent dialogue between individuals' (Moscovici, 1985a). The media play a major role in sustaining, producing and circulating SRs, which cannot be reduced to images inside people's heads.

b they *provide a code for communication*. As a consequence of people sharing SRs, they can clearly understand each other and have free-flowing conversations, since they share a stable version of the world. Communication between people with different SRs is likely to produce conflict.

c they *provide a way of distinguishing social groups*. According to Moscovici, one way of defining a group is in terms of a shared set of SRs, which provide a crucial homogenising force for groups.

SRT was not published in English until the early 1980s, since when research has snowballed, especially in Europe, Australia and South

America, though it has been largely ignored by mainstream North American social psychologists in the experimental cognitive tradition. Potter suggests that one reason for this may be that the latter's pursuit of general laws and processes is directly challenged by SRT's emphasis on the specific content of a culture or group's SR as the main object of analysis.

This has profound implications for how social psychology is conceptualised:

> *It not only requires us to confront individual cultures in all their richness, but also opens up the possibility of a fruitful dialogue with other social sciences, such as anthropology and linguistics.*

(Potter, 1996)

Social constructionism and feminist psychology

For Stainton Rogers et al. (1995):

> *Social constructionism is not a matter of assuming that once you are 'liberated' into seeing that all knowledge is person-made, you will be somehow 'set free' from the very local and contingent conditions that make it and monger it. We are always-ever 'persons of our time and place', deeply and inescapably enmeshed within the practical and very real-looking everyday world. That's the whole point – there is no conceptual vacuum we can occupy where we can be 'outside' the pressing 'social facts' that constitute our understanding of the world. All we can ever do is become – somewhat – disillusioned: begin to recognise the illusions which constitute our 'social realities' as illusions and not as really-real realities.*

Feminist scholars are concerned with trying to identify and challenge those illusory aspects of our social realities that specifically relate to women. According to Nicolson (1995), they have been consistently developing critiques of positivist science for the past 100 years, with momentum and influence gathering especially since the early 1970s.

Part of this feminist critique involves demonstrating how positivist science, far from being value-free, displays a clear bias towards the 'pathologisation' of women, especially in relation to reproductive and mental health (e.g. Ussher, 1992). Nicolson asks why, when there has been no shortage of criticism of the experimental method (e.g. Harré and Secord, 1972), does psychology continue to use it?

Psychology makes its claims specifically to be a science *because* of its methods and its claims to being a value-free science. But, Nicolson argues, *the scientific method is gender-biased*, and she identifies three problems associated with this adherence to the 'objective' investigation of behaviour for the way knowledge claims are made about women and gender differences:

a The experimental environment takes the *behaviour* of the individual 'subject' as distinct from the 'subject' herself as the unit of study.

Therefore, it becomes deliberately blind to the *meaning* of the behaviour, including the social, personal and cultural context in which it is enacted; as a result, claims about gender differences in competence and behaviour are attributed to intrinsic (either the product of 'gender role socialisation' or biology) as opposed to contextual qualities.

b Experimental psychology, far from being context-free, takes place in a very specific context which characteristically disadvantages women (Eagley, 1987). A woman under these circumstances, stripped of her social roles and accompanying power and knowledge that she might have achieved in the outside world (either through a professional role or a particular set of competencies through which she defines her own capabilities), is placed in this 'strange' environment and expected to respond to the needs of (almost inevitably) a male experimenter: she becomes an anonymous woman in interaction with a man who is in charge of the situation, with all the social meaning ascribed to gender power relations.

c Scientists fail to take account of the influence of the relationship of power to knowledge (e.g. Foucault, 1977). How knowledge claims about women's psychology are structured, and the power of dominant social groupings using vested interests to set norms and influence popular knowledge, are also crucial to understanding the development of research paradigms and human socialisation.

Nicolson believes that the priority Western society attaches to science is more problematic in the late 20th century than ever before, because of the relationship of science to the media which influences human socialisation (cf. the role of the media in circulating social representations – see above).

> *Psychology relies for its data on the practices of socialised and culture-bound individuals, so that to explore 'natural' or 'culture-free' behaviour (namely that behaviour unfettered by cultural, social structures and power relations) is by definition impossible, which is a state of affairs that normally goes unacknowledged . . .*

> (Nicolson, 1995)

In the above quotation, 'normally' denotes mainstream, modernist psychology, but, as we have already seen, social constructionism, in its various forms, is concerned with acknowledging this 'state of affairs'. For example, Nicolson quotes Harré (1993), who claims that:

> *Thus, rather than seeking the 'truth' to a research problem, the central theme is that the 'world of human existence does not exist independently of human activity', but is a product of that activity. In particular that world is constructed discursively.*

The view that 'science as knowledge is fabricated rather than discovered' (Fox, 1993) is, according to Nicolson, gaining popularity amongst feminist psychologists.

Although within feminism itself there are many different 'voices', feminism is essentially a reaction to and a product of patriarchical culture (or patriarchy), and one of its significant roles has been to account for women's subordination. Patriarchy commonly refers to the context and processes through which men and male-dominated institutions (including universities and other organisations that foster scientific endeavour) promote male supremacy.

Despite its apparently unrepresentative nature, feminism is relevant to the progress and development of psychological science, primarily as it is consistent with the goal of conceptualising knowledge as a discursive practice, which takes social, cultural and individual aspects of behaviour, experience, thought and emotion into account. At the very least, feminism seeks to *contextualise* women's lives and to explain the constraints, attributed by some to biology, within a social framework: women's lack of social power is made to seem 'natural' by the practice of academic psychology, which has:

> *. . . not only omitted the consideration of women and women's activities, [but] . . . has also validated the view that those activities in which men engage are the activities central to human life. It affirms that women are 'backstage' to the 'real' action.*
>
> (Crawford and Maracek, 1989, in Nicolson, 1995)

Feminist psychologists offer a critical challenge to psychological knowledge on gender issues, by presenting a strong and flexible critical repertoire. They contribute knowledge from other disciplines, which rarely occurs in psychology because, traditionally, it is 'jealous' of its boundaries. According to Nicolson, one source of feminist ideas is post-modern sociology; she quotes the sociologist Giddens (1979), who argues that:

> *There is no static knowledge about people to be 'discovered' or 'proved' through reductionist experimentation, and thus the researcher takes account of context, meaning and change over time.*

Feminist ideas are discussed in Chapters 4 (Prejudice and discrimination), 6 (Aggression and violence) and 8 (Psychology for women).

Psychology and postmodernism

A major figure in postmodern thought within psychology is Kenneth Gergen. He believes that social constructionist dialogues are essentially constituents of the broader, postmodern dialogues. While not all postmodern theorists would consider themselves constructionists, most constructionists have drawn great inspiration from the conversations within the postmodern domains (Gergen, 1995, in Gulerce, 1995a).

Gergen regards attribution theory as a prelude to postmodern psychology: while the former is concerned with the processes by which we come to attribute mental processes, motives, intentions, etc. to people, the latter asks if there *are* any mental processes, etc. Disillusionment with all forms of cognitive psychology led to the view that self-concept, language and psychology as science owed their intelligibility to *relationship*:

> *We can now see that the individual self as an independent agent or bounded entity is problematic, and reconceptualise what we call the individual self as the intersection of multiple relationships. What we have taken to be 'individual decision-making' can better be viewed in terms of the complex relational processes manifesting themselves on the site of what we commonly index as the 'individual body' . . .*
>
> (Gergen, 1995, in Gulerce, 1995a)

For Gergen, a relational orientation is a natural outgrowth of the constructionist, postmodernist concern with representation, texts and language. If these are all viewed as forms of meaning, and we come to see meaning as the outcome of relationships, '. . . then relationships become the font of all that we hold to be "real", "true", or "good" . . .' (Gergen, 1995, in Gulerce, 1995b). The implications of this are profound: we no longer face the puzzle of how the individual mind comes to acquire knowledge of an external world (the critical problem of philosophy since the 17th century and a major concern of present-day cognitive psychology), since instead we speak in terms of, say, 'discursive communities and subcultures', which come to rely on various 'texts' which they come to treat as 'real' or 'objective'.

Perhaps most exciting of all, the relational orientation challenges the investigator to generate new realities, constructions that may be used by people to move their lives in different directions:

> *We cease to function as mere 'mirrors' of the world, as in the old paradigm, and are challenged to be world creators.*
>
> (Gergen, 1995, in Gulerce, 1995b)

(Because this represents such a radical challenge to the individualism of modernist psychology, two chapters in this book are devoted to the topic of 'the Self': Chapters 2 and 3.) Gergen argues for an enriched concept of human science and the generation of alternative realities and practices. This enrichment derives mainly from a social constructionist view of knowledge and action:

> *It has become increasingly difficult to conceptualise psychological processes as being the private possessions of individuals – self-contained in a bounded being. Rather, as we move toward increasing degrees of social saturation within our daily lives, so do we come to see ourselves as increasingly absorbed and shaped by social surrounds. And thus, in psychology, we come to see psychological processes as reflecting cultural life.*
>
> (Gergen, 1995, in Gulerce, 1995a)

For Gergen, postmodernism, as an intellectual movement in Western scholarship, denotes a set of interrelated dialogues on the nature of knowledge, language, politics, the self, pluralism, scientific practice, education, morality and so on. One recurring theme is the loss of foundational rationalities (including methods and presumptions of progress, i.e. the 'modernist' tradition) and the exploration of new visions of the human sciences.

These 'foundational rationalities' are similar to Stenner's (1993, in Stainton Rogers et al., 1995) concept of *grounding assumptions* of modernist social psychology, i.e. taken-for-granted belief in the certainty of empirical and rationalistic procedures without which research could not take place. Critical social psychology challenges these grounding assumptions, the very infrastructure of the discipline, and this represents part of the wave of criticism often brought together under the heading of postmodernism.

As we have noted several times already, the 'voices' that challenge the old paradigm are diverse and dynamic, sometimes agreeing with each other, sometimes not. This makes it impossible to present a definitive list of the characteristics of the new paradigm. However, Smith et al. (1995) identify a number of recurrent themes, many of which we have already identified, and these are shown in Table 1.1.

Table 1.1 Major concerns of the old and new paradigms (based on Smith et al., 1995)

Old	New
Measuring, counting, predicting	Understanding, describing
Causation, frequency	Meaning
Statistical analysis	Interpretation
Reduction to numbers	Language, discourse, symbol
Atomistic	Holistic
Universals	Particularities
Context-free	Cultural context
Objectivity	Subjectivity

Just as the concepts of the new paradigm form a fuzzy set (i.e. it is not unitary), so the old paradigm is, in practice, more varied than Table 1.1 might suggest. The new does not represent a rejection of the old: experiments, quantitative analysis, etc. have a role to play, but not the privileged, almost exclusive status they have enjoyed for so much of psychology's history.

We want to change psychology itself, to lead to the inclusion of ideas and ways of thinking . . . within an expanded, pluralistic discipline . . .

(Smith et al., 1995)

Plan of the book

Each of the nine subsequent chapters follows a similar pattern in the form of a number of recurring headings. One of these, **The story so far**, corresponds more or less to the 'old paradigm'/mainstream/modernist psychology; these sections will outline some of the traditional ways in which the topic under discussion has been discussed and investigated and will, inevitably, assume at least some detailed knowledge on the part of the reader.

Subsequent headings and sections relate to the 'new paradigm'/ postmodernist challenges to the mainstream: **Revisions and reconceptualisations** will mainly reflect theoretical challenges, such as those we have identified above, particularly discursive psychology, social representation theory and other social constructionist approaches, such as feminist psychology. **Implications and applications** focuses on the more practical consequences (actual and possible) of these theoretical critiques, reflecting one of the themes of postmodernist thought.

Other headings will be used, less consistently, in each chapter, reflecting the particular topic being dealt with: it would, perhaps, be opposed to the spirit of postmodernism to impose too rigid a structure, but, more importantly, this is a book *about* postmodern psychology, not a contribution to it.

Finally, to repeat a point made earlier, the new paradigm is not meant to replace the old; rather, it represents an attempt to revise it, extend it and to improve it in the sense of looking at ways in which the discipline of psychology may be changed so as to make it a more truly *human* or *social* science. By de-emphasising the approach of natural science, psychology can perhaps provide a more, not a less, scientific study of human beings.

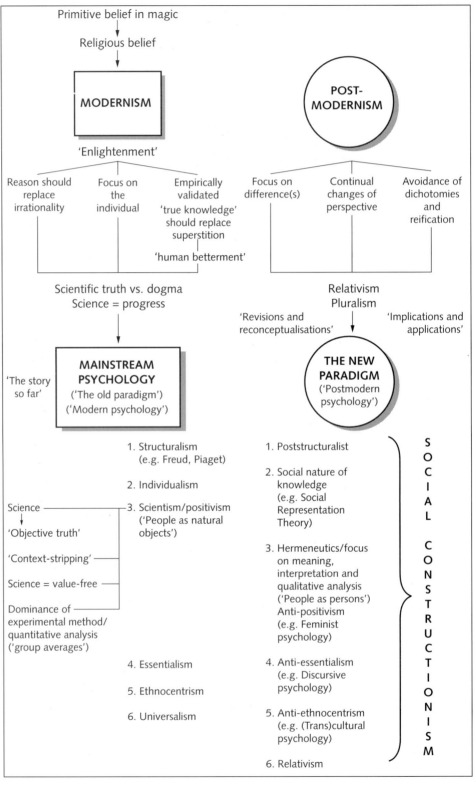

Figure 1.1 A summary of the major features of modernism and postmodernism in general and modern and postmodern psychology in particular, highlighting the major differences

The Self I

One of the central topics in psychology is The Self. Points of focus and terminology may differ between various textbooks and different A-level and undergraduate courses (the self, the self-concept, self-awareness, self-identity, self-esteem, self-presentation and so on (Argyle, 1994)), but there are few general psychology textbooks and courses which do not deal with the topic. It was also one of the first topics to be addressed by the emerging science of psychology before the beginning of the current century (James, 1890, 1892). Intriguingly, it is also one of the 'favourite' topics for coverage with the 'new wave' of discursive/critical social psychologists (e.g. Harré, 1989; Gergen, 1991; Freeman, 1993; Dixon, 1996). As we shall see in this chapter, few areas of psychological research and writing better illustrate the change from the traditional essentialist approach (which sees the objects of our study in psychology as real and having a concrete existence measurable with increasing accuracy by more refined devices and instruments) to a constructivist approach (see Introduction). We will explore the contrasts between these radically different approaches: the former regarding the self as a relatively fixed inner entity which is the true essence of who we are versus an explanation which focuses upon how we 'make a self' through interpersonal processes, discourses and our endeavours to understand and make sense of who and what we are in a complex and subjective world (e.g. Petkova, 1995).

Against this story of unchallenged centrality to psychology, Moscovici (1985) has said: 'If asked to name the most important invention of modern times, I should have no hesitation in saying it was the individual', and cross-cultural writers such as Moghaddam et al. (1993) have shown that the preoccupation with the internal, individualised self is only found in the West – most non-Western cultures are more characterised by collective selves (negotiated and influenced with reference to kin and other social groupings rather than within an autonomous individual).

The story so far

Dobson et al. (1981) say:

> The term 'self' is one of the current century. Previously writers talked of 'the soul', 'nature', 'will' and so on. Its importance has, however, been long recognised.

Bidney (1953), cited in Dobson et al., 1981) suggested that it is the possession of a self-concept rather than language that distinguishes human beings from all other animals. He says that only human beings have the self-consciousness and awareness to stand apart from themselves and consider what they would like to do and become.

JAMES'S I AND ME

It is generally accepted (Burns, 1979) that the term 'self' was introduced into psychology by the first great American psychologist, William James, in one of the most important and influential early psychology texts, *Principles of Psychology* (1890), a book which is over a century old and – at the time of writing – still in print:

> His writing marks the change between older and newer ways of thinking about self. He was strikingly objective in his treatment of the problem and hurled stinging criticism at earlier philosophic notions.

(Burns, 1979)

James argued that the self is comprised of two components, the I and the Me. The I is the inner and centre self, that which is our awareness, that which looks out at all else. The Me, however, is social self – aspects of ourselves which 'we experience and interact with' (Gross, 1996). We may think of it, perhaps a little simplistically, as the Me being what we display of ourselves to others (and in so doing to ourselves as well, of course). Erving Goffman (1959) was later to adapt this schism in his dramaturgical model which shows human life as theatrical with all of us as actors adopting parts and scripts. An analogy would be the actor as self and the performed, social roles as Me's.

For his part, James identified four components of the Me: the spiritual self, the material self, the social self and the bodily self. However, there may be many versions and manifestations of these. He said (1892):

> A man has as many social selves as there are individuals who recognise him and carry an image of him in their minds.

The importance of social processes in the development and nature of the self were considered by two relatively early writers, Charles Cooley (1902) and the symbolic interactionist George H. Mead (1934). We will return to these and consider their contribution to the understanding of the self as a *social* entity in a separate section of this chapter.

ALLPORT AND THE PROPRIUM

Writing in 1955, the influential personality theorist Gordon Allport argued that the term 'self' had become problematic because it had such a variety of meanings and because it produces 'such emotional involvement'. He introduced a new term, *proprium*, which he defined as self as knower, the core self which observes and judges:

> *The self as knower emerges as a final and inescapable postulate. We not only know things, but we know (i.e. we are acquainted with) the empirical features of our own proprium. It is I who have bodily sensations, I who recognise my self-identity from day to day, I who note and reflect upon my self-interests and strivings. When I thus think about my own propriate functions, I am likely to perceive their essential togetherness, and feel them intimately bound in some way to the knowing function itself.*
>
> (Allport, 1955, quoted in Dobson et al., 1981)

Allport contended that there were a number of so-called propriate functions. 'The knower transcends all other functions of the proprium and holds them in view.' The full list of the propriate functions is given in Box 2.1.

Box 2.1 The propriate functions (based on Allport, 1955)

1 Bodily sense: sensations and the sense of self-boundary or enclosedness
2 Self-identity: the realisation of autonomy and the ability to affect the environment
3 Ego enhancement: the value of self-preservation and achievement
4 Ego extension: the extension of the self into the outside world (e.g. through possessions and group membership)
5 Rational agent: the ego function
6 Self-image: the perceived self, comprising two elements – the current evaluation of self and the ideal self
7 Propriate striving: our pursuit of the ideal self

These propriate functions can be viewed as a link back to William James and the components of the Me and a link into contemporary work with the writings of Michael Argyle.

THE 'MAINSTREAM' IN THE 1990s: MICHAEL ARGYLE

One of the most widely read British social psychologists, Michael Argyle originally published *The Psychology of Interpersonal Behaviour* in 1967. He says, in the preface to the recently published 5th edition: 'There have been large sales – more than the rest of my books put together – and translations into many languages, and it has been prescribed reading for many courses.' Argyle is arguably the most notable current exponent of the Essentialist James/Allport line of analysis and writing on the self, its aspects and its functions. He says:

> *People have a need for a distinct and consistent self-image and for self-esteem. This may result in attempts to elicit responses from others which provide confirmation of these images of and attitudes towards the self. The self-image is one of the central and stable features of personality, and a person cannot be fully understood unless the contents and structure of his self-image are known.*

(Argyle, 1994)

Argyle gives his own 'dimensions of the self', which are shown in Box 2.2.

Box 2.2 Argyle's dimensions of the self

1   The self-image   This, he argues, 'contains some enduring aspects and others which vary with the situation and the role being played'. The self-image contains a 'core' (e.g. name, body image, sex and age) and the roles played by the person will be played in a characteristic, individualised style. Argyle is unlikely to endear himself to those sensitive to women's issues, equal opportunities or the unemployed, however, when he says, in writing about the central core:

> *For a man, the job will . . . be central, unless he is suffering from job alienation. For many women, the family and husband's job may also be central.*

2   Self-esteem   This is the extent to which a person values him/herself either absolutely or in comparison with others. Needless to say, in the latter case, the outcome of the comparison depends very much upon whom the person is making the comparison with. Argyle contends that, like self-image, self-esteem too has a core and peripheral aspects (these depending upon specific situations and different role relationships).

3   The ego-ideal   This refers to the person one would like to be and is frequently considered in terms of the 'gap' between what one perceives oneself to be (self-image) and a desired position (ego-ideal). Again, this equates closely with Allport's model of aspects of the self (propriate functions).

4   Integration of the self   This addresses the 'harmony' and consistency of elements of the self. He says:

> *This consistency may take various forms, depending on whether the self-image is based on the attributes of some person, on a set of ethical or ideological rules of conduct, or on an occupation or social-class role.*

In what we have seen so far, Argyle appears to be if not a custodian, certainly an advocate of the James/Allport lineage. However, Argyle's view of the self focuses very heavily on the Me rather than the I (or propriate functions rather than knower). In discussing the 'conditions under which the self is activated', he says:

> *The self is not at work all the time, people are continually trying to discover, sustain or present a self-image. For example, when at home rather than at work, in the audience rather than on the stage, the self-system is not very active.*

> (Argyle, 1994)

To be fair, much of Argyle's writing is in the context of social skills training, but it does appear that, for him, the 'self-system' seems to be largely disengaged when one is on one's own or relatively 'invisible'. The furthest he moves from this is his acknowledgement of 'objective self-awareness' (defined as an awareness of oneself as an object, as seen from outside). As we shall see shortly, this is quite close to Mead's concept of the generalised other, but it is still very much more Me than I. There is little acceptance here of reflexive self-awareness or the inner-eye-looking-out. To this extent, Argyle's contemporary writings are discontinuous with what we have called the James-Allport lineage.

The self in humanistic psychology

Although the term 'humanistic psychology' was not coined until 1958 (by a British psychologist, John Cohen), Carl Rogers had been evolving a 'third force' in psychology (Behaviourism and Psychoanalysis being the first two) for over a decade before this. By the mid-1950s, Abraham Maslow was also making significant contributions to this movement. Although the theories and therapies developed by Rogers and Maslow had significant differences, both were characterised by a great emphasis on the importance of the self. Rogers defined the self as an 'organised, consistent set of perceptions and beliefs about oneself'. It includes my awareness of 'what I am and what I can do' and influences both my perception of the world and my behaviour (Gross, 1996). Both Rogers and Maslow believed that a 'healthy' self was paramount to psychological well-being. Furthermore, they explored the many ways in which people can hold non-veridical self-images, and their therapies focused upon putting their clients in touch with their selves, building a positive regard and acceptance of their self and helping them to realise their full potential. Dobson et al. (1981) say:

> *The concept of self . . . is clearly central to mental health. Its importance was forced upon Rogers, who originally regarded it as a vague, scientifically meaningless construct, by his clients' continual talk about their 'selves' and especially about trying to be their real selves.*

As with all the psychologists who have written about the self described earlier in the chapter, Rogers identified several aspects of the self. He believed the perceived self to be a phenomenological entity, i.e. it is subjective and created/sustained by the individual him or herself rather than defined by some objective reality. Related to the (phenomenological) self-image is self-esteem, but both Rogers and Maslow emphasised that the two may not necessarily be closely related. 'Gaps' between self-image and self-esteem and between the self and our behaviours (for example, doing and saying things which do not accord with our self-image) are examples of what Rogers called incongruence:

> *The self-image of the congruent person is flexible and realistically changes as new experiences occur; the opposite is true of the incongruent person. When your self-image matches what you really think and feel and do, you are in the best position to realise your potential (self-actualise); the greater the gap between self-image and reality, the greater the likelihood of anxiety and emotional disturbance. Similarly, the greater the gap between self-image and ideal-self, the less fulfilled the individual will be.*

(Gross, 1996)

Rogerian therapy is based on the premise that, as we grow and develop, our experiences teach us that love and acceptance by others is 'conditional', i.e. dependent upon us behaving and doing things which others like. This is therefore wholly different to unconditional regard in which others like/love/accept us without qualification, whatever we do or say. Rogers argues that in order to gain love and acceptance from others and earn conditional regard, we learn to behave in ways and do things which are 'not us'. Central to Rogers' client-centred therapy is the need for the therapist to display empathy (seeing the world from the perspective of the client, rather than their own perspective or some objective, 'real' one) and unconditional regard (valuing and accepting the client for what they are, 'warts and all' as it were). One of the major goals of the therapy is that, through these procedures, the client is able to develop positive self-regard and through this, reduce incongruences (for example between self-image and reality and self-image and our ideal-self).

Bandura and self-efficacy

A point which we trust will be becoming increasingly evident is that there is no one field of psychology which has anything like a monopoly on the research and writings concerning the self. This is further illustrated by Albert Bandura's concept of self-efficacy. At almost the same time as Humanistic psychology was making its presence felt as the so-called third force, Bandura was developing social learning theory (early studies with the infamous Bobo doll were made in 1961). It is difficult to imagine two psychological models with less in common and yet – having revised his position on a number of issues (such as the mediating role of cognitive variables upon behaviour) – by the 1980s Bandura too was writing about the self.

Bandura argues that one of the major determinants of what we choose to do, how we choose to do it and the success – or otherwise – of what we do is our belief systems concerning our self-efficacy, i.e. our judgement about our own abilities to achieve specific desired effects. It is important to appreciate that self-efficacy is not merely a reflection of how well we think we have achieved certain things in the past, but is 'instrumental in determining how we interact with our environment and other people' (Hayes, 1994).

Bandura (1986, 1989) identified several psychological processes which are influenced by self-efficacy. These include the following (after Hayes, 1994):

1 Cognition Self-efficacy affects the way in which we think about situations which in turn may well affect our behaviour. For example, our perception of our competence at achieving something will probably have a considerable affect on whether or not we attempt to do it (or how we attempt to do it).

2 Motivation If our self-efficacy beliefs tell us that we can achieve a particular goal or perform a certain task, we are more likely to stick with it or try harder if our original attempts are unsuccessful or if the goal is a distant one.

3 Affective factors If we are confident that we can perform a demanding task (such as, for example, speaking to a large gathering of people), we are less likely to feel anxious or experience stress.

4 Selection We tend to select those situations or tasks which our self-efficacy beliefs suggest we can conquer, whereas we may go to great lengths to avoid those tasks or situations where we fear we will fail or be shown to be incompetent.

Measurement of the self

So far we have concentrated upon theories of the self (and relationships between different aspects of the self, e.g. self-image and self-esteem). Let us now briefly take a look at some of the ways in which psychologists have traditionally measured the self and its components. As we shall see, the variety of approaches is commensurate with the diversity of theoretical positions we have already illustrated (with more to come!).

Burns (1979) dedicates a whole chapter to considering tools and techniques which have been developed by psychologists to measure the self. Space restrictions will not enable us to be so detailed or extensive, but the following should suffice in giving the reader a flavour of the variety of methods which have been (and still are being) used.

For convenience, we have divided them into two overarching categories, clinical and self-reporting. As with any global categorisation of this type, it should be appreciated that the dividing line between the two is not always hard and fast, but in principal at least the latter tend to focus upon offering the individual the opportunity for making responses about how they perceive themselves, their self-esteem, etc., whereas in the former this is explored by the individual and a therapist or psychologist usually working together in a remediation setting.

CLINICAL METHODS

The interview   A good example of this being used would be in Rogers' client-centred therapy which we have briefly discussed already. As we mentioned previously, the aim is for the therapist to facilitate the development of a realistic view of the self and unconditional self-regard by the use of empathy and unconditional regard for the client.

As Coolican (1994) points out, there are many varieties of interviews, mainly differing in terms of the role of the interviewer, the nature of the questions asked, the scope given to the interviewee in how they are permitted to respond and the general purpose of the interview.

At one extreme we have the completely open-ended interview in which the contribution of the interviewer to what is said is minimal. Typically, the interviewer will orientate the interviewee to the topic under consideration (in this case, perhaps their views about themselves) and then largely 'leave them to it', letting the interviewee talk about issues which are important to them. The interviewer would be particularly mindful not to make comments or give cues or signals which might 'lead' the interviewee to say certain things which they otherwise would not. At the other extreme is the structured interview which is effectively an oral questionnaire in so far as all the questions (and the order in which they are asked) are prescribed and the respondent is only allowed to answer in one particular way, often on a numerical rating scale. It would be very rare for the structured interview to be used in a clinical setting, but the open-ended interview is one of the most preferred clinical techniques.

Projective tests

> *These techniques are in direct theoretical opposition to free-response techniques. The workers in this field stress the importance of unconscious factors which, by definition, cannot be admitted by phenomenologists, and claim that projective techniques are necessary to reveal them.*

> (Dobson et al., 1981)

The following technique reported by Adams and Caldwell (1963) illustrates this approach.

A child is given ten model bodies with a number of 'spare parts' (limbs). The child is first asked to indicate which of the ten is most like them and then afterwards to construct their ideal body. By doing this, the psychologist can identify the veracity of the child's body-image aspect of self and also is given an indication of any discrepancy between ideal and actual body-self.

Thematic Apperception Test (TAT)   Here a person is given an ambiguous stimulus, such as a picture or story which is ill-defined or open to a variety of interpretations. The individual is then typically asked to discuss it or to describe 'what happens next'. By requiring the person to place themselves into the picture or the story, it is possible for the clinician to 'read into' their responses many factors relating to their self-image, self-esteem, etc. Note that the form of investigation is indirect, i.e. the individual is not being asked direct questions about themselves but is being given 'opportunities for display'.

Q-sorts

This is a tool that is sometimes used in therapy sessions . . . It is essentially a pack of cards containing a number of statements about 'me'. The client sorts these into a number of categories (for example, 'very like me', 'not at all like me' and so on).

(Cardwell, 1996)

In a study carried out in 1954, Butler and Haigh presented each individual with a hundred statements (e.g. 'I am likeable', 'I am hardworking') and were given the following instructions: 'Sort these cards to describe yourself as you see yourself today, from those which are least like you to those which are most like you'.

In typical Q-sort tasks of this nature, the individual has to place the individual cards in piles along a numerical scale (most usually 1 to 9 with 1 representing 'least like me' and 9 'most like me'). It is important to note that a response constraint is placed upon the individual in that the number of cards which can be placed in each pile is fixed. This results in the production of a normal curve. We have noted on several occasions that this type of 'rigging' may be seen as the production of artefactual psychology (we fix things so that the results 'come out' as want and then take this outcome to be 'reality').

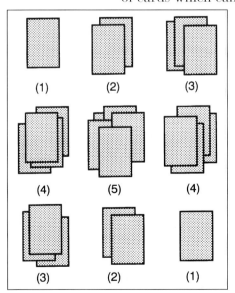

Figure 2.1   Q-sorts. Note the enforced 'bunching' in the middle rows which ensures an overall normal curve response (from Carver and Scheier, 1996)

SELF-REPORTING

Rating scales   Dobson et al. (1981) say:

This is by far the most widely used technique and takes three forms – questionnaires, inventories and attitude-to-self scales. Typically, a number of statements are made, and the subject has to indicate how well each one applies to him.

Note that there are similarities with Q-sorts (responding about self to a number of pre-determined statements), but the nature of the responding is different. Here, there is a simple numerical response (usually on Likert five-point scale) and no restriction upon how often any particular response may be given.

One of the most widely used self-report tests is Osgood et al.'s Semantic Differential. Here, people are asked to respond on a seven-point scale to a number of bipolar opposites according to where they feel they fall between the extremes, for instance kind—cruel; strong—weak.

Free-response methods   These methods are in complete contrast to the projective techniques described earlier in that they are based on the notion that the individual is the only person who has genuine insight and understanding of him or herself. Individuals are given an open-ended task, such as writing an essay about themselves or completing statements like 'I am happiest when ...' and 'Things which I do well are ...'. It is central to this approach that as few constraints as possible are placed upon the responses which individuals can offer. One of the most famous and widely used tools in this category is Kuhn and McPartland's Twenty Statements test in which individuals are invited to make twenty responses to the question 'Who am I?'.

The checklist   This is almost the mirror image of the previous category in that it involves a large number of stimuli (instead of the one question in the Twenty Statements test) and the most limited type of response possible (ticking which of the items on the checklist are true for them). In 1957, Leary devised such a tool with an Interpersonal Checklist. It contained 128 items, and respondents were instructed to tick whichever ones applied to their self and to their ideal self.

Much work has been carried out on the reliability and validity of most of the above measuring techniques. But as we shall shortly see, rather more fundamental questions than statistical ones have been posed with the revisions and reconceptualisations of the self.

Self as a social construction: the early years

Much of what we have examined so far in this chapter would lead the reader to believe that the concept of self held in psychology is that of a stable entity (even if only cognitions and consciousness/awareness) residing in the heads of individuals. This notion has been severely challenged in recent years, as we shall shortly see, but when we consider these 'rewritings of the self' we need to acknowledge two important historical contributions, from Charles Cooley (1902) and George H. Mead (1934). Furthermore, it should be noted that Mead's contribution is far from merely historical; indeed, it could be argued that his ideas are currently more valued and influential than they were at the time of his writing (in the same way that this could be argued for Frederick Bartlett, also writing in the 1930s – see Chapter 7, Memory).

What Cooley and Mead had in common (apart from both being regarded as sociologists by many writers and commentators!) was that both thought it inescapable that the self was substantially social. Although William James had acknowledged the influence of social factors on the self, especially concerning the Me rather than the I, it was Cooley, with his so-called Looking Glass theory of self, who argued against the 'fixed inner entity' concept which has characterised so much of what we have examined so far. He said: 'The self that is most important is a reflection, largely from the minds of others'. He argued, as the name of theory makes clear, that we try to imagine how we look in the minds of those we are interacting with, and this image is reflected back to us, telling us who and what we are. This 'feedback' is seen as fundamentally shaping or creating the self we possess. He said:

> *A self-idea . . . seems to have three principal elements: the imagination of our appearance to the other person; the imagination of his judgement of that appearance; and some sort of self-feeling, such as pride or mortification.*

Thus, he saw this self as having three components, perception, evaluation and affect. The only characteristic missing from the frequently given criteria for attitudes (e.g. Secord and Backman, 1964) was a behavioural component, but then Cooley was writing 11 years before John Watson published his manifesto for Behaviourism, which was to revolutionalise the whole of psychology.

In the same way that neither Rogers nor Maslow coined the term Humanistic psychology, Mead – the pioneer of symbolic interactionism – did not found the term. Gross (1996) explains Mead's position in the following manner:

> *According to symbolic interactionism, human beings act towards things in terms of their meanings; people exist in terms in a symbolic as well as a physical environment, such that the importance of a social interaction is derived from the meaning it holds for the participants. The 'interaction' refers specifically to the fact that people communicate with each other, which provides the opportunity for meanings to be learned.*

Like James, Mead conceives the self to be composed of an I and Me, and argued that the I is a reflexive process (for example, I have self-awareness, consciousness and can interact with myself), but the Me is socially negotiated. For Mead, the individual person and his or her culture are interdependent – one cannot exist without the other.

Mead argues that the self develops through three stages. The first of these is the preparatory stage which occurs during infancy. At this stage, the youngster imitates the behaviour of others but does not really understand or comprehend the meanings or significance of the behaviours. The second stage he called play stage, which is characterised by the acting out of 'whole social roles rather than simple actions' (Hayes, 1994). The child when playing will often refer to him or herself in the third person (such as 'Paul push truck'), which Mead took as indicative of an awareness of our social selves (through the ability to see ourselves 'externally') but that there was a lack of a unified and consistent self. The third and final stage was the development of just such a self, which Mead called the core-self stage (Hayes, 1994).

Figure 2.2   Through play, children develop the ability to see themselves as others see them, rather than only from their own perspective

Through role-playing in play and games, the child is able to build up a Generalised Other, by which Mead means an awareness of how he or she appears and is viewed by others. Through this process, an awareness of the social rules involved in games and a growing appreciation of the meanings located in and transmitted through our language, the child develops the social self. Mead (1934) said:

The self arises in conduct, when the individual becomes a social object in experience to himself. This takes place when the individual assumes the attitude or gesture which another individual could use . . . The child gradually becomes a social being in his own experience, and he acts towards himself in a manner analogous to that in which he acts towards others.

The key factor in casting Mead as the link between traditional self-theories and the revisionists is summarised thus by Gross (1996):

Mead turned James and Cooley on their heads; the self is not mentalistic (i.e. something private going on inside the individual), but . . . is a cognitive process lodged in the ongoing social world.

The Self II

The story so far

Argyle, Allport, Bandura, Eysenck, Mead, Cooley, Freud, Rogers, Erickson, Maslow, Festinger ... the list can go on and on. It is almost true to say that anyone who has published in psychology has written something about the self. By the 1970s, psychology had produced a multitude of theories about the self (or 'personality'), but overall, many felt it had failed in its major pursuit, namely to provide a coherent explanation of what it meant to be human, or to have a self. During this period of 'crisis' in social psychology, many critics argued that the variety of theories on the self, which often started from very contradictory positions, could not be integrated into a meaningful overall theoretical model. Others were less concerned with this fragmentation and more worried about the *asocial* nature of the 'self' in psychological theories. For them, even the more apparently 'social' theories of the self, such as Mead's, were in some respects not sufficiently social (Burkitt, 1991). While in one way Mead's theory brought into focus the importance of others for the self (hence the social context or 'society'), in other ways there was still an aspect of the self, i.e. the I, which was seen as if it was rooted in the person's biological make-up and thus remained as something which lay outside language and culture. For critics, the problem with such views was that once we see an aspect of the self as if somehow 'fixed' (by biology or learning), then this precludes us from any further examination of the social and political context in which people live (Squire, 1989).

In addition, as in Mead's theory, most psychological theories viewed (and still view) 'society' as if it is devoid of any *power relations* and social inequalities. In Burkitt's (1991) words, Mead's failure to identify power relations in society presents us with a model of the self which:

> *... plays down the internalisation of social conflict within the personality through the idea of the 'generalised other'. If society is in conflict, then the generalised values that we appropriate ... will also be, in part, contradictory.*

In other words, it became increasingly clear for many critics that conflict and contradiction are daily experiences in the lives of many people. While much of mainstream psychology tended to turn a blind eye to this possibility, researchers who worked particularly with oppressed groups (e.g. women, black and working-class people) increasingly began to develop the argument that conflict and contradiction were a mark of social oppression, rather than being indicative of inadequacies in one's personality or self. Nonetheless, in the bulk of psychological work on the self, the assumption remained that if there appeared to be a difficulty, it was a problem of the individual. Individuals appeared to be blamed for having 'low self-esteem', 'poor body image', 'neuroticism', etc. Little or no attention was paid to the social world from which they came and within which they continued to exist. Scholars who studied the work of the symbolic interactionist school inherited the view that the selves we are or appear to be are not something which we personally own, but are inextricably interwoven in the fabric of our social milieu. Unlike Mead's work, however, many researchers now began to cast a critical glance on 'society' or on what lay 'outside' and around individuals. Postmodern scholars in particular proposed alternative models whereby the self was not a completed and coherently organised entity. New terminology in relation to the self began to appear emphasising a *self-in-action* (Shotter, 1996), a *self-in-relation* (Hollway, 1989) or an *embedded self* (Sampson, 1990).

Such theorists not only refuse to see the self as if it is 'completed', separated from others and static in some ways, but they also refuse to see 'society' as if it is a harmonious, rather friendly and welcoming entity which is 'out there' and into which individuals fit neatly. Instead, critical psychologists direct our attention to a variety of social practices and institutions in which power operates and affects us all. A cursory look through the terminology employed by mainstream and critical psychology in relation to 'society' is revealing of this difference in approach. Whereas in more traditional psychological theories we find terms such as, *socialisation*, *adjustment*, *adaptation*, *enculturation*, terms which suggest a rather unproblematic entry into 'society', in critical psychology we find other terms – *disciplining*, *coercion*, *regulation* – all of which imply the operation of power.

In addition, the actual term – the self – became somewhat inadequate to grasp the new meanings theorists now attempted to develop. Historically speaking, the term has come to mean something which is inside individuals, which is owned or possessed by them. A much more preferred term in this perspective is *subjectivity*. In order to understand more fully what is meant by this concept, we need to grasp in greater depth how language, and specifically 'discourse', is discussed by the postmodernists. However, for the moment we can begin by saying that subjectivity refers to thoughts and emotions of the individual, to people's sense of themselves and ways of understanding how they relate to the world.

Revisions and reconceptualisations

Let's look now at some of the views on language, or *discourse*, within postmodern perspective and see how these may relate to reconceptualising the self. To remind ourselves what a discourse is, we can say that it is a story which contains widespread, often unquestioned (common-sense) assumptions which tell us who we are and how we should act and feel on the basis of our sex, age, colour, class, physical (dis)abilities, etc. Discourses also *structure power relations*. For example, if we consider traditional discourses about the family which dictate that the man is the 'head' of the family, clearly there is more power invested in the position of being a man than in the one of being a woman in this discourse.

We will return to the relationship between discourse and power later; another important aspect of discourse is that it is *action-orientated* (Edwards and Potter, 1992). In other words, we use particular discourses because they are in some ways useful to us, i.e. they fulfil a function (Potter and Wetherell, 1987). Usefulness and *not* truthfulness is what postmodernists emphasise about discourse. Foucault (1979), for example, one of the founding fathers of postmodern discourse analysis, argues that all discourses we employ are 'equally' true, but they differ in their *usefulness* to different people in different times and places. The implication here is that theories of the self are not so much different from one another in terms of any truth value, but some are more useful than others for different people at different times and places. Another implication of the above point in relation to the question of 'what is a self' is that it is nothing more or less but the stories, or the discourses, we use when we talk about it. Thus, in the words of Harré (1985): 'to be a self is not to be a certain kind of being, but to be in possession of a certain kind of theory'. Discourses, then, (and theories are discourses) are also *constructive* – they construct 'reality'. In our culture, we are so accustomed to the notion that in language we describe, rather than make things up, that it is often difficult to convey what is meant by the concept of linguistic or discursive construction. However, it is often easier to grasp this property of discourse by looking back in history. Thus, for example, few people today would have difficulty in agreeing with the view that 'witches' do not exist or do not represent a 'real' person. However, during the 16th century, many women (estimates vary from 200,000 to millions (Barstow, 1994)) were executed as witches. The idea of the existence of witches was a widely spread, common-sense belief which was shared by the lay and academic person. The concept of witches can be seen as an *object of discourse* – people talked about 'them', defined 'them' in a number of ways, developed practices around identifying witches (such as pricking), developed means of dealing with 'them' (such as torture and extracting particular modes of confessions from 'them'). The belief in witches also meant that particular kinds of 'professions' came into being, and a number of men made their living by being witch hunters, jailers, prickers, executioners and judges. The concept of a witch was held in the minds of many people as 'real' because it existed within the context of a *whole set of social practices* and pre-existing beliefs. Here is an example of the kind of beliefs held at the time. Women were:

> *. . . accused of flying to the sabbat on phallic broomsticks, being seduced by demon lovers, joining in orgiastic dances, kissing the devil's ass, copulating indiscriminately with men, with other women, relatives, demons or the devil himself and giving birth to demon children. Women were believed capable of these acts because of three qualities: being hypersexed, weak-willed and given to melancholy.*
>
> (Barstow, 1994)

Figure 3.1   Torturing a 'witch' to confess (15th/16th-century etching)

Now, while 'witches' were something made-up in language, the ensuing social practices led to a situation where real things happened to the bodies of those seen to be witches; people were tortured and many times were also burned alive. Constructions of the self, then, are not merely 'only words'; they have real implications for how people are viewed and treated by others. While we may fancy that in modern times we have moved away from such 'superstitions', we only have to remind ourselves of the representations of the Jews in Nazi propaganda and the ways in which these were used to justify mass murders during the Holocaust. Even more recently, the so-called 'ethnic cleansing' in former Yugoslavia has been an example of nationality being similarly used to justify inhumane practices. These are examples not only of how identities are made up or constructed in language, but also how these are maintained by practices. For postmodernists, language is constructive. Whether we talk about a person as a 'witch', as a 'Jew', as 'disabled', as 'intelligent', etc., we are not talking about some real entity, but about an object of discourse, the reality of which is more or less convincing to us, depending on the time we live in and on the social practices surrounding us. The self is also treated in this way.

Anthropologists have been among the first to demonstrate how the self is constructed differently in different cultures. Moreover, on the basis of this and other cross-cultural work, it begins to appear that our Western conceptualisation of the self is rather 'peculiar' (Geertz, 1984). In our culture, we tend to think that people have individual characteristics, such as extroversion or introversion, high or low self-esteem, external or internal locus of control, masculinity or femininity and so on. As we have also seen from the previous chapter, many psychologists themselves have been involved in attempts to articulate and define such characteristics and also to develop instruments with which these can be measured. However, a brief perusal of anthropological and cross-cultural research presents us with a picture showing that, in many other cultures, people do not seem to think of the self as something which belongs solely to the individual, made up from a variety of distinct and sometimes unique characteristics. To greater or lesser degree, such cultures place the individual within the context of other, larger, social, religious and even cosmic explanations. To put it another way, a self cannot be understood in such cultures by focusing solely on individuals. In one study, for example, Harré (1983, cited in Potter and Wetherell, 1987) explains how the Maori people of New Zealand see individuals and the world around them as if they were permeated by cosmic forces, where people become invested with a special power, called *mana*, due to the specific circumstances of their birth. Individuals' subjective experiences (such as fear, anger, grief) are understood *not* in terms of personally owned characteristics, but are seen as the result of the ebb and flow of such forces. In other words, while we in the West tend to seek the causes of why people are and behave the way they do within themselves, the Maori culture provides answers to such questions by focusing on external explanations.

There is also a more collectivist (rather than individualistic) understanding of the self in other cultures. This can be observed in studies which examine the ways in which people account for their behaviours. Strauss (1973) points out that the Cheyenne provide explanations of specific behaviours which are 'generally in terms of relationships with other persons, not in terms of the inner core of traits of "personality" '. Miller (1984) makes similar observations. Whereas Americans offer traits as explanations to particular behaviours, Indians appear to look at context in order to do the same. Thus, for example, an American is likely to say, 'he is insecure' and an Indian, 'there is no one about'; and where an American tends to attribute a characteristic to an individual, 'she is kind', an Indian person tends to look at the same issue in more relational terms, 'she listens to my problems'.

What such examples illustrate is that in different societies and historical circumstances, the self is understood in different ways and that our current Western understanding is one among many. Moreover, as researchers like those above have argued, the way in which we think of the self in the West is to see each person as an owner of herself or himself. Macpherson (1962) has referred to this type of modern self with the concept of *possessive individualism*. Critics argue that our views on the self are not any more true than other people's, but that it is a construction which fits our society and historical circumstances. Just as in our consumerist and capitalist society we can possess cars, computers, land, etc., we can imagine possessing and being in control of our abilities, minds, feelings and so on. Our current concept of the self cannot be universalised to other cultures since it will not be 'useful' to them. Take, for example, Japanese culture, where the self is defined in more inclusive ways and where characteristics that are seen to be in place *between* rather than within individuals are valued. Cousins (1989), for instance, discusses the Japanese concept of *amae*. This refers to a positive interdependency which exists between people such as husband and wife, employer and employee, teacher and pupil. Given this cultural context, we can see how we cannot generalise to other cultures, such as Japan, our own concept of the self. Our Western models of the self, with their emphases on autonomy, independence and separation from others, will be at odds with the much more relational and collective notions about the self in Japan, and may even appear 'wrong' and 'abnormal'. In other words, what most postmodern researchers have contributed to the debate about the self is that in order to understand how and why people talk about the self, we need to place the debate within a social and historical context. Now let's look at the second issue which we raised at the opening of this section: the issue of power relations.

Power relations

Let's take some examples and explore in greater depth the ways in which discourses about the self may function in the interests of the speaker (i.e. we shall be looking at politics with a small 'p'). At the same time, we'll look at how the same discourses might function on a broader cultural level, protecting the interests of dominant groups in power (i.e. politics with a capital 'p'). In the west, the invitation 'tell me about yourself' is perhaps most often encountered during initial romantic dates. In such situations, a person may present an account of her or himself in such a way as to 'impress' a possible future partner, i.e. one of the functions of the self-story is simply to 'impress'. What is deemed to 'impress', however, will typically vary from one sex to another, since, as many theorists have pointed out, Western discourses are *gendered*, i.e. discourses of masculinity and femininity instruct the sexes differently (Hollway, 1989). Thus, for example, a man may attempt to impress a potential partner by telling his story in such a way that he appears 'strong' or 'brave'. However, discourses are not pure, and issues around class, race, age and so on intersect. This means that cultural constructions around categories such as race can be also evoked. There is a long Western tradition which constructs black male (and female) sexuality as if somehow 'more' than that of whites. Thus if the speaker is a black male in the above hypothetical romantic encounter, there would be cultural discourses around the so-called 'nature' of black male sexuality which would be easily available for him. Many critics have argued that such constructions of black sexuality have emerged in a *particular historical context* and have functioned to oppress black people of both sexes. Thus, historically speaking, the argument that black males have 'greater' sexual drive which is somehow less controllable and less 'civilised' (as compared to white males) has been used to justify oppressive practices such as lynching and disproportionate (as compared to white men) representation of black men in prisons for sexual crimes (Searles and Berger, 1995). Despite this 'larger' political function of the discourse, in everyday life black men will have at their disposal social constructions which positions them as 'more sexual' (than white men) and may use these to their more immediate, 'micro' ends, i.e. to impress a potential partner. In other words, what postmodern critics argue is that the dominant discourses we enter may, as Foucault argued, offer us an identity with certain 'pleasures', while at the same time these very discourses may work towards the reproduction of the existing unequal social relations (in this case between black and white people). Thus one of the main implications of postmodernist research for those who are concerned with practices of social inequality has been that, since mainstream discourses function ideologically (i.e. to preserve existing power relations between groups of people), then *identity is a political issue*. Below we expand upon this particular implication of postmodern thought.

Implications and applications

In general terms, there are three main areas in which insights gained from postmodernism have influenced psychology. Firstly, many researchers have felt that up until now we have been asking the wrong questions (Crawford, 1995) and that there is a need to change the 'subject' of the discipline (Henriques et al., 1984). In relation to the study of the self, the new questions asked shift away from the study of 'individual' to the social construction of the self. Texts, written or spoken, become the focus of investigations. Along with the change in research questions and different types of data (i.e. texts) come new research methodologies, such as 'deconstruction' and discourse analysis. Such methodologies examine discursive cultural heritage and the 'meaning of difference' (Hare-Mustin and Marecek, 1990). As we suggested in the section above, available constructions of differences in identity among different groups of people are not neutral and innocent, but are value laden and are implicated in the reproduction of existing power relations. In other words, researchers who examine the 'meanings of difference' also tend to address political questions. This 'politicising' of the discipline differentiates many postmodern scholars from those working within the parameters of more traditional psychology. Below, is a working example of a form of textual analysis which illustrates many of the above points.

The second implication of adopting the postmodern perspective involves our understanding of subjectivity and, more specifically, addresses the question of how we came to be, feel and think the way that we do, given the discursive and social practices of our culture and the specific locations which we occupy in it.

The final 'application' of postmodern insights which we discuss in this chapter relates to efforts to 'invent' or 'construct' new forms of subjectivities which are more self-consciously engaged in current political debates.

Who is speaking? Beginning textual analysis

When examining discourses about the self, we pointed out that the ways in which the self is talked about are *functional*. We also pointed out that discourses are never purely descriptive; they are not presenting a picture which is, as Sampson (1993) puts it, 'God's view from nowhere'. Thus, the argument goes, discourses about the self are *from a point of view* and *to a particular end*. The question then arises: how do we know who is speaking? One way in which this question is addressed by critical researchers is to look at the content of a text and examine what kind of person is represented in positive terms, or as the 'norm', and what kind of person is represented in negative terms, or as the 'other'. Let's see how this is done in a particular text.

In 1906, Otto Weininger wrote an influential book called *Sex and Character*. Like many writers before and after him, Weininger argued that his theory was about real differences between women and men – and, of course, if we are to believe what he says, women and men would end up with very different types of selves. A man, in the author's view, is potentially capable of being a 'genius' because he:

> *. . . embraces the whole world in himself and therefore understands everything and everybody. His memory is continuous and universal . . . His mind is of intense alertness. His thoughts are all articulate and clear; he has a 'universal appreciation'. He is the creator of his own moral law. His will is directed towards the realisation of values. His feelings, like his thoughts, react to the slightest of stimuli, that is his sensibility equals his intellectual power. He is intensely aware of his uniqueness, and therefore values human personality above all else . . . His universal memory, his all-embracing mind, his soul . . . and his ardent desire for immortality makes him transcend time.*

On the other hand, a woman by definition cannot be a genius, since he believed that:

> *Woman's thoughts are never distinct and articulate, [they are] unclear, half-conscious images in which thinking and feeling are intertwined. Hence her sentimentality . . . which, however, never attains the degree of deep emotion. Woman's judgement is uncertain . . . Woman lives unconsciously and only receives her consciousness from man . . . She lacks the power of discrimination between true and false . . . because . . . her memory is short. The fact that woman remembers only her amorous experiences – but these with great detail – is another proof of the limited sphere and the nature of her interests . . . she does not conceive of the value of truth. She knows neither the moral nor the logical Imperative. She has no relation to the Law nor does she know of a duty to herself . . . Her deficient memory prevents her from having any exact relation to time or . . . Eternity. She therefore cannot take the proposition of identity . . . she is not, she is nothing.*

(Klein, 1971)

For many contemporary readers, the above extracts may come across as an onslaught of insults on women and a glorification of men. However, a critical reading of such texts in academia would usually begin with questioning the scientific validity of the author's claims. How does the author know, for example, that 'woman's thought are never distinct and articulate'? On what scientific evidence can we base assertions such as claiming that man's 'universal memory, his all-embracing mind . . . reflects the whole world'? What, indeed, is the precise definition of an 'all-embracing mind'? While science and its methods of investigation are often viewed as the very tools which we have at our disposal to fight prejudice, postmodernists argue that the situation is not that simple. In many cases, quite the reverse may indeed happen, i.e. we use 'science' to test and give credibility to existing (often prejudiced) systems of beliefs (Kitzinger, 1990). 'Science' itself is viewed as a discourse which re-tells, in acceptable ways, existing cultural constructions, along with their underlying values. Thus for example, more recent work on styles of perception, according to which women tend to be context-dependent and men context-independent thinkers (Witkin, 1978), can be seen to represent a more fanciful and convincing (to the modern mind) reproduction of Weininger's view that man's 'thoughts react to the slightest of stimuli', whereas 'woman's thoughts are never distinct and accurate'. For researchers doing discourse analysis, then, a critical reading of a text will *not* draw on the conventional scientific criteria. This is because, for postmodernists, 'science' is just another discourse which is as 'true' as many others. What may be interesting for such researchers is to see how meanings from older texts (such as Weininger's) are reproduced, as well as elaborated on or altered or dropped altogether in new discourses. In other words, postmodernists tend to venture into history and examine the ways in which their specific object of investigation has been constructed in varying socio-historical conditions.

Another way in which critical analyses of a text are conducted is to look for *omissions* in the text, the consideration of which would undermine or make the presented argument unsustainable. While gaps and omissions in texts today are associated with the work of postmodernists, critical scholars have always drawn on this method. Viola Klein, for example, from whose book the above extracts were taken, criticises Weininger by pointing out one such omission. While Weininger seemed bent on denigrating women, Klein points to another, and in her time more pervading, construction of women, namely the idealisation and glorification of women, which he does not consider. She writes:

> *There is still another problem arising out of Weininger's conception of woman: if women really are so inferior, how is it possible that they were adored and glorified by the greatest spirits of humanity? How could a being, devoid of any qualities, be the inspiration of genius of all times?*

A third strategy employed in critical analysis of a text involves the examination of what kind of binary oppositions are employed in it. Table 3.1 shows some examples of such oppositions from Weininger's texts.

Table 3.1 Binary oppositions based on Weininger's texts

Men	Women
• are conscious	• are unconscious
• have a good memory	• have a bad memory
• are morally superior	• are morally inferior
• are intelligent	• are unintelligent
• are independent	• are dependent
• are logical	• are illogical
• can make good judgements	• are not capable of good judgements
• have a distinct identity	• have no identity
• have a broad range of interests	• have a narrow range of interests
• strive to transcend time	• are not interested in immortality
• are capable of being a genius	• are not capable of being a genius

It is clear from Table 3.1 that women are not constructed simply as different from men, i.e. as beings in their own right who happen to be different, but are shown *in relation* to men as their opposite which is also a *negative*. The opposites used to construct male and female identities are mutually dependent on one another for meaning. Male (positive) identity is in *debt to*, or swims in glory but for the representation of, women as an 'other'. As Virginia Woolf once said, such texts represent an example of how, in academic writing, men have constructed 'woman' as a mirror in which they are reflected back to themselves twice their own size. However, since men are represented in positive terms and women negative ones, we can say that Weininger's text is written from a male point of view. It is actually amusing to see men being represented as God-like creatures with 'all-embracing souls' and with 'ardent desires for immortality' who, like a God, can live for ever. The crescendo of this incredible ego trip is only to be achieved by a construction that plunges womanhood into the depths of 'nothingness', for woman, Weininger says, 'she is not, she is nothing'.

Some of the implications of postmodern perspective in relation to the study of the self are that the perspective has equipped us with certain means with which to demonstrate how 'identity' is put together. The three points which we raised here are that in order to understand 'who is who' today, we need to delve into the past and see how particular 'types' of identities were formulated in particular conditions and how these may have been altering through time. We can also address the question of how a particular type of an identity is maintained by the ways in which certain views are omitted (see also Sampson's (1993) discussion of the 'absent presence'). Thirdly, we also illustrated how identity is put together by the use of binary oppositions. This list of deconstructive strategies is not exhaustive, but it does illustrate one of the main implications of postmodernism for the study of the self, namely that the perspective ends up telling us what a 'self' is not, rather than what it is. For some writers, 'deconstructing the subject of psychology', i.e. the person, has been worrying in so far as the approach raises questions about the very identity and future existence of the discipline. (If psychology has nothing concrete to say about the 'individual', then what is psychology?) Other writers find only 'deconstructing' the self dissatisfactory. Some such as Edward Sampson (1990) argue that psychologists also need to offer 'reconstructions' of the self. However, they have done so tentatively, avoiding universal claims and, like Foucault, acknowledging that any theories we propose (or construct) will be rooted in current ways of life, and in time might be just as subject to the deconstructive criticisms of others. So what, after all, does it mean to be a human being from a postmodern perspective?

From subjectivity to politics

In an excellent new book, *Understanding the Self*, Stevens et al. (1996) remind us that humans exist on a number of planes, all of which are intertwined in a rather complex way. Thus, for example, we live in *social worlds* whose rules and regulations embrace us and to which we respond and also create. In addition, we are all born in separate and different bodies. Our experiences of life are *embodied*, in so far as we experience the world and others through our bodies. A colour-blind person, for example, would relate to and experience the world in a very different way from someone with the ability to see colour – an ability, which, like so many other ones, able-bodied people take for granted (for an informative case study, see Oliver Sacks' (1995) discussion of an artist who lost his ability to perceive colour). Thirdly, each individual goes through life meeting and interacting with different people and has a *unique life story*. These different histories contribute to an endless diversity in human experience. Recently, there has been a revival in psychology exploring life histories and autobiographies (e.g. Coupland and Nussbaum, 1993; Josselson and Leiblich, 1995). Finally, since the work of Freud, many psychologists have argued continually against mainstream 'ego' psychology, pointing to the more *unconscious* aspects of our experiences.

Bearing in mind these different planes on which we exist, it is not surprising that both mainstream and critical theoretical accounts of the self are multiple and variable. Different researchers have tended to focus on one of these different areas or have combined aspects of one with others. The postmodern perspective tends to exclude psychoanalysis (and thus the unconscious), and it has also little to offer in terms of biological models of the self. It does, however, offer many insights in relation to the ways in which the social and the personal intersect on the level of subjective experiences.

Let's now look at how the discussion presented so far in this chapter can be embroidered and developed further into a tentative picture of subjectivity. In the first place, we can say that our subjective sense of being is a product of our culture and times. The stories which we narrate about ourselves will be in some ways 'functional' for us. Just as the ways in which constructions of the self differ across cultures and times, so the ways in which we talk about ourselves in the course of our daily lives may vary. This *variability* in accounts of the self need not be viewed as something negative, simply related to interest functions for the person involved. As human beings, we *relate* and *engage* with others primarily through the use of language. Cosslett (1994), for example, illustrates how, in the process of her research on women's experiences of childbirth, she herself appeared rather different with different women. Since human experience is multifaceted and complex, we can draw on and highlight different aspects of it while interacting with others. Cosslett discovered that with women who had had a more joyful experience of birth, she offered accounts of her own experiences of childbirth which emphasised the positive aspects. On the other hand, with women who had had a more traumatic time, she offered more negative accounts. When we relate to others, we search through our own experiences for ways of connecting. Through sharing of meaning, we construct and participate in a 'joint' reality with others (Shotter, 1996). And again, this is not to say that we 'lie' or that we are 'two faced' or 'inconsistent', as mainstream psychology has often claimed. Rather this somewhat chameleon quality of our use of language makes it possible for us to relate to the many people we meet in life and to *experience a sense of belonging* (Shotter, 1996). However, if we accept that experience of shared meanings and a sense of belonging makes people happy in our modern world, this may not be easily achievable. Gergen (1991), for example, argues that modern society, with its technological advances and explosion of information, *saturates* us with many different notions about lifestyles and identities so that our subjective experiences are *contradictory* and *fragmentary*. For Gergen, as well as Shotter (1993), experiences of conflicts and contradictions around notions of identity appear to be an inevitable part of living in contemporary Western cultures. Thus, while mainstream psychology has sought to discover internal and systematically organised self, critical psychologists point to current cultural conditions which make contradiction rather than consistency a feature of subjectivity.

Mainstream psychology also tends to talk about the development of the self as if one is going through a number of linear stages where the passage from one stage to another seems fairly unproblematic and logically organised. But is it like that? In everyday life we use language which suggests that we experience emotional upheavals. Hence people say: 'I was messed up', 'screwed up', 'off my head', 'on the brink', 'fucked', 'I cracked', 'was on the verge of a breakdown', 'went through a downer', 'was in the pits', 'was a mental wreck', etc. There are many times in life when we experience dilemmas, and these tend to be in the context of what happens in our lives *with* others. During such moments of crisis we search for new answers which eventually enrich and elaborate the narrative of our self-stories. For Josselson (1995), 'Moments of crisis represent nodes of change in which the individual becomes other than he or she was', and which are 'personal keys to meaning-making, the place where the person's self-understanding is put to a self-imposed test'. Such experiences of our lives are perhaps more often represented in other than psychological literature. In literary novels, for example, we often witness the main protagonists going through emotional upheavals and ultimately changing *via* their entanglements with the lives of others. Josselson argues that, during crisis, the self is in a *dialogue* with others and is presented with the opportunity to enter and understand the subjectivity of some other person. In turn, this enriches our own story of the self. Like Sampson (1993), she argues for a psychology which understands the self more in terms of a process during which we are dialogically engaged with others. As it is, 'psychologists are locked into their own language systems and cannot represent another's world view' (see also Sampson's notions of psychology's monologism below). No wonder many students come to feel that psychology is 'boring'!

Crisis in life cannot be predicted in the manner that traditional psychology has attempted. For example, who could have predicted the recent revolution in Eastern Europe or the war in Yugoslavia, events which brought crisis to the lives of millions of people. Critical psychologists prefer to see both the world around us and the 'self' more in terms of 'flux' than set structures. Mark Freeman's (1993) book *Rewriting the Self* is a collection of essays exploring ongoing transformations of life histories. In traditional psychology, the past and the present in a person's life often appear cut off from one another. Socialisation theories, for example, tell us that we 'learn' attitudes or behaviours and then we 'become' what appears to be the end product of this past. This view obscures how, at every point in life, we continue to have new experiences with which we re-order and reinterpret our past. Thus becoming a student, getting a new job, losing a loved one, getting married, becoming a parent and so on are some of the countless events that happen to people all the time. Many of these events lead us to re-examine our past, give new salience or a new interpretation to memories that were 'always there' and 'forget' others. In addition, our personal histories are interwoven in some larger cultural context. Changes in Eastern Europe, for example, led to the demise of communism. History text books underwent drastic rewriting and reinterpretations. New books appeared on the market showing how the communists 'had lied', and new 'truths' documented previously hidden atrocities, such as Stalin's for example. At the same time, ordinary people also began to re-write their own life histories. In interviews with Bulgarian women after changes in the country, Petkova (1996) found that aspects of one's past that were unspeakable during communism now became not only something to be written into one's life history but also something to be proud of. Thus, for example, incidents of communist wrongdoings, implications of members of one's family in practices of resisting communism were now spoken about, emphasised and elaborated. Just as in everyday life we connect to specific others, we also 'stretch out' of our more individual histories to connect with the histories of the masses or the culture. Thus postmodernism continually represents a vision of the self where our subjective experiences are *embedded* in a flux of relationships, culture and times. If we take this view on board and see connections everywhere, the issues of personal and social change collapse into one. However, the notion of the 'embedded self' is not the same as the concept of 'belonging' introduced here earlier. To have a sense of belonging means to have an effect on the outcomes of interactions we have with others, be they on the level of the family (i.e. micro) or of the culture (i.e. macro). For Shotter (1996), what is meant by 'belonging' is being in a position to have a voice in the making and re-making of our worlds.

However, our world comprises of hierarchically structured institutions whose very existence is made possible by the proliferation of discourses which facilitate practices of exclusion and inclusion. As Shotter (1996) points out, belonging is not always up to us or in our power. We have seen earlier here how discourses about the 'nature' of masculinity and femininity, for example, ensure the exclusion of one sex (usually women) from certain categories, themselves discursively constructed, such as a 'genius'. Weininger's account of what it is to be a woman acts to 'silence' and exclude; for women, according to him, have nothing to say with their defective memory, inability to articulate feelings and to relate to moral and legal issues. Thus, the question becomes: how, if one is living in a culture which is not welcoming to members of one's group, is one to participate in that culture?

Perhaps some answers lie in the struggles of oppressed groups, such as the black movement in the United States during the 1970s. At this time of political activism in academia, 'psychology of nigrescence' appeared. What characterises nigrescence is that black people began to write about themselves and about how it feels to live in a culture to which you could not easily, or at all, belong. Nigrescence thinkers developed their own theories for the development of a black self. Cross (1971), for example, delineated five stages of nigrescence, which Mama (1995) summarises in the following way:

1 Pre-encounter   During this stage, the person is influenced by racist ideologies so that one experiences self-hate and a sense of inferiority.

2 Encounter   This stage comments on certain shocking social events which allow the person, perhaps for the first time, to see his or her condition differently.

3 Immersion–Emersion   This is typified by a struggle to remove the old perspectives and in the process may include 'a glorification of African heritage, either/or thinking blacker-than-thou attitudes' and a 'tendency to degenerate white people'. This is a dramatic stage whose effects level out in time.

4 Internalisation   Here the conflicts between old and new views acquire a level of resolution and people become more self-confident, open and non-racist.

5 Internalisation-Commitment   During this stage, many people become political activists.

While in some ways this theory resembles 'white', traditionalist theories of the self, in that it presents a linear model of development and a self who is a coherent, stable unit, it is nonetheless written from the point of view of one who is existing in a discriminatory and unfriendly social world; that is, unlike the typically 'white' theories which, as we discussed at the beginning of the chapter, see nothing wrong with 'society'.

However, writing from the point of view of being black is not easy given that Western linguistic and academic traditions have been built over many centuries by social practices which have best protected the interests of white people. Perhaps most pernicious of all, at the heart of this tradition lies strong individualism which, as we discussed at the beginning of the chapter, ends up seeking faults within individuals or specific underprivileged social groups, while at the same time it turns a blind eye to social context. However, it appeared increasingly that there was no one theory which could capture once and for all what a self is, be it black or white, female or male. Mama (1995) observes that 'old knowledges are seldom entirely dispensed with but can be reactivated . . . whenever conditions permit'. Thus while nigrescence psychology asserted that oppression damages black people, it was to be replaced at different times and places with the same old 'white' view that black people are oppressed because they are damaged. Given this ongoing dynamic between social struggles and visions of the self, many critical writers began to seek an academic tradition which can capture the complexity of such interactions. Shotter (1996) and Mama (1995), for example, are both concerned that we develop *bridging concepts*. Rather than doing that, so far, we have tended to present the individual as a frozen unit, a statue behind which an ever-changing external world passes by. What critical psychologists are struggling to say is that we are all in the picture and at the same time we are also its painters. Mama (1995) offers the concept of *positionality* as one such 'bridging concept'. She uses it to investigate simultaneously the dynamic between the 'individual in the picture' and the 'individual as the painter'. Similarly to Hollway (1989), she proceeds from the notion that existing discourses which we utilise to talk about ourselves position us as particular types of person in relation to others. In this sense, we are already 'constructed' (or defined) over our heads, so to speak, as to who we are. There are, however, different discourses between which we move, and for members of groups defined as 'others' (such as black people), the multiplicity of such discourses appears greater. Let's take an example. The extract below is from a conversation held between the author herself (Amina) and two other women:

ANGELA: *I think most black people are schizophrenic, though, in that they have to . . .*

THERESA: *I was just about to say that, because I rap in patois when I rap in St Lucians, and I sort of use a different patois when I rap with West Indians who are not St Lucian.*

AMINA: *And you talk and project yourself very differently – well, I do anyway – when I am with English people compared to being with Caribbean people or West African people.*

ANGELA: *And what do you become when you are with English people?*

AMINA: *I become more English. That whole aspect of myself just takes over.*

ANGELA: *I don't know. I do with certain English people – that's how I get certain jobs and shit like that – because I know I've got to play the game at the interviews, but with other English people I can be what I want. I think I've got so many different personalities – well, not personalities – it's the same personality but different ways of expressing that.*

The point illustrated by this extract is that to exist as an 'other' means to be in a world which is not your 'oyster'. It means to be in a situation in which you are continually aware of how different discourses construct you this way and that way, so that you may feel 'schizophrenic'. As Mama points out, the existing psychiatric language (e.g. 'schizophrenic', 'personality'), while it is available and people will use it casually as one of her participants does, is unsatisfactory. Its negative connotations imply a failure within individuals. However, what the women above are sharing concerns the usual (therefore normal?) conditions of existence for many black people. Each of the women, despite their differences, has found herself in a situation where not re-positioning herself, or not altering her identity, has meant exclusion (and thus not getting a job, earning a living). While 'fragmented subjectivity' may be a human condition, particularly characteristic of our times, nonetheless the shifts in identities illustrated above are more specific to the lives of those outside the norm of white, male, heterosexual, middle class. Such shifts, as Mama points out, are experienced on a subjective level as if 'contradictions in oneself' lead to anxiety and discomfort. The chameleon aspect of language which allows us to connect with humanity, and which obviously the speakers above have all practised, is work which is devalued and made invisible. Dominant discourses about the 'individual' which seek out stable and unchanging personality characteristics end up pathologising efforts to belong to a human community. A form of analysis which takes seriously what participants in research have to say about their own lives illuminates the effects of dominant discourses and helps us to redress the question from 'who am I?' to 'what are we all doing?'.

Conclusion

To sum up some of the main points, we can say that critical work on the self in psychology was fuelled in the first place by the view that Western theories explaining the self tended to ignore the importance of the social and historical conditions in which people existed. Developments in the study of language, which are at the centre of postmodernist work, used the concept of discourse to 'bring the social' into the psychology of the 'self'. Starting from the assumption that discourses are useful and functional, such theorists point out that, since different cultures exist in different conditions and are organised in different ways, then the ways in which the self is viewed will also vary. Anthropological and cross-cultural research has produced evidence to support this view, namely people across the world regard the 'self' in different ways, simply because they live differently. The typical notions about 'what is a self' which originate in the West are not the most 'advanced' ones, or the 'right' ones; they are just Western. Moreover, if generalisations of any kind are to be made, it appears that our ideas about the self are more unusual than most other people's. While other cultures tend to talk about the self in more collectivist and relational terms, by contrast Western views on the self tend to be 'individualistic'. It is not so much that someone is, say, decisive, autonomous, rational, caring, nurturing, sexy, with low or high self-esteem, intelligent, dumb, etc.; it is simply that in the West we have developed a way of speaking and a vocabulary which tends to explain why people act the way they do by focusing on the individual.

The implications of postmodern critique were discussed in relation to the development of new research questions in psychology which involved new methodologies, i.e. textual analysis informed by poststructuralist understanding of language. While these methodologies often lead to deconstructing popular accounts of the 'person', they also bring a number of insights which can be utilised to inform a new understanding of what it means to be a 'self'. Most importantly, the perspective presents us with a view whereby human beings and their identities are inextricably interwoven in culture, history (both personal and collective) and ongoing relationships with immediate others. While we argued that 'belonging' to a human community and being able to effectively participate in its making is desirable for all, we also outlined some of the main difficulties of such a possibility at present. Existing social practices and discourse mutually support one another and ensure the exclusion of different categories of people from the power structures in Western cultures. While the process of entry into mainstream culture is fraught with difficulties, the work of critical scholars (often deriving from the experiences of marginalised social groups) has contributed to the production of what Shotter (1996) calls 'critical tool making'. Such tool making may contribute to social changes as well as to new ways of understanding human subjectivity. These new ways will require a departure from established academic traditions, and currently are a 'genre' yet in the making. It would be nice to conclude this chapter with something like: 'and this is how the politics of identity can be successfully resolved'. Instead we hope to have proposed a new way of viewing the whole issue about the self on which we can all work together, for as Mama (1995) says, 'How does one end the beginning of something?'

Prejudice and discrimination

4

Introduction

According to Littlewood and Lipsedge (1989), every society has its own characteristic pattern of normative behaviour and beliefs. (See Chapter 9.) It must, therefore, deal with the threat which comes from those inside who deviate from those norms, as well as the threat posed by outsiders. 'Our' group (whether it be class, nation, race, etc.) is partly defined by those we exclude from it. However outsiders are supposed to differ from us, they are seen as an undifferentiated mass with a number of individual variations.

Even if they are not seen as physically dangerous, outsiders are threatening simply because they are different; their existence challenges our belief in our society as the 'natural' way of living, of normality. So, in order to confirm our own identity, we push the outsiders even further away, and '. . . By reducing their humanity, we emphasise our own' (Littlewood and Lipsedge, 1989).

How do we achieve this? Groups which are technologically less developed than we are tend to be seen as excessively cruel and 'sexual' (too little discipline), while those which are more advanced are seen as mindless automatons (too much discipline). Some societies see their neighbours as cannibals or witches or lunatics – the 'standardised nightmares of the community' (Littlewood and Lipsedge, 1989).

But at least outsiders are usually fairly easy to identify. This makes the 'outsiders in our midst' potentially even more dangerous, since they must first be identified before they can be isolated.

> *Accusations of witchcraft occur when the relations between people are ambiguous . . . Racist ideas in America came to full theoretical development only when slavery was ending. German anti-Semitism was directed against the hidden outsider who lay concealed within. Official racism in Britain worsened as immigrants have become British rather than consenting to remain migrant labourers.*
>
> (Littlewood & Lipsedge, 1989)

Definitions of who the outsiders are (both internal and external) change over time and according to political and economic circumstances. For example, war between European nations has usually resulted in black-white differences being shelved and 'our blacks' being accorded a temporary white status (Fanon, 1964). Foucault (1967) suggests that, in the early medieval period in Western Europe, the lepers were the victims of this terror of internal contagion, attention then shifting to those with VD, and later to the mentally ill. The leper house became the psychiatric hospital.

Clearly, some of these outsiders are more easily identifiable than others: racism and sexism reflect fairly obvious, visible and innate biological differences, while lepers *become* highly distinguishable as a result of disease. By contrast, the mentally ill are, generally, much more difficult to detect (at least by the non-professional); it is usually their behaviour, rather than their appearance, which is distinctive, and sometimes only their expression of private, subjective experiences 'gives them away'. Even less visible are gay men and lesbians (except for the few who conform to the popular stereotypes of effeminate males and butch females), whose status as outsiders can be camouflaged by leading 'normal' heterosexual lives as husbands and fathers, etc. By contrast, blacks cannot 'pass' as whites, or women as men, quite so easily. (An intriguing exception is the case of Anatole Broyard, one of America's leading literary critics, who died in 1990. It was recently revealed that he was black, but his light skin helped him to conceal the fact from the literary world, as well as from his own children!) (Kemp, 1996.)

Ironically, it is only when gay people make themselves visible ('come out of the closet') that they can begin to win their rights as human beings (Doyle, 1983). In 1973, the American Psychiatric Association passed resolutions removing homosexuality from its official list of mental disorders, followed a year later by the American Psychological Association. This demonstrates the influence of ideological and political forces on scientific definitions of 'reality': homosexuality was now *demedicalised*, no longer defined as a psychological abnormality. Nothing had changed objectively, only psychiatrists' and psychologists' *perceptions* of it!

While homophobia (the irrational fear and extreme intolerance of homosexuality) has primarily *religious* roots (the pre-Christian Jewish and early Christian condemnation of sex outside marriage and for any purpose except reproduction, even as an expression of love between husband and wife) (Doyle, 1983), racism has

Figure 4.1 Aphra and Dawn are lesbians who perform professionally with the group Divy Deak (an anagram of Dyke Diva), dressed as gay men. They describe themselves as 'reverse drag queens' (photo © Debbie Humphry)

different roots. While often seen as having originated in the political need for exploitation of resources and/or labour during slavery and colonialism, the strength of present-day racism cannot be adequately explained in terms of political and economic factors (Fernando, 1991).

Fernando (1991) believes that racism has been socially constructed over hundreds of years and that its origins are lost in the history of Western culture. Although evident predominantly in Western societies dominated by white people, racism has spread all over the world with the global spread of Western influence, through education, advertising, propaganda, political manipulation, economic pressure and the ordinary 'common sense' of the layperson. It is an integral part of Western culture, especially in the English-speaking countries and those involved in imperial domination of non-European peoples.

Although racism, in a broad sense, refers to anti-Semitism in Europe, and conflicts between Tamils and Sinhalese in Sri Lanka, Catholics and Protestants in Northern Ireland, and between Bosnian Serbs, Croats and Muslims in the former Yugoslavia, '. . . the contrast between victimiser and victim, exploiter and exploited, oppressor and oppressed, is at its starkest between Europe and Africa – black and white . . .' (Howitt and Owusu-Bempah, 1994).

The story so far

Defining terms: individual attitudes vs social practices

Psychologists usually agree that while *prejudice* refers to an *attitude* held by an individual, *discrimination* refers to some aspect of a person's *behaviour*; in other words, while the former is essentially private and internal, the latter is essentially public and external. Just as it is important to distinguish between them, so it is also important to understand the *relationship* between them. If they are, indeed, different, is it possible to find one without the other, and if so, does it follow (and does it make sense) that discrimination can be seen as a form of action which, while performed by individuals, reflects social forces and influences which lie *outside* the individual and are more powerful than the individual actor? In other words, if you do not have to *be* prejudiced (attitude) in order to perform prejudiced deeds (behaviour), might not those deeds be understood as *conformity* with social and cultural norms which demand discriminatory behaviour?

If so, the emphasis begins to shift away from the individual towards the society of which the individual is a member. According to Fernando (1991), we should distinguish between *racism* and *racial prejudice*, the former relating to society, the latter relating to the individual. By attributing racism to individuals ('racist' and 'racially prejudiced' are often used synonymously), the focus is put squarely on individuals as the 'culprits'; it follows from this perspective that, in order to remove or reduce the harmful effects of racism/racial prejudice, all that needs to be done is to change the attitudes and behaviour of certain individuals. Could it be that the terms we use to name and describe behaviour reflect our beliefs and assumptions about its nature and causes? If individuals are properly described as 'racist', for example, the implication is that racist societies are simply those composed of (large numbers of) racist individuals; this is a form of *reductionism* which clearly fails to distinguish between individual prejudice and social ideology.

Racism refers to an ideology, dogma or political stance which reflects the traditions and history of that society (Fernando, 1991). While racial prejudice may be regarded as the counterpart within the individual of society's racism, they are not one and the same. According to Wellman (1977, cited in Fernando, 1991), an attitude like prejudice must be seen within its 'structural context' – the distribution of power within the society, political constraints arising from external influence, rivalries between social classes, etc.

> *And once racial prejudice is embedded within the structures of society, individual prejudice is no longer the problem, it is* racism *that is the active principle. Racism is then essentially about 'institutionally generated inequality' based on concepts of racial difference; although it affects the behaviour of individuals, 'prejudiced people are not the only racists'.*
>
> (Fernando, 1991)

What we have said about racism and racial prejudice, also applies to other 'isms', such as *sexism* (inequality and discrimination based on gender), *ageism* (inequality and discrimination based on age) and *heterosexism* (inequality and discrimination based on sexual preference or orientation). These are commonly given (e.g. in psychology textbooks) as examples of *prejudice*, i.e. attitudes held by individuals, but in line with Fernando's distinction, they should all be regarded as ideologies, characteristics of a whole *society*.

While the term 'racially prejudiced' exists as a perfectly valid alternative to 'racist' when describing individuals, the equivalent terms 'sexually prejudiced' and 'age prejudiced' are both uncommon and clumsy. In the case of heterosexism, the individual counterpart is *homophobia*, the fear of homosexuals. These terms are both relatively uncommon, but they at least help to keep apart the social and individual levels.

The authoritarian personality: racism as racist individuals

Perhaps the best known and most influential reductionist theory of racism is the *authoritarian personality* (Adorno et al., 1950). According to Adorno et al., a combination of very strict and punitive and unloving parenting produces a personality structure which is predisposed to very strong proingroup and anti-outgroup feelings. However, Adorno et al. themselves recognised that the *content* of prejudiced attitudes is derived from society; in other words, it is society which defines the outgroups, the legitimate targets for discrimination.

According to Wetherell (1996), Adorno et al. were not suggesting that personality and child-rearing practices *cause* authoritarian, racist and fascist ideologies. However, such ideologies, which reflect prevailing social and economic circumstances, become especially attractive to the authoritarian personality, i.e. there is a mesh between an individual's character and the philosophy of life that he or she finds sympathetic among those on offer in a particular historical period. They argued for a complex interaction between psychological factors and socio-cultural conditions.

Similarly, Brown (1985) sees their research as describing:

> *. . . how and why certain individuals become* potentially *fascistic and ethnocentric. But precisely because they defer to authority such people are liable to* conform *to societal norms and would project their aggression on outgroups which are already perceived as such in their society.*

Conversely, if societal norms of prejudice and discrimination are sufficiently powerful, many people may engage in discriminatory behaviour who do not possess most or any of the characteristics of the authoritarian personality, so that, in practice, cultural or societal norms may be much more important than individual personality in accounting for ethnocentrism, outgroup rejection, prejudice and discrimination.

Despite their recognition of the influence of social ideologies, Adorno et al. focused on the prejudiced personality – the prejudiced individual rather than the 'prejudiced society', racial (and other kinds of) prejudice rather than racism (and other 'isms'). For example, attention is drawn away from institutionalised racism, such as apartheid in the 'old' South Africa. Something which needs to be understood at a societal level is being 'reduced' to the activity of individuals, and in the process the evils of society are being transformed into the psychological abnormality of individuals.

According to Wetherell (1996), the concept of the authoritarian personality is too unidimensional to grapple with the personal and social history which results in an individual espousing extreme racist views, such as those advocated by the British National Party (formerly the National Front). She cites Billig's (1978) study of the National Front, in which he concluded that in order to understand such an organisation, a multi-layered approach is needed: political allegiance is highly complex and personality is only part of the overall picture.

The authoritarian personality is presented as abnormal, very extreme and inflexible in the way the world is construed, having to deal with unusually intense repressed resentment and hostility (towards the parents) through displacing and projecting it onto others (minority groups in general). If prejudice and discrimination are manifestations of individual pathology, the investigator need look no further; society is not implicated. As Rattansi (1992) puts it, 'The mode by which the discourse of *prejudice* consigns racism to a form of irrationalism is, at bottom, a *pathologisation* of the individual subject . . .' By stressing the irrationality of racism, Adorno et al. obscured the *specificity* of racist sentiments, their orientation to a particular social context and to the pressing political issues of the day (Wetherell, 1996).

Why do particular minority groups in particular historical periods become the targets of racism? Although Adorno et al. saw the authoritarian personality as being prejudiced 'through and through' (i.e. hostile towards minority or out-groups in general), the focus was very much on racism, fascism, anti-Semitism and other extreme political attitudes. Since their research was undertaken, 'new' forms of prejudice have been identified (sexism, etc. – see above), while old forms are said to have mutated from explicit to implicit, so that racism is now much more subtle and covert. However, what has *not* changed over the years is the model: the metaphor is still of an individual disorder; for example, 'In modern racism, the overt symptoms have changed, but the underlying disease remains' (Brehm and Kassin, 1990, cited in Stainton Rogers et al., 1995). Although racism in the USA and UK may have become more subtle among the 'politically correct' from whom social psychology student participants are drawn, this is hardly true of those cultures in general (Stainton Rogers et al., 1995).

While we may describe individuals within a particular society as *xenophobic* (a *morbid* fear of foreigners, comparable to fear of insects or agoraphobia), such descriptions do not tell us why a society as a whole is racist (Littlewood and Lipsedge, 1989).

> *Racist attitudes may be manifest as a highly articulate set of beliefs in the individual, but they are also found in less conscious presuppositions, located in society as a whole . . . Racism is the quite specific belief that cultural differences between ethnic groups are of biological origin and that groups should be ranked in worth.*
>
> (Littlewood and Lipsedge, 1989)

Again, if it is individuals who are prejudiced (by virtue of having an abnormal personality which manifests itself as hatred of outgroups, etc.), how is it possible for a whole society to be racist? By definition, the authoritarian personality is a theory of prejudice based on *individual differences*, so unless every member of society can be described in this way (in which case the differences have been removed), how can such a theory account for society's racism?

Posing the question at all demonstrates the limitations of the theory, in particular its reductionist nature: it is *not* meaningful to explain whole societies in terms of the characteristics of its individual members, and it is even more absurd to try to reduce a whole society to the characteristics of just *some* of its members (i.e. those with an authoritarian personality)!

Racism is not a disease or a delusion, for in a racist society such beliefs are highly adaptive. In a racist society, the racist is the normal individual. To single out the most prejudiced, those who most accurately reflect the social view, and to call them mentally ill, is to find a scapegoat. We excuse ourselves by using the very mechanisms for which we condemn the racist. Everybody who benefits by racism in a racist society is, in some measure, a racist.

(Littlewood and Lipsedge, 1989)

Prejudice and discrimination in psychology, psychiatry and biology

The classification of people into racial types based on physical appearance has a long history in Western culture. While skin colour has been the most popular characteristic used for this purpose, others have included hair form, facial characteristics and skull shape and size. Darwin's (1859) theory of evolution introduced a concept of 'race' which differed from its predecessors. By analogy with his description of numerous 'races' within each species of animals, the idea developed that, while human beings as a whole constitute 'a species' with fertile mating within it, individual (human) 'races' represent 'varieties' or 'subspecies', each being partially isolated reproductively from the others (Banton, 1987, cited in Fernando, 1991).

While this view allowed for the continual modification and development of races (rather than seeing them as static sets of inherited characteristics), in his *Descent of Man* (1871) Darwin talked of the likely extinction of 'savage races' because of their inability to change habits when brought into

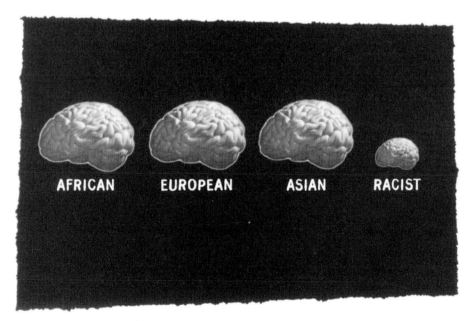

Figure 4.2   Poster from the European Youth Campaign against Racism and the Commission for Racial Equality

contact with 'civilised races', he then joined Galton in calling for the control of how different races breed in order to ensure the survival of the latter.

20th-century genetics at first described different races in terms of blood types, but this proved unreliable. More recently, scientific advances have enabled geneticists to identify human genes that code for specific enzymes and other proteins. However, these attempts have also proved to be of little value: the genetic differences between the classically described races (European, Indian, African, East Asian, New World, and Oceanian) are, on average, only slightly higher (10 per cent) than those which exist between nations within a racial group (6 per cent), and the genetic differences between individual human beings within a population are far larger than either of these (84 per cent) (Fernando, 1991).

Although 'pure' races are no longer identified with any confidence, the traditional view persists that people resembling each other in obvious physical ways, such as skin colour, belong to a 'race' that represents a genetically distinct human type. Anthropologists, biologists and medical people are all guilty of perpetuating the myth, despite the widely held belief that 'race' has ceased to have a scientific meaning. While geneticists occasionally use it as shorthand for something like 'large, long-isolated, inbreeding population or gene-pool', this is *not* race as popularly understood. 'Race' is a *social*, not a biological category:

> *Any theory that puts Colin Powell, Shirley Bassey, Maya Angelou, Frank Bruno and Snoop Doggy Dogg in the same 'isolated inbreeding population' cannot have much going for it. Humanity is a single gene-pool, parts of which were relatively (rarely completely) isolated for longer or shorter periods of time.*
>
> (Richards, 1996)

Similarly, Wetherell (1996) argues that 'race' is a social as opposed to a natural phenomenon, '. . . a process which gives significance to superficial physical differences, but where the construction of group divisions depends on . . . economic, political and cultural processes . . .' She points out that many writers prefer to put quotation marks around 'race' to indicate that we are dealing with one possible social classification of people and groups rather than an established biological or genetic reality.

Scientific theories of racial differences, especially physical anthropology in the 18th and 19th centuries, were used to justify the colonial exploitation which was in full swing at that time. For example, in Hunt's Presidential Address to the Anthropological Society of London in 1853 (cited in Fernando, 1991), he declared that (a) the Negro is a distinct species from the European, using intelligence as one criterion; (b) similarities between the Negro and the ape are more numerous than between the European and the ape; (c) the Negro becomes more humanised when in his natural subordination to the European than under any other circumstances; (d) the Negro can only be humanised and civilised by Europeans; (e) European civilisation is unsuited to the Negro's needs and character.

Scientists from a wide range of disciplines, including the new science of psychology and the somewhat older branch of medicine called psychiatry, contributed to the 'proof' of the superiority of white races over all others. According to Fryer (1984, cited in Fernando, 1991), virtually every scientist and intellectual in 19th-century Britain took it for granted that only people with white skin were capable of thinking and governing.

As these sciences developed, so racism became integrated into scientific thinking. Nowhere was this more evident than in the attempt by psychologists to demonstrate, objectively and scientifically, the intellectual inferiority of blacks, beginning with the Army Alpha and Beta tests of IQ given to American soldiers during the First World War. Nobles (1976) sees the study of 'Negro' intelligence as among the worst abuses of scientific psychology to date.

In a famous case in America, the National Association for the Advancement of Coloured People sued Wilson Riles (Superintendent of Public Instruction for California), the Californian State Board of Education and the San Francisco School Board, over placement of five black children into classes for the educable mentally retarded (EMR). The Plaintiff's complaint was that the placement had been based largely on standardised IQ tests which are racially and culturally biased against black children. Judge Peckham decided in favour of the Plaintiff (1980):

> We must recognise at the outset that the history of the IQ test, and of specific educational classes built on IQ testing, is not the history of neutral scientific discoveries translated into educational reform. It is, at least in the early years, the history of racial prejudice, of social Darwinism, and of the use of the scientific 'mystique' to legitimate such prejudices.
>
> (Peckham, 1979, quoted in Hilliard, 1992)

IQ tests were consequently banned as a criterion for placing children in EMR classes in California.

The IQ test can be regarded as an ideological weapon, used by a white-dominated society to oppress minority groups, especially (but by no means exclusively) American blacks (African Americans) and people of Afro-Caribbean origin in the UK. As scientists, psychologists responsible for the construction and use of IQ tests are meant to be, and are seen by society at large to be, objective and value free. However, as Gould (1981) most convincingly demonstrates, their theories and instruments have too often been dangerous reflections of their own personal motives and racial, class and sexual prejudices.

The attempt to present racist views as scientific 'fact' is revealed in the (not very subtle) form of 'scientific racism'. Chris Brand, a psychologist at the University of Edinburgh, whose book *The g Factor: general intelligence and its implications* was withdrawn by the publisher (John Wiley) in April 1996 before publication, denies being a 'racist' while being 'perfectly proud to be a racist in the scientific sense', i.e. a believer in the view that race and psychology have deep links (most likely genetic). According to Brand (quoted in Richards, 1996), 'You won't find any psychologist of repute who has said anything different [than that black people have lower intelligence] since the turn of the century'. However, according to Richards (1996), dozens of psychologists of unimpeachable repute (including Bartlett, Freud, Piaget and Skinner) have either disagreed or, more commonly, not even been interested in the question. Some who have agreed turn out not to have been so reputable after all. For example, Cattell was pro-Hitler in the 1930s, a ruthless racist eugenicist all his life, who even contemplated genocide ('genthenasia'). Brand is simply wrong!

So if, as Richards believes, the race-IQ debate is scientifically dead, why does it refuse to lie down and be buried? According to Tucker (1994, *The Science and Politics of Racial Research*, cited in Richards, 1996) and others, it is financed by far-right-wing agencies such as the Pioneer Fund (founded by the US Nazi millionaire Wickliffe Draper in the late 1930s), which has awarded huge grants to Jensen and Shockley in the US, Rushton in Canada and Lynn in Ulster.

According to Howitt and Owusu-Bempah (1994), instead of asking 'who are the racists in psychology?', we should ask 'who is not racist in psychology?'

> *Psychology breathes in the air of racism. A misplaced and unfounded trust in the independence of psychologists from racial bias takes its toll in that the profession regards racism as the evil work of a few ... Psychology continues to treat racism largely as something apart from itself, something the discipline studies, and not what it does ...*

The sexist nature of psychology is demonstrated in a variety of ways, including the biased nature of the study of sex differences (e.g. Unger, 1979) and discrimination against women within psychology itself. According to Paludi (1992), for example, the history of psychology is the history of the contributions of men, with women psychologists being kept largely invisible, despite their enormous contribution, both historically and currently.

One manifestation of this is the devaluation (by men) of the areas of psychology in which women are traditionally more numerous and which they seem to prefer, compared with the traditionally 'male' areas. The former include person-oriented and service-oriented fields such as educational, developmental, clinical psychology and counselling, while the latter are the academic-experimental areas, including learning and cognitive psychology, which are regarded (by men) as more scientifically rigorous and intellectually demanding (Paludi, 1992). Could it be that women are 'channelled' into certain fields of psychology, which then are defined as 'inferior' simply because they are populated mainly by women? Certain individuals act as *gatekeepers*, determining the career paths of others; in the case of psychology, the gatekeepers are usually men.

A classic demonstration of racism within psychiatry are the two diagnostic categories proposed by the American psychiatrist, Cartwright, in 1851, at the time of slavery, meant to apply exclusively to black people: (a) *Dysaesthesia Aethiopis* was a disease which afflicted all 'free negroes' without a white person to direct and take care of them, 'the natural offspring of negro liberty – the liberty to be idle, . . . wallow in filth, . . . indulge in improper food and drinks'. Symptoms included breaking, wasting and destroying everything they handle, tearing or burning their clothing, stealing from others to replace what they have destroyed, and apparent insensitivity to pain; (b) *Drapetomania* was, quite simply, the disease which caused slaves to run away (Fernando, 1991). (Racism in psychiatry is further discussed in Chapter 10.)

Revisions and reconceptualisations

Social Identity Theory: doing what comes naturally

Ironically, one of the major attempts to address the limitations of the authoritarian personality theory, namely Social Identity Theory (SIT) (Tajfel and Turner, 1979) has itself been criticised on the grounds that it presents racism (and other forms of prejudice) as 'natural', helping to justify it. Stemming from Allport's (1954) claims that stereotypes are 'categories about people' and that 'The human mind must think with the aid of categories', Tajfel (1969; Tajfel et al., 1971) saw the process of categorisation as a basic characteristic of human thought. SIT implies that the tendency towards in-group favouritism is natural and in-built. This will manifest itself in situations (such as the minimal group experimental procedure) where there is the opportunity to distribute 'rewards' to unknown, unidentified others who resemble each other only in the most superficial and arbitrary ways and where there is no explicit or institutionalised conflict or competition between the groups.

If intergroup hostility is natural and built into our thought processes as a consequence of categorisation, then racism, conceived as a form of intergroup hostility (or in-group favouritism), may also be construed as natural; in terms of the distribution of resources, racism is thus justified as the norm ('charity begins at home') (Howitt and Owusu-Bempah, 1994).

Of course, Tajfel never intended SIT to be seen as a justification of racism; indeed, he was a life-long opponent of racism, having lost his family and community in the Holocaust. Taken out of context and elevated to the status of a universal human characteristic, SIT is easily *misrepresented* as an explanation and justification of racism (Milner, 1991, cited in Howitt and Owusu-Bempah, 1994).

According to Howitt and Owusu-Bempah (1994), the issue is not whether people do often favour their own group at the expense of others, but what is meant by the claim that this is natural (which Tajfel seemed to believe required no explanation). If we accept that out-group hostility and in-group favouritism are 'natural' once groups have been so categorised, then the problem is not justifying the hostility/favouritism but explaining how out-group categories (the 'us's' and 'them's') are created and continue despite major changes in the characteristics of out-groups and the dominant 'host' nation. How are in- and out-groups socially generated and maintained?

Wetherell (1996) believes that SIT emphasises the 'ordinariness' of racism and its continuity with other forms of group behaviour. Intergroup conflict is *not* seen as a psychopathology or the result of irrational prejudice, but as a form of behaviour involving complex psychological states which are also central to more positive group actions, such as developing a sense of solidarity with others, group loyalty, cohesiveness and national belonging. Racism is only inevitable given a particular social context where 'racial' categories become significant and acquire meaning as group divisions. These categories are not natural but become powerful as a result of social history.

Discursive psychology: racism as racist talk

According to Wetherell (1996), the derogatory categorisations and group stereotypes that form the substance of racist talk are best seen as rhetorical and communicative acts, as opposed to primarily perceptual or cognitive phenomena. Instead of constituting errors, biases and shortcuts in people's information processing, group descriptions and stereotypes are developed as part of stories and accounts which are *ideological* in nature, i.e. they need to be understood in terms of the patterning of social relations, power and inequalities within a society.

> *To understand the forms group descriptions and categorisations take, the social psychologist should look first to the nature of the broader patterns of communication in which group categorisations are embedded rather than to the structure and modes of operation of the human mind.*

> (Wetherell and Potter, 1992)

This way of looking at racist talk is central to *discursive psychology*. Like social representation theory (see Introduction), discursive psychology is a *social constructionist* approach, but instead of being concerned with how people make sense of their worlds through simplified representations, discursive psychology is concerned with how people construct versions or accounts of the world in the course of their practical interactions and how these accounts or versions are established as solid, real and independent of the speaker. In saying and writing things, people are performing *actions*, i.e. people use language and discourse in order to achieve particular goals and purposes.

According to Potter and Wetherell (1987), attitudes do *not* exist as a coherent, relatively permanent orientation to an issue or object (which is how they have, traditionally, been understood); when people are interviewed about an issue, what they say does *not* represent something inside their head. This radically different view of attitudes was based on the analysis of transcripts (*discourse analysis*) from two interview studies, one about race relations in New Zealand, the other about the police handling of a riot. In both studies, individuals' accounts typically showed considerable *variability*, i.e. at various points in the interview, depending on what question the interviewer was currently asking, respondents gave answers that appeared to be quite incompatible *if considered to be manifestations of the same underlying attitude* (such as attitudes towards the Maoris).

Instead of taking what people say as an expression of internal states or underlying processes, Potter and Wetherell believe that we should look at what people are doing with their talk, what purposes their accounts are achieving; and since a person may be trying to produce different effects at different points in the interview, it is not surprising that we find the variation in their answers that we do. What people say is intentional, socially directed behaviour which performs certain functions for them.

Having said this, we nevertheless all draw upon the same tools from the toolbag from time to time (Burr, 1995). These tools are what Wetherell and Potter (1988) call *interpretative repertoires*, which represent a consistency in accounts which is *not* located at the level of the individual speaker and which enable people to justify particular versions of events, excuse or validate their own behaviour, fend off criticism and otherwise allow them to maintain a credible stance in an interaction.

For example, Potter and Reicher (1987, cited in Burr, 1995) analysed the way that 'community' and 'community relations' were used in different accounts of the St Pauls' riot in Bristol in 1980, in local and national papers, TV reports, records of parliamentary proceedings and transcripts of interviews with some of those involved. Different accounts, from different sources, used the 'community' repertoire to achieve different effects. For example, sometimes the riot was portrayed as a problem of 'community relations': the police were represented as forming part of a wider community suffering from difficulties in interpersonal relations and trust. Alternatively, the repertoire was used to characterise the event as an open conflict between the 'black community' and the police.

By using the repertoire in these contrasting ways, those giving the accounts could 'warrant' different versions of the event and motivations could be attributed to participants and blame apportioned, as well as solutions proposed. The 'community' repertoire, therefore, can be seen as a collection of metaphors and linguistic devices which could be drawn upon by almost anyone in order to produce a particular, desired representation of an event; these are a *social* resource, available to all those sharing a language and culture (Burr, 1995).

Similarly, Wetherell and Potter (1988) identified three repertoires used in the New Zealand study. One of these, the *culture-fostering* repertoire, presents the view that Maori culture should be encouraged and protected, both for the sake of its uniqueness and distinctiveness *and* in order to provide Maori people with a sense of their own history and cultural roots. This is based on the notion that Maoris lack something that ought to be regained: they are culturally deficient. So what function does this serve for respondents?

> *Firstly, it seems to make sense of another commonplace understanding that Maoris have a deprived social position and are discontented, through using the idea of rootlessness and loss of identity. In this lay sociology, people without roots – those who have 'lost' their identity in some way – do not perform well and are likely to agitate. Secondly, in using the notion of cultural deficit, speakers can effectively place Maori problems elsewhere, removed from their own responsibilities and actions. In this way speakers can convey that they themselves are in no way to blame for these problems . . . Respondents virtually never characterised the inclusion of Maori culture in a way which involved active effort or change on their own part; effort and change was depicted as a Maori problem and duty.*
>
> (Wetherell and Potter, 1988)

These respondents were concerned with positioning themselves acceptably with regard to the moral rules and expectations of their culture:

> *The person is therefore located as an actor or performer in a moral sphere, a person whose prime aim in construing her or his account is to construct herself or himself and her or his actions as morally justifiable.*
>
> (Burr, 1995)

Just as we noted earlier that psychology as a discipline tends to see racism as 'out there', something to be studied by it but not a problem within itself, so Wetherell (1996) maintains that the white reader (and author) of writings on racism is often assumed to be beyond racism, to be considering the actions of other people who are different from us.

The social constructionist perspective questions any such simple construction of identity, that we are either all 'good' or 'bad', 'liberal' or 'illiberal', 'racist' or 'anti-racist'. We need to ask about *all* the internal dialogues and cultural narratives from which identities are constructed and the effects of privilege and disadvantage on these possible identities.

Identity is always in production, a *continuing process* rather than an already accomplished fact. While 'race' is an important marker, it interacts with other identities (such as gender, class and sexuality); each of these involves complicated communities of interpretations, but the dividing lines between these have become more blurred and there is increasing awareness of the *diversity* of people's social positions.

> *These distinctions [race, gender, etc.] are important ones because each is massively socially significant, yet it is also clear that identity is more complicated than 'race' or ethnic group membership* per se.
>
> (Wetherell, 1996)

Applications and implications

According to Paludi (1992), in response to the neglect of women's contributions to psychology and to the recognition that women's history has the potential to transform women's self-understanding, a subfield of *women's history in psychology* has evolved in recent years. This draws on Lerner's (1979) model, namely (a) finding lost or overlooked women and putting them back into the history (*compensatory history*); (b) noting women's contributions (*contribution history*); (c) noting how history is constructed through a male (*androcentric*) perspective and reconstructing it from the perspective of women (*reconstruction history*).

In 1973, the American Psychological Association (APA) formed the Division of the Psychology of Women, which, in turn, has a Section on the Psychology of Black Women as well as Committees on the Psychology of Latinas and Asian-American Women. In her Presidential Address to the APA in 1987, Bonnie Stricklund pointed out that women now constitute about one third of all employed psychologists and more than half of those gaining PhDs in psychology each year. She predicted that psychology will become the first science to be 'feminised', i.e. it will have more women than men. This, she claimed, will allow the investigation of a set of research problems that weren't consistent with, or couldn't be solved by, the *androcentric paradigm*, such as women's friendships with other women, rape, sexual harrassment, battered women, eating disorders and sexism in psychopathology (Paludi, 1992).

Far from advocating that psychology should be value free, objective and 'scientific', many feminist psychologists argue that we should stop denying the role of values and recognise that psychological investigation must always take wider social reality into account. Research is always based on biases and underlying values. Many have called for a new, *value-laden approach to research*; until and unless psychology 'comes clean' about its values and biases, it will never be able to reflect adequately the reality of its subject matter, i.e. human beings.

> . . . *just as there is no . . . [APA] . . . division on the psychology of men or white people, there is no special topic area called heterosexual studies . . . 'Psychology', the official entity, values those experiences that are white, male, heterosexual, young, middle class, able bodied and North American; thus has the universe of 'human behaviour' been defined. 'Special topics', including lesbian and gay issues, have been defined as of special interest only, not in the core curriculum in reality or emotionally.*
>
> (Brown, 1989, quoted in Paludi, 1992)

Feminist research insists that researchers become actively involved in the research process, taking the perspective of the participants; they are not detached investigators but become an integral part of the whole process (Paludi, 1992).

Another term for 'North American' in Brown's list of valued experiences above is *Eurocentric* (or *Euro-American*), which refers to a set of general guiding principles, fundamental values and customs, and psychobehavioural modalities which, together, make up the individual's *world-view* (Nobles, 1976). The world view is reflected in the individual's self-concept which, according to Nobles (1976) and others, is fundamentally different for African Americans (the *extended* self, reflecting the *Afrocentric* world view) compared with those from a white, American or European (Anglo-Saxon) background.

> *. . . there is a growing awareness that existing theories and research in psychology do not sufficiently consider the uniqueness of the experience of African Americans. One explanation for this phenomenon is the faulty assumption that Eurocentric psychological theories and research can be blindly applied across a variety of cultural groups.*
>
> (Burlew et al., 1992)

The much cited article by Nobles (1976), referred to above, was originally presented to the National Association of Black Psychologists in America in 1974. That Association was established in 1968, and one of its major goals is 'to develop an approach to psychology that is consistent with the experience of black people'. It has played an important role in stimulating and contributing to the body of literature on the psychology of African Americans (Burlew et al., 1992). The *Journal of Black Psychology* was founded in 1974.

According to Watson (1973, cited in Fernando, 1991), black psychology is concerned with three main areas: (a) providing a picture of black family life that is different from the one presented by conventional white wisdom, stressing the strengths within it and its way of making out in the world that blacks live in; (b) highlighting the excessive numbers of black people being diagnosed as mentally ill and, in so doing, exposing white racism as the cause of black mental illness; (c) questioning the validity for black people of established IQ tests and devising new tests geared to black experience.

In American psychiatry, black professionals have formed an association, the Black Psychiatrists of America (1973). Although there is some concern in the UK about racism in psychiatry, this has not led to the adoption of any particular strategies to counteract it. However, the Transcultural Psychiatric Society (UK) changed its constitution in 1985 to specify opposition to racism as a primary objective, and in 1987, the Royal College of Psychiatrists established a committee to consider 'problems of discrimination against trainees, other doctors in psychiatry and patients on the grounds of race'. Biennial Reports of the Mental Health Act Commission (1987, 1989 – a sort of Government inspectorate) have identified the needs of black and ethnic minorities as a priority, quoting the effects of racism on black people (Fernando, 1991).

A radical pro-Afrocentric and anti-Eurocentric viewpoint is taken by

Baldwin (1992), who sees black psychologists as perpetuating the domination of Eurocentric theories and models, either by applying them directly in trying to explain black people's psychological reality, or by trying to 'blackenise' them to make them seem more relevant. Either way, he argues, black psychologists commit the fundamental 'self-destructive' error of failing to look to their own 'African' reality to give intellectual direction and inspiration to their own theoretical developments.

As for clinical psychology, the 'Euro-centric-oriented training' which black psychologists receive, has virtually made them incapable of providing any type of truly culturally relevant mental health or psychological services to black people. Often, this takes the form of treating black people as if they were 'white people in black skin' (Baldwin, 1992). (See Chapter 10.)

He urges black psychologists to work towards the liberation of black people from Western oppression and to help them to move towards positive black mental health, the highest level of which is the vital psychological orientation called African self-consciousness.

Interpersonal relationships

5

Setting the scene

'One of the most important aspects of psychology – and social psychology in particular – is the study of relationships we have with others' (Humphreys, 1996). Little wonder, then, that there are few current social psychology textbooks which do not deal with this topic, many dedicating considerable coverage to it. However, it is only in recent times that the topic has gained sufficient respectability to have its own journals (for example, the British Journal of Social Relationships). To quote from Humphreys (1996) again:

> ... *it is only recently that this topic has been regarded as worthy of study. Perhaps psychologists previously believed that the dynamics of relationships such as friendship, love and family ties and feuds could not easily be studied by the scientific method or that they were somehow too trivial to be of importance to academics and intellectuals. Relationships were regarded as being too much 'of the real world' or too populist.*

We will use the term 'interpersonal' rather than 'social' relationships here for two reasons. Firstly, the term 'social' could be taken to include relationships between a person and a non-human other (e.g. a pet or, more contentiously, an 'ego-extension' such as material possessions or things we produce). Secondly, 'interpersonal' conveys a connotation of intimacy which has characterised much of the research, as we shall shortly see. This contrasts with more macro social relationships, such as group membership.

What then is a relationship? Argyle and Henderson (1985) say, 'The easiest way to define relationships is in terms of regular social interaction over a period of time, together with the expectation that this will continue for at least some time in the future'. Argyle, Henderson and Furnham (1985) distinguished 22 forms of relationship and discovered that all of them were to be found in Italy, Japan, Hong Kong and Britain. Argyle (1992) contends that the most important forms of relationship are:

- friendships;
- marriage and 'other kinds of cohabitation';
- parent–child relations;

Figure 5.1 Psychological research into social relationships has typically focused upon those deemed important in Western cultures (such as the romantic couple) rather than those which are important in non-Western cultures (often, the extended family)

- siblings and other kin;
- work relations, especially between mates and with supervisors;
- neighbours.

As we shall see later, although numerous relationships may be found to exist in many different cultures, their importance varies greatly between different cultures. For example, Moghaddam et al. (1993) and Segall et al. (1990) argue that, whereas in Western cultures romantic love in dyads (two-person 'groupings') is viewed as one of the most prominent, valued and sought-after relationships, in the majority of non-Western cultures greater emphasis is placed upon family ties and responsibilities and kin.

Let us conclude this initial orientation by asking why relationships should be so important to us. Argyle (1994) argues that humans (as well as non-human animals in the case of the first six factors given below) have the following needs, all of which can be satisfied in relationships:

- biological needs (e.g. eating and body comforts);
- dependency (e.g. help and support);
- affiliation (shown by physical proximity and smiles, etc.);
- dominance (e.g. being allowed to take the lead in decision-making);
- sex;
- aggression;
- self-esteem and ego-identity;
- other motivations which affect social behaviour ('needs for achievement, money, interests and values').

Another account is given by Howitt et al. (1989) who offer a list of functions which may explain why we struggle to maintain close personal relationships despite the pain that they can cause (see Box 5.1).

Box 5.1   Howitt et al.'s (1989) account of the human need for relationships

Security   Knowing we can turn to someone on whom we can rely makes us more confident about exploring unknown situations. It helps to remember that there are people who care for us.

Self-worth   The knowledge that others value us, almost no matter what, makes it easier to accept ourselves.

Expressing feelings   When we are upset, we find it comforting to discuss and express our feelings.

Social comparison   Comparing our views on a problem with those people who care for us may help us to decide on what action to take.

Advice elicitation   Close others, with whom we are willing to share a little of ourselves, may provide inspiration as well as practical help.

Sense of well-being   Being with our favourite people may create a sense of feeling good or well-being. Having a good time may make us feel good about ourselves and distract our minds from pondering on difficulties.

Clearly there are overlaps with the list of factors given by Argyle. What is evident is that relationships are one of the central aspects of the quality of human life. It is rather surprising therefore that it did not become a central research theme in (social) psychology long before it did and that much of the research to date has been characterised by a desire to straitjacket relationship research into highly contrived explorations such as those requiring students to rate the attractiveness of another student (with whom they have been randomly paired) and seeing how this affects their desire for another 'date' (what else can one 'go on' with such limited information and exposure?) and cutting published wedding photographs in half and judging the attractiveness of the brides and grooms and correlating the results to see if people marry others of judged equal attractiveness to themselves. Furthermore there has been an unjustifiable concentration upon short-term studies of the initial aspects of relationship formation with no long-term follow-through and a neglect of non-heterosexual dyadic relationships (Humphreys, 1996). Let us continue by examining in more detail some of these 'peculiarities' of focus.

The story so far

Let us take a different view of 'dominant' accounts. Instead of examining what has been written in mainstream psychology texts let us, for a change, examine a different type of exposure. In Britain, one of the major 'exposures' of academic psychology is via A-level syllabuses and examinations. For example, in 1996 over 22,000 candidates entered for the AEB examination alone (and there are two other Boards also offering A-level Psychology). It is therefore important to appreciate the influence of the A-level syllabuses in terms of what students of psychology in Britain learn about the subject.

The syllabus which has dominated the world of A-level Psychology for the last decade (1986–1997) focuses upon interpersonal relationships through 'Theories and determinants of affiliation and attraction' (AEB 0651, I C.2). The two best-selling books written to this particular syllabus – Gross (1996) and Hayes (1994) – both carry substantial sections on interpersonal attraction (substantially less on affiliation), and this in turn has also given a particular view of how psychologists have studied interpersonal relationships to many thousands of psychology students. (In fairness, it should be pointed out that both of these textbooks also dedicate considerable space to other topics related to this field, such as theories of social relationships.) Many other new social psychology textbooks (e.g. Hogg and Vaughan, 1995) and new editions of well-established 'best-sellers' (e.g. Baron and Byrne, 1994) also accord prominent and detailed coverage to attraction as one, if not the, principal components of interpersonal relationships.

The situation is further compounded by the fact that, notwithstanding more recent writings (e.g. Wood and Duck, 1995), two of the most widely published and read British social psychologists, Michael Argyle and Steve Duck, have also written about interpersonal relationships through almost exclusively essentialist and realist (see Introduction) research and reviews of principally 'mainstream' relationships (e.g. heterosexual dyads, Western families and same-sex friendships).

Affiliation

Cardwell (1996) defines affiliation as 'the tendency for people to seek the company of others. It is also seen as a motivational variable, in that people differ in their need to affiliate'. He adds:

> *People may affiliate for a number of possible reasons:*
> * *to avoid loneliness that may exist in the absence of a social network of friends and relatives;*
> * *to reduce anxiety, either because others provide a source of information that might reduce our anxiety, or because others provide emotional support;*

*We started sneaking around and going out late at night and no one
else knew. I didn't tell any of my friends . . . We got along great,
sexually and emotionally, though she said I didn't express my
feelings enough . . .*

Thus, by having a 'double' life, Frank has managed to position himself as a
subject in two contradictory discourses. By compartmentalising and
separating his 'love' time from his 'sport' time, he has achieved a way of
dealing with the contradictions between the two. In so far as by daytime he
is 'one of the lads' and by night-time a 'Romeo' of a kind, Frank's self is
de-centred. In the same way, his friendship with the 'boys' and 'love'
relationship with the girl are worlds apart. To talk only in terms of
'satisfaction', as mainstream psychology has tended to do, is to ignore the
conflicts which are introduced between the two by our inevitable location as
subjects in contradictory discourses, as illustrated above.

Applications and implications

In a number of ways, the implications of a postmodernist perspective for
the study of human relationships are evident from the discussion so far.
Thus, for example, the notion that we cannot claim universal truths has
lead to two main trends of research on the topic. Firstly, critical
deconstructive work has been employed to illustrate points of view
embedded in theories claiming universal status (e.g. O'Connor's (1992)
work on women's friendships). Secondly, during the last decade, much
scholarly work has been accumulated which is increasingly more sensitive
to the diversity of human relationships when the social, economic and
cultural positioning of those investigated is taken on board. We have seen,
for example, with Franklin II's (1992) study how black men's friendships,
while developing characteristics like no other types of friendships, make
sense and are relevant to people existing in these very sociopolitical
conditions. In this way, one implication of the postmodern perspective is
that it frustrates the development of theories which, while claiming
universal status, speak from a white point of view and end up labelling in
negative ways the kind of relationships that 'others' develop.

The notion that human relationships are structured in language (rather
than purely described by it) has contributed to a change in research aims,
types of data and methodologies employed. Thus, for example, new
research questions have begun to examine cultural discourses in order to
illustrate how what is 'attractive' is already scripted in our discursive
heritage. In this way, who is attracted to whom becomes not an individual,
sex-specific characteristic, but can be seen as an outcome of a dialectical
dialogue between cultural categories and the people who embody them
(Tseëlon, 1995). The focus on language has also lead to examining more

specifically what people do with it. Thus, for example, we saw from Appel's (1983) study how specific linguistic devices are employed by beauticians to tacitly accuse women of failing to look after themselves and be beautiful. Such studies are illuminating because they illustrate how the 'beauty myth' is sustained and reproduced in day-to-day linguistic practices. In addition, since language and *not* the 'individual' is the focal point of investigation, the scope of psychological research areas has broadened. Areas, such as historical texts, literary genres and a variety of media materials, previously seen as 'belonging' to other disciplines, are now also relevant to psychologists (e.g. Coward, 1984; Tseëlon, 1995).

The view that we inhabit a complex social world and that in some ways we participate both on micro and macro platforms has led researchers to keep a 'dual focus' while conducting their research. Thus, for example, we saw how Holstein and Gubrium (1994) were able to illustrate how the family discourse was incorporated in a debate between a father and his son to achieve their various, more personal goals. At the same time, the authors were able to illustrate how we can trace and locate such discourses to larger, or macro, institutional settings. Thus, while mainstream research has tended to strip away social context, postmodern studies tend to be sensitive to the 'profound contextuality' of any investigated matter.

Just in the way postmodernists have argued against the notion that the self can be 'integrated', 'coherent', an entity-like object, they have also directed attention to fragmentations, contradictions and conflicts embedded in personal relationships. Drawing on Hollway's (1989) work, we outlined three main cultural discourses which Western people deploy to organise and structure heterosexual love relationships. Since these are incommensurable, they have implications for the contradictions and inconsistencies in people's lives.

Aggression and violence

Introduction

While many psychologists, as well as scientists from other disciplines such as biology and ethology, see *aggression* as 'natural' and normal, a form of behaviour shared by most animal species, human and non-human alike, *violence* is something altogether different. Crime statistics include a category for 'violent crimes' (but not 'aggressive crimes'), the public is warned about approaching certain escaped prisoners because they might be dangerous (i.e. violent), Mary Whitehouse condemns sex and violence on television (not sex and aggression). It is also worth noting that only human beings are described as displaying (or being capable of) violence; the natural form of this kind of behaviour is aggression, while violence implies an aberration, something destructive and pathological. So how have they been defined?

A widely accepted way of distinguishing between them is in terms of their *outcomes*. So, according to Campbell and Muncer (1994), for example, aggression encompasses a variety of verbal and emotional as well as physical attacks, sharing the actor's intention to hurt or control the victim who wishes to avoid these outcomes; violence produces actual bodily

Figure 6.1   The aggressive behaviour displayed by this pair of eagles is usually seen as natural and normal, while violence (actual or threatened), which often involves the use of specially manufactured weapons, is a uniquely human aberration

injury and is subject to criminal prosecution. Similarly, Archer (1994) says that, while 'aggression' concentrates on the act, 'violence' focuses on the consequences. Importantly, what they have in common is the intent of harming someone.

Again, while aggression can be symbolic (e.g. verbal), violence denotes 'a form of human aggression that involves inflicting physical damage on persons or property' (Moyer, 1976). For Berkowitz (1993), violence refers to an extreme form of aggression, a deliberate attempt to do serious physical injury.

Perhaps the major objection to distinguishing violence from aggression in these ways is that it detracts from the *psychological* aspects of violence. Howitt and Owusu-Bempah (1994) discuss psychological violence in the context of racism (see Chapter 4). They begin by asking: if racism is abhorred for its most violent extremes, how do we construe the effects of racism which doesn't leave corpses? Just what do we think the experience of racism is like for the victim?

The horror of physical extermination and the sterilisation of millions carried out throughout the world, in the name of eugenics, shouldn't detract from the *psychological* violence and oppression of racism. Oppression and racism have a personal urgency and immediacy for black people; their daily encounters with racism do not encourage them to approach the subject with the cold detachment that white academics do (even those who have themselves been the victims of discrimination, such as Adorno et al. and Tajfel – see Chapter 4). Racism, anti-Semitism, sexism and other forms of oppression, together with their associated adverse psychological and social effects, are almost never seen as violence, even when they are intentional. But they are often perpetrated *unconsciously* and, as we saw in Chapter 4, are so much part of the fabric of society that their existence is (genuinely) not recognised by the majority of those who belong to the groups accused of perpetrating them.

From a psychological point of view, the most flagrantly unsatisfactory aspect of such definitions is that they negate or invalidate the victim's definition of what constitutes a violent act. Black writers are more likely to take this into account. For example, Bulham (1985, quoted in Howitt and Owusu-Bempah, 1994) defines violence as 'any relation, process or condition by which an individual or a group violates the physical, social and/or psychological integrity of another person or group'. From the victim's perspective, racism inhibits human growth, limits productive, living, and causes death; it matters very little, if at all, whether or not the perpetrators are conscious of or intend the psychological harm they inflict (Owusu-Bempah, 1985, in Howitt and Owusu-Bempah, 1994).

The story so far

Theories of aggression: innate drives or environmental triggers?

Traditionally, psychological *theories* have attempted to account for aggression (as opposed to violence), and this is true also of theories that derive from other disciplines, such as ethology. According to Campbell and Muncer (1994), theories have fallen into two categories: *instrumental* and *expressive*.

Instrumental theories focus on the *consequences* of aggression in terms of social and material rewards gained by the actor as a result of his or her aggression; these may include coercive power, social control, normative approval, self-esteem, management of identity, plus a variety of other social and material rewards, including territory, money and peer approval. Campbell and Muncer maintain that in recent years, instrumental theories have become so widely accepted that they seem self-evident; but their uniqueness can be seen by comparing them with *expressive theories*, which focus on the build-up of drive, stress and arousal which is discharged through aggressive action.

Freud (1920, 1923), Lorenz (1966), Storr (1968) and Dollard et al. (1939) were particularly concerned with the motivational component that energises and potentiates the behaviour. For example, both Freud and Lorenz saw aggression as instinctive, such that aggressive energy builds up in the individual human or non-human animal and, if not expressed in some way (directly or indirectly, such as through sublimation) will eventually 'spill over' and be discharged; in other words, aggressive behaviour is spontaneous (it will happen when aggressive energy has reached a certain threshold) and does not occur in response to environmental stimuli.

Dollard et al.'s *frustration-aggression hypothesis* was intended partly to 'translate' some of Freud's psychoanalytic concepts into learning theory terms. While agreeing with Freud that aggression is an innate response, Dollard et al. argued that it would only be triggered by frustrating situations and events. However, it soon became apparent that the frustration-aggression hypothesis, in its original form, was an overstatement. It has subsequently been revised by several psychologists in a variety of ways, from a variety of theoretical perspectives. For example, Miller (1941), one of the original authors of the theory, claimed that frustration is an instigator of aggression but situational factors (such as learned inhibition and fear of retaliation) may prevent actual aggressive behaviour from occurring; hence, frustration is not a sufficient cause of aggression. Bandura (1973) argued that frustration might be a source of anger, but frustration-induced arousal (like other types of arousal) could have a variety of outcomes, of which aggression is but one; whether it actually occurs is more the result of learned patterns of behaviour triggered by environmental cues.

Berkowitz's modification of the frustration-aggression hypothesis, in some ways quite similar to Bandura's, concentrates more on the discharge mechanisms by which the aggressive drive is converted into aggressive action: what are those environmental cues that trigger learned patterns of behaviour? According to Berkowitz (1966), frustration produces anger; to be converted into actual aggression, what is needed are certain *cues*, environmental stimuli associated either with aggressive behaviour or with the frustrating object or person. Aggressive or violent behaviour is, at least partly, a reaction to specific features of the surrounding situation which 'pull out' responses that heighten the strength of the behaviour. This happens either when the environmental stimuli have an aggressive meaning for the aggressor and/or when they somehow remind the aggressor of decidedly unpleasant experiences (the *aggressive-cue theory*).

In a series of experiments designed to test the aggressive-cue theory, Berkowitz used the same basic paradigm in which participants are told, upon arrival, that they will be paired with another person (a confederate) in a study concerned with the physiological reactions to stress. To do this, they will be asked to offer a written solution to a problem. Stress will be introduced by their solution being evaluated by their partner, who will deliver between one and ten electric shocks to them (according to how they evaluate the solution). After completing their solutions, half the participants receive a single shock, while the rest receive seven (all fairly mild), the lower number of shocks indicating a very favourable evaluation. Following this first stage, participants take their turn in evaluating the confederate's solution, either after seeing a violent film (*Champion*, depicting a brutal prize-fight and starring Kirk Douglas) or a non-violent film (showing highlights of an exciting track race) or in the presence of objects that are/are not associated with violence (such as a shotgun and revolver or badminton rackets and shuttlecocks respectively). Aggression is measured as the number of shocks delivered by the participants.

The findings of several experiments using this paradigm suggest that people's actions towards others are sometimes influenced in a relatively thoughtless, automatic way by particular details of the immediate situation: the mere physical presence of weapons, even when not themselves used in the performance of aggressive actions, may still increase the occurrence of such behaviour. But is there any reason to doubt the validity of the paradigm?

Evaluating the aggressive-cue paradigm: reducing the social to the individual?

According to Stainton Rogers et al. (1995), giving someone an electric shock can only be claimed as an index of aggression if participants see it as such; pressing a button *isn't* an inherently aggressive act. For this to count as a measure of aggression, it is not sufficient that the experimenter defines it in this way; participants need to be given a plausible storyline which, as we saw above, took the form of 'feedback' about the quality of performance on a problem-solving task. But is there any guarantee that it is actually interpreted in this way? Participants could equally well consider that they are engaging in a necessary, if troubling, 'pro-social' act ('being cruel to be kind') as opposed to an aggressive one; alternatively, some participants may have suspected that the shocks weren't real (based on familiarity with Milgram's experiments which had taken place three or four years earlier). Either way, the paradigm lacks *internal validity* (Stainton Rogers et al., 1995). What about its *external validity*? According to Stainton Rogers et al. (1995):

> *... much is being stretched in assuming that pressing buttons in a laboratory, and, say, mugging an old lady in an alleyway are determined by essentially the same cause-and-effect process.*

Given that aggression has no objective or fixed meaning, trying to construct ways to measure it objectively is highly problematic; to study aggression in the laboratory requires an operational definition (of the independent and dependent variables) which becomes both narrow and of dubious representativeness, even in terms of the theories being tested. It has been estimated that 65 per cent of laboratory studies of aggression have used the administration of electric shocks as their main index of aggression.

> *It is not just in its atypicality as a context for aggression that the laboratory context should be troublesome (e.g. few subjects are drunk, few subjects know their victims) but also in terms of the constraints upon behaviours enacted within it. For obvious reasons, ethics committees cannot allow even the possibility of murder!*
>
> (Stainton Rogers et al., 1995)

(A further aspect of the lack of external validity of the experimental paradigm is the almost exclusive use of *male* participants. This is discussed further below in relation to feminist research into male violence towards women.)

According to Stainton Rogers et al., far from being 'very preliminary results', experiments like those of Berkowitz contain actionable lessons over aggression in real life. Indeed, Berkowitz (1972) used the frustration-aggression hypothesis in attempts to explain civic unrest and rioting in the USA: aggressive and destructive behaviour displayed in riots are consequences of the frustration caused by social disadvantage, and arousal is caused by environmental factors such as a rise in ambient temperature and the presence of aggressive cues (such as police carrying weapons).

> *Although historians might be able to demonstrate a variety of connections between economic crises and civic unrest, it is hard to believe that these are best explained by people in a rioting crowd all simultaneously experiencing high levels of frustration, and all coincidentally chancing upon the same target on which to act out their aggression.*
>
> (Stainton Rogers et al., 1995)

Explanations in terms of the arousal of innate drives and responding to environmental cues have the effect of sanitising and de-politicising acts of protest (such as the Chinese students in Tiananmen Square in 1989) (Stainton Rogers et al., 1995), as well as removing them from their proper and particular social and historical context. This can be seen as one form of *reductionism*, such that behaviour which needs to be understood at a more general level (social/political/historical) is explained at a more particular, specific level (innate drives, etc.); the latter, by definition, are properties of individuals. (See Adorno et al.'s authoritarian personality theory of prejudice, Chapter 4). Billig (1976) makes this point by saying that explanations based on the frustration-aggression hypothesis, although they incorporate factors and cues in the environment, are basically individualistic/individualising explanations: they ignore the *socially constructed* nature of the appropriate target for aggression as well as the socially defined repertoire of aggressive acts (again echoing criticisms of Adorno et al.'s account of prejudice).

Again, the fact that most theories and explanations emphasise processes within the individual (*intrapersonal/intrapsychic*) and interpersonal acts of aggression (as opposed to *intergroup* aggression), whereby the frustrated ambitions of groups within society are reduced to individual frustrations, can be linked to a conservative ideology designed to maintain the status quo (Billig, 1976). The emphasis on emotional factors has led to a neglect of social circumstances, but even more so to a neglect of addressing the socially constituted nature of aggression; psychologists' decisions about which aspects of aggression to study have produced a focus on phenomena which do not require them to examine their own ideological position and the society they live in (Stainton Rogers et al., 1995). Stainton Rogers et al. (1995) also make the point that such explanations are guilty of the fundamental attribution error (Ross, 1977).

Revisions and reconceptualisations

The football hooligan as 'just following rules'

An alternative social-psychological explanation, which emphasises the sociological within social psychology, is the ethogenic approach used by Marsh et al. (1978) in their study of football hooliganism (*The Rules of Disorder*): we cannot simply assume that we can understand the aggression of another by viewing aggressive acts from the outside:

> *... the best, though not necessarily the ultimate, authorities as to what the action 'actually' is are the actors themselves. In their accounts are to be found,* prima facie, *the best interpretations of what went on, from the standpoint of the problem of the interpretation of action. This follows almost directly from the fact*

that the actors were the ones who intended the action in the first place.

(Marsh et al., 1978)

They adopted a phenomenological approach, which involves using a variety of techniques (mainly participant observation and interviews, both formal and informal) to gather self-reports of behaviour, in an attempt to uncover the rules which football hooligans attribute to their behaviour. However, they did not take fans' accounts at face value: much of the content was expressive (designed to promote a dangerous and exciting image as opposed to accurately describing events).

Marsh et al. were less concerned with aggression or violence as such and more concerned with trying to interpret the social lives of particular segments of contemporary young people. Arguing that all human beings need to achieve personal dignity, a sense of self-worth and personal identity, they claim that certain sections of young people in contemporary British society are deprived of the means of achieving these within the conventional worlds of school and work. So they are forced to turn for their achievement to the world of their own sub-culture, for such sub-cultures provide a forum for 'a sense of belonging and prestige'.

For urban young men in particular, it is the football terraces that allow for the emergence of sub-culture rituals. The ritual 'warfare' between rival groups of supporters allows the construction of alternative social hierarchies, within which those who are destined to fail in conventional terms (school, work, etc.) may be successful. Confrontation between rival supporters is usually symbolic and consequently non-violent; such symbolic battles include the parading of gear (scarves, boots, denim jackets), the yelling of chants and the chorusing of football songs. Rival fans who follow their group's rules quite carefully can avoid real physical harm to themselves or others. For example, chasing the opposition after a match ('seeing the others off') does not inevitably end in violence, since part of the agreed code is not to actually catch anyone.

However, confrontation does move beyond the merely symbolic (though probably less often than the media would have us believe) and physical injuries are sustained (occasionally, even fatalities). The point is, however, that, as far as Marsh et al. are concerned, *all* such confrontation, whether ritualised or violent, is governed by rules; far from being lawless, random behaviour indicating a mob's loss of control, rules exist to ensure that aggression (which they see as an underlying human

Figure 6.2 Soccer hooligans showing lawless, uncontrolled aggression, or football supporters engaging in predominantly ritualised, rule-governed behaviour?

predisposition) is kept within certain bounds but at the same time providing the means by which reputations can be made and defended.

Seen in this light, soccer hooliganism is a kind of staged production. Much of what appears to be aggression simply is not; rather, it is part of an identity-enhancing symbolic display, a cultural drama. Marsh et al. were less concerned with aggression as such than with explaining the reasons why certain social behaviours will appear to be aggressive and described and defined as such, both by the participants and the wider social group. While aggression may be a taken-for-granted human predisposition, what society defines, recognises and problematises as aggression may well be a set of functional activities dressed up as a cultural drama:

> *If we look for the explanation of aggression within the individual actor, rather than addressing the complexity of the cultural drama, we fail to recognise the social, political and economic factors which are involved in such social activity.*

(Stainton Rogers et al., 1995)

Soccer hooliganism can also be understood in more social terms. For example, Murphy et al. (1990, cited in Hogg and Vaughan, 1995) describe how soccer arose in Britain as an essentially working-class sport and how, by the 1950s, working-class values to do with masculine aggression had already become associated with the game. Government (seen as middle class) attempts to control this aspect of the sport can backfire because they enhance class solidarity and encourage increased violence that generalises beyond matches. This sort of explanation points towards an analysis in terms of intergroup relations and the sub-cultural legitimation of aggression (Hogg and Vaughan, 1995).

Another feature of Marsh et al.'s study of soccer hooliganism was the view that human social life is a product of interaction between sequences of actions and talk about those actions: 'Everything we do can be redone by talk'. In other words, a range of *discourses* of aggression emerges which permits us not only to think in different ways but to conduct ourselves in different ways (Stainton Rogers et al., 1995). This represents one of the ways in which aggression is *socially constructed*: there are no objective 'facts' about aggression (or anything else), only accounts, interpretations, ways of talking about it and attempts to represent it. (See the section below on social representations of violence.)

Sociobiology and the evolutionary psychology of male violence

According to Gilbert (1994), there are two broad, polarised positions within Western society, regarding the explanation of male violence:

- We are, by nature, basically aggressive/violent and selfish; there is in all of us a beast waiting to get out. Furthermore, these traits are somehow more basic and more at the core of the male mind than, say, love, compassion or morality.

- Our violent/destructive behaviour owes much to the environment and to distortions and deprivations of socialisation.

Current evolutionary approaches suggest that this polarisation is misleading (e.g. Buss, 1991; Trivers, 1985).

According to Daly and Wilson (1994), every living creature has been shaped by a history of Darwinian selection, as has every complex functioning constituent part of every living creature. The complex functioning parts of living creatures that psychology is primarily concerned with is their 'minds'. But minds are 'private', so the data of psychological science can only be the mind's behavioural manifestations, and psychological hypotheses can only be claims about the processes and mechanisms that produce individual behaviour (the 'psyche'). *Evolutionary psychology* is 'the science that studies the psyche in the light of current knowledge and theory about the evolutionary processes that created it' (Daly and Wilson, 1994).

Evolutionary psychology (new social Darwinism or 'neo-Darwinism') is a development of *sociobiology* ('The systematic study of the biological basis of all social behaviour'; Wilson, 1975), according to which, as part of human beings' broader adaptation to the environment, males and females are equipped with instincts and physical attributes for particular types of activity and responsibility (Durkin, 1995). Evolutionary psychologists contend that sociobiologists often ignore the mind's role in mediating the links between genes and human behaviour. According to Cosmides and Tooby (cited in Horgan, 1995), the mind consists of a number of specialised mechanisms or modules, designed by natural selection to solve problems faced by our hunter-gatherer ancestors, such as acquiring a mate, raising children and dealing with rivals; the solutions often involve emotions such as lust, fear, affection, jealousy and anger.

While evolutionary psychology is mainly concerned with universal features of the mind, it also maintains that natural selection has constructed the mental modules of men and women very differently as a result of their divergent reproductive roles. According to Thornhill and Wilmsen Thornhill (1992, cited in Edley and Wetherell, 1995), human sexual psychology is *dimorphic*, i.e. the respective adaptations differ in men and women. The sexes differ in their feelings about whether, when and how often it is in their interests to mate; because women are more selective about their mates and more interested in evaluating them and delaying intercourse (since the fitness costs of any single act of intercourse, i.e. its effects on the chances of her genes being successfully passed on to her offspring, have always been greater for women), men, to get sexual access, must often try to overcome the female resistance. The use of violence by men can be a very effective means of controlling the reluctant woman.

According to Thornhill and Wilmsen Thornhill's 'rape adaptation hypothesis', during human evolutionary history there was enough directional selection on males in favour of traits that solved the problem of forcing sex on a reluctant partner to produce a psychological tendency specifically towards rape. One 'design feature' of male sexual psychology is the man's ability to remain sexually competent in the face of a woman's resistance; this presumably reflects past fitness benefits of pursuing and achieving intercourse despite female resistance. Not only does this hypothesis recast an oppressive form of behaviour in a much more positive light (it is 'adaptive'), but it also represents it as a natural characteristic of men ('they can't help it'). Not surprisingly, it has been condemned as not simply trying to explain men's sexual coercion, but *justifying* it (Edley and Wetherell, 1995).

Feminists especially would be repelled by such a proposal. Ironically, they also *share* with evolutionary psychologists the view that male violence (sexual and non-sexual) cannot be dismissed as pathological (see the discussion of Marc Lepine below), but for very different reasons. For evolutionary psychologists, all forms of violence are seen as evolved adaptation, a form of self-interested competitive behaviour benefiting *individuals* (as opposed to the whole species) (Daly and Wilson, 1994).

While Lorenz (1966) saw aggressive behaviour as evolved adaptation, he argued that aggression between conspecifics (members of the same species) that resulted in the serious injury or death of one or other of the animals to be indicative of pathology or 'mishap'. He effectively ruled out the considerable evidence that animals are often killed by members of their own species as being relevant to the study of aggression as adaptive, and helped thereby to promote the view that human beings are unique as a species in their murderous tendencies.

However, evidence of widespread animal conflicts is exactly what an evolutionist would expect to find (Daly and Wilson, 1994). The human evidence that is cited in support of the adaptive nature of violence includes the relationship-specificity of human violence; circumstances that elicit it are threats to fitness (the ability to survive in order to pass on one's genes to one's offspring), and the targets of violence are generally not merely those who are available but those with whom the aggressor has substantive conflict and, hence, something to gain from subduing them.

Competitive conflict is predominantly a same-sex phenomenon; same-sex rivals are usually more similar in the resources they desire than are opposite-sex individuals. In particular, opposite-sex individuals are often the 'resource' being competed for, especially in male–male conflicts. Sexual rivalry is a universal and sometimes deadly source of conflict in humans; a substantial proportion of homicides can be seen as the outcome of dangerous confrontational competition amongst men (typically aged between 15 and 34; Daly and Wilson, 1990; Wilson and Daly, 1985; 1993b) over women (Daly and Wilson, 1988a).

Men also assault their wives, the very resource for which rivals compete. The use of a credible threat of violence can effectively deter rivals, but it can also deter a wife from pursuing courses of action that are not in the man's interests. As genetically unrelated individuals, the interests that they have in common are usually confined to the welfare of their joint offspring. Likely sources of marital conflict predictive of substantial fitness consequences in human evolutionary history include sexual infidelity (and the risk of men's cuckoldry, i.e. being father to another man's biological child), desertion, and conflicts over allocation of parental effort. Although male violence towards wives is universal, the *contexts* in which it occurs are remarkably few: infidelity, her unilateral decision to leave, 'disciplining' a 'too independent' wife and male sexual jealousy:

> *. . . the particular cues and circumstances which inspire men to use violence against their partners reflect a domain-specific masculine psychology which evolved in a social milieu in which assaults and threats of violence functioned to deter wives from pursuing alternative reproductive opportunities, which would have represented substantial threats to husbands' fitness by misdirecting parental investment and loss of mating opportunities to re-productive competitors.*

(Daly and Wilson, 1994)

Consistent with this interpretation is the finding that men kill their estranged wives more often than estranged wives kill their husbands (Daly and Wilson, 1988b). Daly and Wilson concluded that jealousy is the leading motive in spousal homicide: males are interested in protecting their own gene pool from being mixed with those of others ('If I can't have her, nobody can').

While these data are consistent with an evolutionary view, other interpretations would also fit these data. For example, marital dissatisfaction has been found to correlate highly with serious partner abuse. Alcohol and drug abuse have also been found to correlate significantly with severe spouse abuse (Pan et al., 1994, cited in Wilson et al., 1996) as has low socio-economic status (Straus et al., 1980, cited in Wilson et al., 1996).

As far as *parent–offspring conflict* is concerned, genetic relatedness predicts reduced conflict and enhanced co-operation, because the genetic posterities of blood relatives co-vary in direct proportion to the degree of relatedness, i.e. the closer the blood tie, the more genes are shared and hence the greater the incentive to help the relative to survive in order to produce offspring with those genes. In support of this prediction, a study by Daly and Wilson (1982) of homicides in Detroit in 1972 showed that co-residents biologically unrelated to the killer (spouse or not) were 11 times more likely to be murdered than co-residents who were genetic relatives.

Similarly, evolutionary psychologists would predict that the risk of maltreatment of stepchildren would be greater than for genetic offspring. Supporting evidence comes from findings that step-families are over-represented in child-abuse samples (Daly and Wilson, 1981; 1985; 1987; 1993), samples of child homicides perpetrated by parents (Daly and Wilson, 1988b), samples of children dying before age 15 (Hill and Kaplan, 1988, cited in Daly and Wilson, 1994) and samples of children suffering head and other injuries (Wadsworth et al., 1983; Ferguson et al., 1972; both cited in Daly and Wilson, 1994).

According to Daly and Wilson (1994), there are a number of circumstances where we would expect some reluctance to invest in a newborn, including:

- doubt over the offspring being the putative parent's own;
- indications of poor offspring quality and reduced reproductive value;
- extrinsic circumstances (such as food scarcity, lack of social support, needs of older but still nursing offspring) making it unlikely that a child would survive during human evolutionary history.

The great majority of ethnographic accounts of infanticide in non-industrialised societies reflect one or other of these categories (e.g. Daly and Wilson, 1984; 1988a; Wilson and Daly, 1993a), as do variations in risk of physical and sexual abuse of own offspring (Daly and Wilson, 1981; 1985).

As we shall see later in the chapter, there is a cross-culturally universal sex difference in the human use of physical violence, whether it be fist fights, homicides, warfare or the slaughter of animals (e.g. Daly and Wilson, 1988a). According to evolutionary psychologists, the competent use of violent skills contributes quite directly to male fitness: both successful warriors and game hunters have converted their success into sexual, marital and reproductive success.

> *Men have evolved the morphological, physiological and psychological means to be effective users of violence.*
>
> (Daly and Wilson, 1994)

Again, as we shall see later on, young male adults are the principal perpetrators of potentially lethal violence, as well as its main victims. Why? For Daly and Wilson (1994), the answer lies in the social demands and agenda that faced ancestral men and women in particular life stages. Young men were both especially formidable and risk-prone. In the foraging (hunter-gatherer) societies in which the human psyche evolved, the young man who would acquire a wife had to display powers in hunting, warfare, the capacity to defend his interests, to women or any young man who might hinder or facilitate his ambitions. Compared with other male mammals, young adulthood is particularly competitive among humans because human social complexity can make the consequences of differential performance in that stage enduring and hence even more crucial.

Changes in muscle strength at puberty, as well as superior male motor performance (especially strength and quick energetic bursts, as distinct from balance and precision) make young men psychologically specialised to embrace danger and confrontational competition. As car drivers, they both underestimate objective risks and overestimate their own skills, compared with older drivers. Men's suicide rates also maximally surpass those of women in young adulthood (Daly and Wilson, 1994).

Violence and gender: expressive and instrumental representations

According to Campbell and Muncer (1994), when men and women talk about violence, two very different representations are made. For women, *expressive* concerns feature prominently, that is, they are primarily about the discharge of anger, with the actor being portrayed as out of control as if she were possessed by some demonic force. For men, by contrast, *instrumental* concerns predominate, focusing on how aggressive acts are directed at physically overcoming or subduing the challenger, with the actor needing to maintain a level of control in order to achieve that goal.

Campbell and Muncer believe that part of gender socialisation entails the acquisition of appropriate *social representations* of specific phenomena, including aggression (see Introduction), and findings from studies of the causes of domestic violence are consistent with this gender difference. The predominant explanation of why men beat their wives (based on largely American research) is that they need to maintain power and control. Such violence is more common where there are status differentials in education and occupation which place the husband in an inferior position. Attempts to assert or maintain control over decision-making, social relationships, family finances and spouse's freedom of movement have all been identified as salient factors in wife-beating, as well as attempts to compensate for power deficits outside the home.

Bowmaker (1983, cited in Campbell and Muncer, 1994) maintains that male sub-cultures play a role in supporting wife-beating: men who are most integrated into peer sub-cultures which support patriarchical dominance of the family are more severe in domestic violence.

Developmentally, exposure to violence as a child is a powerful predictor of adult domestic violence: boys from violent families acquire an instrumental theory of violence through modelling and vicarious and, ultimately, direct reinforcement (e.g. Bandura, 1973).

> *The literature, then, is very largely in agreement that male violence in the home is an instrumental act aimed at asserting or maintaining control, and that men who beat their wives are most likely to be those who, in terms of marital power structure, personality, sex-role adherence or peer-group affiliation, have a particular sensitivity to issues of male control.*

(Campbell and Muncer, 1994)

As far as the causes of aggression by wives is concerned, the primary responses to the well-replicated findings that similar percentages of women and men admit to at least one act of serious violence in the preceding year (e.g. Archer and Ray, 1989; Marshall and Rose, 1987; both cited in Campbell and Muncer, 1994) are to question the validity of the measures, minimise the importance of this area of research or to assert that violence by wives is a defensive response to male-initiated violence.

If women view aggression as an expressive act involving loss of self-control (as opposed to an attempt to control others), then they are most likely to show aggression when stress and frustration are high and/or when self-control is low. Both these elements of the female 'violence equation' are affected in marriage: 'push' forces are heightened in the domestic arena. Men's violence increases regularly as a function of stress, but women's violence remains considerably lower than men's until a high level of stress is present, when their violence shows a dramatic increase. Women seem to suppress their stress more effectively until some critical level is reached (Campbell and Muncer, 1994).

Archer and Lloyd (1985) agree with feminist writers who claim that violence is a *male* (rather than a human) problem. For example, there are still vast sex differences in overt acts of violence as reflected in homicide statistics, violent crime, accounts of violent acts in public, major acts of violence in a domestic context, and the use of violence by organised groups (police, army, politically motivated groups outside the law) (Archer, 1994). However, as we noted above, women *do* commit acts of violence: approximately 40 per cent of family homicides are committed by women (Campbell and Muncer, 1994), and homicide statistics for the USA (but not other countries) show almost as many husbands are killed by their wives as vice-versa (Archer, 1994). However, the men killed by their wives are more likely to have been wife beaters (60 per cent) than the women killed by their husbands were likely to have been husband-beaters (15 per cent). Moreover, women who killed in marital relationships differed from other women in abusive relationships who didn't kill in terms of the extremity of their *husbands'* behaviour (including murder threats and physical attack) (Brown, 1987, cited in Campbell and Muncer, 1994). Similarly, in a study by Dobash et al. (1992, cited in Archer, 1994), almost all the wives who killed their husband were motivated by self-defence, often following years of physical violence at the hands of their husband. Men's motives are usually very different, often jealousy related.

From an expressive aggression perspective, the salient dimension of a woman's experience is the traumatic build-up of stress: an intolerable level of stress results in loss of self-control which leads to lethal violence ('I can't take this any more'). From an instrumental aggression perspective, the salient dimension of a man's experience is loss of control of his spouse: several studies of men's accounts of why they killed their wives suggest that there is an escalating series of events in which she fails to obey orders or challenges his self-esteem and power ('Do what I tell you to do') (Campbell and Muncer, 1994).

It could be argued that instrumental aggression is prototypical, i.e. it represents a 'best instance' or ideal case of what aggression means (especially when 'violence' is being discussed as opposed to 'aggression'). If, as we have seen, expressive aggression often takes the form of self-defence or the response to an intolerable build-up of stress caused by another's violence, and if this is typically the kind of violence displayed by women, and if instrumental aggression, more typically displayed by men, is motivated by the need for power and control and the wish to inflict harm upon the victim, then 'aggression' denotes the latter rather than the former.

This analysis of the term is consistent with the observation that 'most acts of aggression which may result in injury or death (and fear of these) are carried out by males, and in particular young males' (Archer, 1994).

> *The position adopted by most authors is that a critical assessment of the present evidence indicates that men commit the bulk of the serious cases of physical violence towards women and children, and of course are largely responsible for sexual aggression. If we add to this the much higher rate of within-sex violence by males than females, it more than justifies singling out male violence . . .*
>
> (Archer, 1994)

So, not only can aggression/violence be taken to denote instrumental aggression when not otherwise qualified, but it can also be taken to denote a characteristically male form of behaviour (when not otherwise specified); hence the feminist belief (alluded to earlier) that violence is a *male* problem, rather than a human problem.

Feminism and the politics of masculinity

From a feminist perspective, what defines men is their power in relation to women, their advantages and privileges. The possession of power cannot help but have crucial consequences for those who possess it; inevitably, men's characters and psychologies will be structured and shaped through this relationship with women (Edley and Wetherell, 1995). More importantly from a practical point of view:

> *Feminism has provided a context in which many women, throughout the world, have been enabled to name their experiences of violence and abuse and speak openly about them ['breaking the silence'] . . .*
>
> (Kelly, 1988)

Cherry (1995) cites the case of Marc Lepine who, in 1989, murdered 14 female students at the University of Montreal before killing himself. Inevitably, the media, as well as social scientists and others, speculated as to the motive for the killings. For many feminists, the answer was horrifyingly clear: Lepine had made a political statement that pushed violence against women to its ultimate expression, namely, mass murder. His suicide note revealed the very real link between gender and aggression in his troubled mind: it was followed by a 'hit list' of 19 radical feminists, but instead of murdering high-profile feminist activists, he acted against women engineering students whose inroads into a male-dominated world might just as easily have fed his rage.

Lakeman (1990, cited in Cherry, 1995), a feminist activist, analysed the media's tendency to avoid viewing Lepine's actions as the expression of male violence towards women and the women's movement. They individualised the murders, portraying him as a madman acting out a brutal scenario. By asking 'Is there a little bit of him in all men?', an analytic framework is generated that contextualises Lepine's actions in the study of men's daily lives and the cultural construction of masculinity (Cherry, 1995).

Sexuality and male violence

One of the main achievements of feminism has been to draw attention to the strong and uncomfortable links between male sexuality and male violence. For example, the combination of desire, sexual climax and murder is almost entirely a male preserve:

> *There has never been a female Peter Sutcliffe (the Yorkshire Ripper).*
> *Women have committed very brutal murders; they have killed*
> *repeatedly; they have killed at random. But in all the annals of*
> *recorded crime, no woman has done what Peter Sutcliffe did (or Jack*
> *the Ripper, or Christie, or the Boston Strangler).*
>
> (Cameron and Fraser, 1987 (*The Lust to Kill*), quoted in Edley and
> Wetherell, 1995)

According to Cherry (1995), traditionally, questions as to why men violate women's bodies and their lives were answered in an individualised way, and blame was often located within women themselves. This is an example of 'blaming the victim', which, in turn, can be explained in terms of the *just world hypothesis* (Lerner, 1965; 1980), according to which we believe that when 'bad' things happen to people, it is because they are in some way 'bad' people, so that they have at least partly 'brought it upon themselves', i.e. people get what they deserve. For example, in identifying common myths and stereotypes about sexual violence, Kelly (1988) says that in the case of domestic violence, there is a mythical belief that some women are masochistic, seeking out violent men, and if they don't leave their violent partner, it can't be that bad ('they enjoy/want it'); women provoke men by nagging, not fulfilling their household 'duties', and refusing sex ('they ask for/deserve it'); it only happens to working-class women, women who are 'bad' housewives, or those who saw or experienced violence as children ('certain kinds of women or in certain kinds of families'); it wasn't violence, only a fight; ('they tell lies and exaggerate'); if they had fought back, the man would have stopped: they are abused because they are weak and passive ('if they had resisted, they could have prevented it'); and the perpetrators witnessed or experienced abuse as a child or under extreme stress due to pressure of work or unemployment ('the men who do it are sick, ill, under stress or out of control').

However, theorising male violence towards women has evolved since the late 1960s, when feminists began a systematic study of rape. Before then, rape was studied from a perspective of individual psychology and mental health, bolstered by psychoanalytic writings, studies of the psychopathology of imprisoned rapists and the new field of victimology (Clark and Lewis, 1977, cited in Cherry, 1995). Accordingly, rape was seen as sexually motivated and female precipitated. Throughout the 1970s, many feminist researchers developed their work alongside and outside mainstream social psychological thinking and research, partly as a result of the omission of women as participants and targets in the experimental studies of aggression, such as those of Berkowitz (see above). Cherry (1995) proposes a number of reasons why feminist researchers did not simply add women to the highly stylised aggression paradigms of the 1960s and early 1970s:

- A simple 'add women' approach wouldn't provide detailed information about the range and commonness of experiences women have with male violence – you have to listen to women who have experienced it. A shift from laboratory to survey and interview methods better suits the knowledge required and marks a substantial shift in scientific practice among feminist researchers.
- Knowledge gained from talking to women challenged the idea that male violence towards women has much in common, both *quantitatively* and *qualitatively*, with intra-sex violence (male–male/female–female) and/or female violence towards men.
- By conducting studies that reduce the experience of violence in women's lives to a laboratory paradigm that stresses antecedent-consequent (IV-DV) relations, there is an implicit agreement to an investigative practice that produces generalisations about female-precipitated violence, i.e. men's violence towards women is legitimated as 'natural' reactions to provoking stimuli (women's behaviour, such as frustrating men's wishes, etc.). Women's accounts of violence suggest that their alleged 'frustration' and 'attack' are not precipitators of male violence but *rationalisations* that men use *after* the fact of violence. Once again:

  > *Exclusive reliance on modes of inquiry that stress mechanistic thinking lessens the likelihood that male aggression involving women will be explored in the context of masculine identity and its connections to legal, political and economic privilege.*

  > (Cherry, 1995)

- Research 'for women's sake' (rather than for its own sake) names the phenomenon 'male violence towards women' and begins to explore the experiences of violence in women's lives. Describing the phenomenon as 'the experimental analysis of interpersonal aggression' provides a gender neutrality which obscures women's experience.

Throughout the 1970s, analysis of rape from the victim's point of view emerged as a competing theoretical framework to previous work. For example, Susan Griffin's article *Rape, The All-American Crime* (1971, cited in Cherry, 1995) argued that rape is *not* a sexual crime but a violent, political act; the threat of rape functions as a form of social control which affects all women. A 'male protection racket' exists whereby individual men are supposed to protect women from all other men; women become dependent on the goodwill of their male protector and more vulnerable to abuse by him. Seen as an aspect of close male–female relationships, rather than an aspect of the generalised phenomenon of 'aggression', feminist research distinguished between different 'types' of rape, such as date and marital.

During the late 1970s and 1980s, research began to document the incidence of a number of forms of sexual violence, including rape, domestic violence, child sexual abuse, sexual harassment and violent pornography; rape no longer had a privileged place, as the full range of men's use of force and coercion was recognised (Cherry, 1995; Kelly, 1988). Myths, such as those described above regarding domestic violence, function to minimise the assaults and reveal underlying attitudes which may have as much impact on how women and girls see their own experiences as on how others respond. They help to create stereotypes about which men commit sexual violence, which females it happens to and offer a causal explanation; they may deny the violence, normalise it, pathologise the offender and/or the victim, all of which will deflect responsibility from men and undermine women's and girls' experience.

Kelly's (1988) feminist definition of sexual violence is aimed at countering such myths and stereotypes:

> *... any physical, visual, verbal or sexual act that is experienced by the woman or girl, at the time or later, as a threat, invasion or assault, that has the effect of hurting her or degrading her and/or takes away her ability to control intimate contact.*

Culture and male violence

According to Goodwin (1994), the wider *cross-cultural perspective* on relationship aggression has been rarely explored. For example, it is only Americans who 'date': the term is uncommon in the UK and even less meaningful in cultures where 'dating behaviour' is not permitted. Cross-cultural contextualisation is important because aggression in the relationship has different *meanings* in different cultural contexts, and it is a way of testing different theoretical perspectives.

For example, the strong ethos of social exchange in the US (a strongly *individualist* culture) may lead certain men to feel that, once they have kept their end of the bargain (paying for a meal/driving her around in an expensive car), she should keep hers (i.e. sex); failure to do so may cause him to feel justified in sexually assaulting her (Gordon and Donat, 1992, in Goodwin, 1994). But in most *collectivist* cultures, the value of direct social exchange is less evident, with interaction governed by broader values reflecting the collective goals of the community (Leung, 1988, in Goodwin, 1994).

Again, women in individualistic societies are often caught in a double-bind, being both attracted to their partner and having to deal with the possibility of unwanted advances (Burgoyne and Spitzberg, 1992, in Goodwin, 1994); this often produces equivocation, misunderstanding and potential aggression. Such problems are, of course, less likely to arise in societies where outside parties closely supervise or regulate premarital interactions (such as Muslim countries) (Goodwin, 1994) and may explain why rape is reported less often amongst Hispanic women in the USA who usually originate from the collectivist cultures of South America (Sorensen and Siegel, 1992, in Goodwin, 1994).

Both definitions and social judgement of sexual assaults have also varied historically. For example, during slavery in Colonial America, it was considered 'impossible' to rape a black woman because of her inherently 'sexual' nature: there were no penalties for abuse of black women by white men. Furthermore, black women were seen as possessions; the legal framework encouraged sex between black women and white men (but not, of course, between black men and white women) as a means of producing more slaves. According to Goodwin (1994):

> *Seen in this context, it is not surprising that African-American women, even nowadays, are less likely than white Americans to report sexual assault to the relevant authorities, anticipating a lack of community and societal support if they do so, a pessimism supported by the evidence from police and courtroom procedures . . . At the same time, African women are more likely than their white counterparts to see sexual assault as an inevitable part of their lives. This may encourage them to make less effort to guard against its occurrence, thus perpetuating the risk of attack.*

Applications and implications

According to Cherry (1995), published work on violence from a feminist perspective intentionally links with direct efforts to seek change for potential and actual victims, grounding its generalisations in the concrete lives of women speaking out against violence. At the same time, the analysis of sexual violence as a continuum (rape, wife battering, child sexual abuse, etc.) raises a question about services for abused women and children: should we continue to develop services which focus on specific forms of sexual violence (e.g. refuges for battered women and rape crisis lines) or should we develop services based on women's needs? (Kelly, 1988).

In practice, some provision already exists for addressing a range of forms of sexual violence, as in Rape Crisis Lines which counsel women who were abused as children, who have been sexually harassed and, sometimes, who are being abused by their partner. Women living in refuges may have been raped by the abusive man; they may have also been sexually abused as a child or have discovered that one or more of their children has been sexually abused. Kelly (1988) believes that feminist activists should discuss ways in which services could be more integrated, at least locally.

The kind of theorising that feminists have been developing over the last

25 years is finding its place in men's consciousness-raising groups, social activism groups and academic communication. In reviewing research on the social psychology of rape, Cherry (1983, in Cherry, 1995) discovered how little was written about the use of violence in men's lives compared with work on women's experience of and resistance to victimisation. In general, the study of men *as* men has been missing in the analysis of violence towards women, except for those few men imprisoned and in psychiatric institutions.

In 1975, Susan Brownmiller published *Against Our Will: Men, women and rape,* in which she looked at the extensiveness of rape in wartime, using the Vietnam War, including the My Lai massacre, as one of the most horrific examples. In 1981, an entire issue of the *Journal of Social Issues* was devoted to the study of rape, including an article by Malamuth on how men assessed the likelihood that they would use rape under various conditions. Malamuth located 'rape proclivity' (natural tendency/pre-disposition) as an aspect of social learning theory and the processes of behavioural inhibition/disinhibition. Feminist theorising and research suggests that it is better located in the dual frameworks of gender role and power-dominance relations.

Rape proclivity means something at both a psychological and societal level (i.e. society's tolerance of both the abuse of power and the abuse of women as legitimate targets). (There are some very important parallels here with sexism in particular – of which sexual violence is a manifestation – and prejudice/discrimination in general: see Chapter 4.)

While there remains a relative silence about rape and other forms of sexual violence from a male perspective, there are the beginnings of a psychology of men and men's studies, in which a well-articulated account of violence in men's lives becomes possible (Cherry, 1995).

Memory

The story so far

The birthdate of contemporary (i.e. empirical as opposed to philosophical) psychology is generally taken to be 1879 (O'Neil, 1968) when Wilhelm Wundt established the first psychology laboratory, in Leipzig. In North America, William James had the same idea at much the same time but did not put it into practice, and so the birthplace of the modern discipline was Germany rather than the USA.

The Ebbinghaus tradition

With the new psychology less than a decade old, Hermann Ebbinghaus began a series of experiments into memory, and thus we can see that memory was one of the first topics (along with perception and learning) of empirical psychology. The title of his ground-breaking book, *Memory: A contribution to experimental psychology*, published in 1885 – a mere six years after the opening of Wundt's first psychology laboratory – left the potential purchaser in little doubt where Ebbinghaus was 'coming from'. It transpired that the methods which Ebbinghaus used to study memory helped establish a manner of carrying out research and gathering data which was to dominate cognitive psychology in particular and much of psychology in general until the 1960s (Cohen, 1990) or the 1970s (Hayes, 1994): the rigorous laboratory experiment. Furthermore, Ebbinghaus established into the newly born science of psychology a major theoretical orientation which once again dominated cognitive psychology well into the second half of the 20th century: Associationism.

Cohen (1990) puts this into historical context thus:

> *Early ideas about memory arose out of the assumption that all learning and memory is based on the* association of ideas *or sensations that occur close together in time. These views were developed in the 17th and 18th centuries by the British Empiricist philosophers, in particular Locke, Berkeley and Hume. Relying on their own introspections, they observed that when experiences occur together . . . they become associated and are remembered together.*

The strength of the learned association is determined by the frequency with which the experiences occur together and by the vividness of the sensations.

It was these notions which Ebbinghaus seized upon and studied experimentally. He took the laboratory to be a 'sterile' and 'pure' environment in which learning and memory from previous experience in the 'real world' could be eliminated. He believed that only by studying memory in this unsullied environment could such 'confounding' variables as meaning, motivation and previous experience be nullified. This supported a paradigm (psychological positivism) which has only relatively recently come under scrutiny and challenge (see Introduction).

Ebbinghaus argued that the only way to study memory in a 'pure' sense was to work with novel data which could not have been encountered before and hence could not be part of already existing associations (the much dreaded contamination factor), and so he developed thousands of nonsense syllables (such as ZEJ). Clearly no one would have ever been exposed to these before. He also felt it was essential to carry out his work as objectively as possible and endeavoured to control and standardise his experimental procedures as far as he possibly could.

One feature of his experimental work in memory did not have a lasting legacy, however. For almost all of his experiments he worked alone and used himself as the subject (although he was occasionally aided by a laboratory assistant). This idiographic (as opposed to nomothetic) approach has only rarely been subsequently used in cognitive psychology. Let us consider a typical Ebbinghaus experiment in order to savour the flavour of his work.

Ebbinghaus was interested in the way in which memory is affected by the passage of time. Common sense might tell us that we remember things which have occurred further back in our experience. It was consistent with the spirit and purpose of the new scientific psychology that this should be tested experimentally. Ebbinghaus used sets of eight lists, each of which contained 13 nonsense trigrams. He read them through from beginning to end until he could recall them accurately without hesitation. He then retested himself on recall from the lists. He carried out the first testing 20 minutes after retention and his last testing was a month (31 days) after retention.

The DV measure – with time being the IV – was the number of trials needed to re-learn the material as a percentage of the number originally needed. The results showed that, as the interval between the original learning increased, so did the amount of re-learning which was required. Ebbinghaus had showed that most forgetting occurs within one hour of learning; after that, the rate of loss increases but at a gradual rate. For example, the rate of re-learning is roughly the same after one day as it is after two, around 70 per cent re-learning needed (compared to 40 per cent after one hour). By 744 hours, the figure had reached 80 per cent.

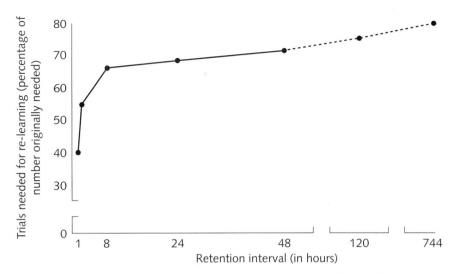

Figure 7.1   Ebbinghaus's results showing how delay before recall can influence forgetting (from Ebbinghaus, 1885)

As we have noted above, this laboratory/experimental methodological orientation almost totally dominated not only memory research but the majority of cognitive psychology until very recently. The legacy of Ebbinghaus has been a significant one indeed.

Two types of memory?

Another early psychological writer, William James, provided another of the cornerstones of memory research when, in 1890, he argued that there are two forms of memory: primary and secondary. Once re-designated short-term and long-term memory, these were the central features of what has come to be called 'structural models of memory' (Hayes, 1996). The most influential version of this has been Atkinson and Shiffrin's (1968) modal (or multistore) model of memory. This contends that memory can be understood as a flow (and loss) of information through three stages which are differentiated by their placement in the sequence, the ways in which

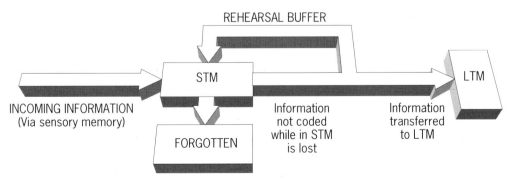

Figure 7.2   Atkinson and Shiffrin's multistore model of memory (based on Atkinson and Shiffrin, 1971, and taken from Gross, 1996)

they operate and their capacity. The three modes are sensory memory, short-term memory and long-term memory. A truly phenomenal amount of research within cognitive psychology has been carried out exploring the different memory stores and their characteristics, for example, ways in which information is encoded within the different modes, how it is stored and retrieved (or is lost/inaccessible), how storage capacity and retrieval can be enhanced and the multitude of processes and events which adversely affect memory.

Cohen (1990) argues that this model is illustrative of the information-processing approach. She says:

> *The information-processing approach follows the Ebbinghaus tradition in using formal laboratory experiments. However, its theoretical framework has been derived from communication science.*

The emphasis on channel capacity, system efficiency and information wastage and loss is entirely consistent with the concerns of information-processing and communication science which emerged after the Second World War.

The notion that memory can best be understood through structural analysis has, over the last 25 years, been challenged, both at a conceptual and empirical level. Gross (1996) considers three 'major attempts' to modify and revise Atkinson and Shiffrin's model: Tulving's (1972) work on episodic and procedural memory; Craik and Lockhart's (1972) work on levels of processing and Baddeley and Hitch's (1974) model of working memory. Although it should be clearly appreciated that the manner of the modification or revision forwarded by these three challenges were significantly different (see Gross, 1996, for elaboration and discussion), it can be said that all of them challenged the adequacy of a structural model. For example, Tulving demonstrated that long-term memory is not a single entity but several, differentiated by how they operate (episodic memory being highly personalised, 'autobiographical' memory; semantic memory being general, factual knowledge about the world). Craik and Lockhart also challenged the passivity of the structural model and emphasised the importance of the amount and type of activity carried out by the individual as the key determinant of how well something is remembered. Whereas Tulving challenged the notion of a unitary long-term memory, the working-memory model (Baddeley and Hitch, 1974; Baddeley, 1981; 1986) contested short-term memory as unitary. This model shares with the other three challenges the notion of activity and adds purpose, i.e. what is memory for? It is proposed within this model that short-term memory is 'overseen' by a central executive (which is essentially an attentional system) which organises and deals with three sub-systems which differ by what they do and the 'units' they work with. These are the articulatory loop (which processes verbal information and acts as an 'inner voice'), the visuo-spatial scratchpad (spatial/verbal and 'inner eye') and the primary acoustic store (phonemic non-lexical and 'inner ear').

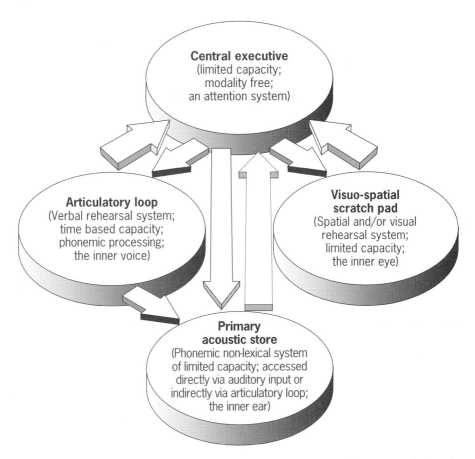

Figure 7.3   The working-memory model (based on Cohen et al., 1986, and taken from Gross, 1996)

All of these challenges were significant and consequential, but all were located within the Ebbinghaus tradition. The constructivist tradition, however, was completely different.

The constructivist tradition

Cohen (1990) and Hayes (1994; 1995) write about an alternative history and tradition in memory research, one which is 'much more at ease with real-life experience' (Hayes, 1995). We may call this different tradition *constructivism*. It differs from associationism both conceptually and methodologically. In terms of the former, constructivist theories contend that memory is far from being passive recording of data which can be retrieved 'intact'; instead, they view memory (in all aspects, e.g. encoding, storage and retrieval) as dynamic and constructed. Memories, it is argued, are not like old photographs (literal and objective records of past events) but constantly 're-made' and reinterpreted. When we engage in recall from memory, what we have is not a literal representation of a stimulus but a 're-constituted' account which re-draws it, paying close attention to some features of it whilst completely ignoring others. If Freud believed that the present is a product of the past, then constructivists believe that the past is always a product of the present.

Let us illustrate this by reference to something which has affected many of us at some time in our lives: being betrayed by a close friend or lover. Now, let us ask ourselves a critical question: when we re-appraise this person having been betrayed or jilted by them, do we just regard them in a negative light but hold on to the image of them being previously wonderful (as we once thought), or do we 'shoot the new image backwards' (they always were capable of deceit, betrayal, etc., but we simply didn't see it until it was too late). My vote definitely goes to the latter.

The methodological differences are also considerable. Rather than studying memory (and other cognitive processes) in the sterile and pure (unsullied, as we called it earlier) environment of the psychology laboratory, Bartlett took his psychology into the 'real world' and generally used qualitative (words and images) methodologies rather than quantitative ones which focused on numbers and frequencies. Cohen (1990) puts it thus: 'This approach focuses on meaningful material rather than lists of nonsense syllables and seeks to study the operation of memory in more natural situations'.

Bartlett's most famous study, the recall of a story entitled The War of Ghosts, well illustrates his approach. He presented a wide variety of people with the story given in Box 7.1.

Box 7.1   The War of Ghosts

One night, two young men from Egulac went down to the river to hunt seals, and while they were there, it became foggy and calm. Then they heard war cries, and they thought, 'Maybe this is a war party'. They escaped to the shore and hid behind a log. Now canoes came up, and they heard the noise of paddles, and saw one canoe coming up to them. There were five men in the canoe, and they said, 'What do you think? We wish to take you along. We are going up the river to make war on the people'. One of the young men said, 'I have no arrows'. 'Arrows are in the canoe,' they said. 'I will not go along. I might be killed. My relatives do not know where I have gone. But you,' he said, turning to the other, 'may go with them'. So one of the young men went, but the other returned home. And the warriors went on up the river to a town on the other side of Kalama. The people came down to the water, and they began to fight, and many were killed. But presently the young man heard one of the warriors say, 'Quick, let us go home: that Indian has been hit'. Now he thought, 'Oh, they are ghosts.' He did not feel sick, but they said he had been shot. So the canoes went back to Egulac, and the young man

> *went ashore to his house, and made a fire. And he told everybody*
> *and said, 'Behold I accompanied the ghosts, and we went to*
> *fight. Many of our fellows were killed, and many of those who*
> *attacked us were killed. They said I was hit, and I did not feel*
> *sick.'*
>
> *He told it all and then became quiet. When the sun rose he fell*
> *down. Something black came out of his mouth. His face became*
> *contorted. The people jumped up and cried. He was dead.*
>
> (Bartlett, 1932)

After giving the story to people to read, he tested their ability to recall it at increasingly long intervals, the first being 15 minutes after the reading. The longest interval he ever used was ten years! Typical mistakes in story recalls included omission of detail, alterations of emphasis (focusing on some aspects to the detriment of others), changes of sequence, rationalisations (where additional material is introduced to 'make sense' of the story) and personalisations (where re-telling was influenced by the person's own reaction to the story, such as revulsion to 'something black came out of his mouth').

Comparing the Ebbinghaus and Bartlett traditions

What, then, were the principal differences between these two traditions and what have the consequences of these been for recent psychological work in the field of memory, remembering and forgetting? Before we can answer this question, it is important to note that Bartlett's interests and research focus changed considerably between 1916, when his Fellowship thesis at Cambridge University and first academic paper were submitted and published, and 1932, when his most famous and influential book, *Remembering*, was published (Douglas, 1980; Shotter, 1990; Rosa, 1996). This view is, however, somewhat contested by Middleton and Crook (1996).

Bartlett himself said in 1936 that he enrolled at St John's College, Cambridge, 'largely because Rivers was there, and my interests were turning strongly towards anthropology. However, I decided to read moral science first, and that is how I came into the Cambridge Psychological Laboratory'. Rivers had been the psychologist on the famous anthropological study of the Torres Straits (1898/1899). Bartlett added that it had been Rivers who had 'told me that if I wanted to be an anthropologist, I must be a psychologist first, and specifically I must know the psychological methods' (Bartlett, 1937). Rosa (1996) says, 'It is my belief that Bartlett, for a time, was torn between these two disciplines'.

The account Rosa gives is of someone, initially drawn to the social and cultural, who increasingly, as his career in psychology developed, found it necessary to be more faithful to the mainstream of psychological individualism and essentialism. Douglas (1980) puts it powerfully thus:

> *The author of the best book on remembering forgot his own first convictions. He became absorbed into the institutional framework of Cambridge University psychology, and restricted by the conditions of the experimental laboratory.*

Shotter (1990) adds: 'And in such circumstances, he came to treat remembering as that tradition demanded: as wholly an inner process'.

It is fascinating to read the accounts given of Bartlett's early writings (1916–1921) (Rosa, 1996), the possible pinnacle of his articulation of his cultural psychology (his first book, *Psychology and Primitive Culture*, was published in 1923 (Shotter, 1990)) and the arguments for and against in change of 'position' in *Remembering* (Middleton and Crook, 1996).

The account given below focuses upon the early/middle Bartlett although, despite what has just been said, much of it was still evident in *Remembering*. Let us begin by considering the following summary of the differences between the Ebbinghaus and Bartlett traditions with which Bartlett opens *Remembering*:

> *(Bartlett) rejects the Ebbinghaus tradition of memory research. That tradition . . . sought to separate out all the 'noise, of individual differences among memorising subjects and thereby treating them to a comparable 'starting level'. The well-known device was to use short and meaningless written material. Bartlett questions the strategy of paralysing accompanying human responses to material used in that sort of memory research. He comments, 'such isolation is not to be secured by simplifying situations or stimuli and leaving as complex an organism as ever to make the response'. He doubts the general appropriateness of such a strategy which loses 'the special character' of human action to render situations sensible for the purposes of current and future concerns. He argues that the improvised setting of experiments moulded in the Ebbinghaus image do not offer us stripped-down psychological capacities such as memory. They offer instead just another context in which 'as complex an organism as ever' will make a response. His insightful commentary on psychological experimentation builds on his analysis of the importance of understanding the experiment as socially located as any other setting.*

(Middleton and Crook, 1996)

Box 7.2 chronicles some of the key differences between the two traditions. We will build upon many of these in our Revisions and reconceptualisations.

> **Box 7.2 Key differences between the Ebbinghaus and Bartlett traditions**
>
> - They both used the experimental method (exclusively in the case of Ebbinghaus) but in different manners.
> - They worked with very different types of materials.
> - They held different views concerning the appropriate location of memory research for example, ecological concerns and remembering as everyday life.
> - They held different views regarding the location of memory itself: is it inside the head or a dynamic interaction between the person and their social environment?
> - They held different conceptions of memory: is it passive or active?
> - They held conflicting views on the importance of interpretation and context.
> - They disagreed on the question of what 'good memory' is defined by: is it accurate recall or function and accountability?

Revisions and reconceptualisations

1   Ecology, culture and cross-culturality

We have already mentioned that Bartlett was drawn to Cambridge by the presence of W. H. Rivers, who had been the psychologist on the anthropological study of the Torres Straits at the turn of the century and in his early writings one of his principal concerns was with 'conventionalisation' (1916). We may regard this as the cultural form in which text, symbols and meaning are 'stored' and represented, and how this is affected when 'transferred' from one culture to another. Given his concern with this, with anthropology and with culture, it would seem entirely consistent with his position that psychologists should regard similarities and differences between cultures as significant.

Bartlett (1932) argued that memory skills in preliterate cultures develop differently, if not better, than those in literate cultures. The vein of empirical research into this field does not appear to be great, but a good summary of interesting studies and findings is given in Segall et al. (1990). We could speculate that in cultures with a strong oral (as opposed to written) tradition, certain forms of memory may be significantly greater, as this is the way in which their cultural tradition is 'carried' and sustained.

Studies have been carried out into eidetic imagery (photographic memory). In an early study, Doob (1964) investigated the incidence of eidetic imagery in a 45-person sample of the Ibo people of Nigeria (male/female; children/adults; urban/rural) and found their performance 'dramatically higher than that normally found in the West'. Furthermore, this was found to be more pronounced in the rural rather than urban peoples. Doob suspected, on the basis of these results, that this outcome may be related to a difference from 'Westernisation' and carried out further studies (1966; 1970), but did not find conclusive or systematic outcomes. Studies carried out by Sheehan (and colleagues, e.g. 1972) on Australian Aborigines have also provided inconsistent results. This variability was largely a function of the isolation of the community studied. In a 1972 study a greater incidence of eidetic imagery was found in isolated as opposed to relatively highly concentrated communities, but a later (1973) study disconfirmed the hypothesis of a relationship between isolation and incidence of eidetic imagery by finding a low incidence in a community which was even more isolated than the one in the previous study where the incidence had been high!

Segall et al. present a summary of a complex series of studies carried out on the Kpelle in Liberia. Much of the research would appear to be clearly located within the associationist tradition, and the results support the conclusion that schooling was closely related to successful recall. It is worthy of note that the negative differential between the Kpelle and the Americans was reduced when the former were allowed to use their own categorisation systems in the studies as opposed to having them provided for them.

The studies most supportive to Bartlett's position would appear to come from the research carried out in cultures with a strong oral tradition. Segall et al. (1990) summarise the research thus:

> *Ross and Millsom (1970), for example, suspected that the reliance on oral tradition that is characteristic of African societies might make Africans more likely to remember details in orally presented stories than a comparable group of Americans. Both groups were university students, one in Ghana and the other in New York. The researchers tested retention of the themes in stories read aloud. They found that, in general, the Ghanian students recalled the stories better than the New York students. The sole exception was one story told in 17th-century English. The Ghanaian performance was especially impressive, since they both heard and reproduced the stories in English, which to most of them was a second language.*

What then can we conclude from these various studies? Certainly there are no easy, 'clean' outcomes, but there is no clear evidence for the notion that memory is invariant across cultures. Furthermore, Bartlett would no doubt have been intrigued by the Ross and Millsom findings which showed differences in favour of the non-Western peoples when using the serial reproduction technique which he popularised.

2   Remembering as everyday life

It is no exaggeration to say that, beginning in the late 1960s, Ulric Neisser (1967; 1976; 1979) turned around much of cognitive psychology in general, and memory research in particular. In his book *Cognitive Psychology* (1967/1979), which largely triggered the so-called cognitive revolution, he said: 'The present approach is more closely related to that of Bartlett's work than any other contemporary psychologist'.

Perhaps the best illustration of Neisser's work is his analysis of the 'Watergate-case memory' of John Dean (1981; 1982). John Dean had been counsel to the American President Richard Nixon, and his testimony was one of the central features of the legal case. Dean initially displayed remarkable feats of recollection through what was called retrospective recollection whereby he 'thought himself' back into situations. However, when, at a later stage, tapes of the critical meetings became 'available', it became evident that his literal recall had in fact been fairly poor: the mass of detail which he recalled had been substantially erroneous. But Neisser (1981) said:

> There is a deeper level at which he (was) right. He gave an accurate portrayal of the real situation, of the actual characters and commitments of the people he knew, and of the events that lay behind the conversations he was trying to remember.

An early anticipation of this shift in focus in how we determine 'accuracy' in remembering was given by Bartlett back in 1932 when he said, 'In a world of constantly changing environment, literal recall is extraordinarily unimportant'. This is not to say 'anything goes', rather that accuracy may be defined in many ways other than literal recall, and many other dynamics, such as the use of memory and the manner in which it is used and contested in everyday life, are arguably just as important (although one could hardly imagine Ebbinghaus agreeing with this!).

Neisser (1982) identified what Edwards and Potter (1995) call 'three kinds of truth', these being:

- verbatim recall (literal recall of detail, such as, for example, being able to retrieve and reproduce the Lord's Prayer or multiplication tables faultlessly);
- recall of gist (a more holistic level of 'accuracy' in which 'themes' and 'story-lines' are judged to be correct – although this may be difficult to determine in practice – but recall of detail is often erroneous);
- repisodic memory (an even more holistic level at which recurrent themes are located across different occasions and recall is 'embedded' in recollection or construction of motives and purpose).

Neisser argued that although Dean's remembering was substantially inaccurate at the first level, he was increasingly accurate at the gist and repisodic 'levels'.

The reader may well have noticed that, as this chapter has progressed, the dominant term for the phenomenon under scrutiny has changed from *memory* to *remembering*. This is deliberate, as both Neisser and Bartlett placed great emphasis (in contrast to Ebbinghaus) on the active nature of remembering. From 1920 onwards, Bartlett consistently used the term 'effort after meaning' when describing human activities such as remembering, and this captures well the nature of what we may presume Dean was 'doing'. This emphasis upon active selection, sense-making and interpretation frees the individual from what Bartlett called 'chronological determinism' (1932).

Although they feel that Neisser did not go 'far enough' (more of this shortly), Edwards and Potter (1995) argue that 'Neisser's (1981) "ecological" analysis of the memory of John Dean was in three ways a welcome departure from much previous memory research'. The three ways being:

- it examined memory in a natural context;
- it switched emphasis to a 'functional' view of memory (in attempting to make sense of the pattern of his (Dean's) personal goals);
- ('crucially', they say) it changed the way in which veridicality is defined and assessed ('studying memory for its accuracy rather than its inadequacies').

Notice, once again, how Bartlett 'anticipated' Neisser's work when he said:

> *The actions and reproductions of everyday life come largely by the way, and are incidental to our main preoccupations. We discuss with other people what we have seen, in order that they may value or criticise our impressions with theirs. There is ordinarily no directed and laborious effort to secure accuracy. We mingle interpretation with description, interpolate things not originally present, transform without effort and without knowledge.*

> (Bartlett, 1932)

Let us stay with the notion of veridicality and interpretation just a little longer.

REMEMBERING: RIGHT OR WRONG?

As we have mentioned above, the Bartlett tradition, in contrast to the Ebbinghaus tradition, contends that 'literal recall' is not everything. Shotter (1990) discusses the dynamic of justification whereby much of remembering in everyday life is concerned with contesting accuracy in social situations (for example, convincing others that our own recollection of a particular event, such as a wedding, is the accurate one). Once again, we see 'other' activities (other than passive recall, that is) 'embedded' in remembering. Discursive psychologists have argued that we need to recognise that variability and contestation in accounting should not be regarded as a problem (for example, by trying to find the 'truthful' version) but 'as a resource in the interactive and constructive accomplishment of socially located action' (Potter and Wetherall, 1987, cited by Middleton and Crook, 1996). To put it crudely, the social negotiation and contesting should be seen as part of the process of remembering – where accounts are challenged, changed and reformulated in the telling – rather than the pulling of fixed traces out of the heads of participants. After heated negotiation of what happened at the wedding, the recollection of events will never be the same again for any of those involved in the 'discussion'. Shotter (1990) adds to this when he writes:

> *Not only are we working . . . within a framework of social accountability, such that we have a responsibility to others (and to ourselves) to formulate in our 'efforts after meaning' a justifiable memory account, but the accounting practice involved has a rhetorical structure of (implied) criticism and justification to it.*

MEMORY: IN THE HEAD OR IN A SOCIAL DYNAMIC?

Critical to the information-processing and (to a lesser extent) the reformulated cognitive approach (e.g. the work of Neisser – illustrated above – and Loftus) is the notion of memory being an in-the-head entity (consistent with essentialism, discussed in several other contexts in this volume). For the discursive psychologists (whose arguments we shall shortly address), it is framed in social action. Bartlett's position was intermediate between these two. Rosa (1996) explains it as follows:

> *He explicitly argues against any type of reduction to simplicity, be this either individual, or social, or a mixture of both. This point of view is clearly stated in his first book . . . where he criticised the dissolving of the individual in a set of psychological 'processes' . . . The question, he wrote, is how to connect individual actions with social antecedents and consequences.*

However, according to Rosa, Bartlett 'connect(ed) social practices and cultural materials with psychological processes and personal experience, while keeping psychology a biological science, and using the experimental method'. For Bartlett, one of the key interfaces between the individual and the social in remembering is schema, which is generally regarded as one of his greatest contributions to psychology. He defined it as an 'organised setting' for all the activities we have identified as being part of dynamic remembering, and it is critical to his notion of 'sense-making'. For Bartlett, schema 'does not only provide us with a means of understanding the unitary nature of mental life; it is also a means whereby people's mental functioning may be located as sociocultural activity' (Middleton and Crook, 1996).

Shotter (1990) argues that between 1923 and 1932, Bartlett lost his emphasis on the social nature of remembering, but even when Bartlett later turned heavily to the experiment as his dominant methodology, he still regarded this as illustrative of social influence. He regarded the experiment as an 'emergency' situation to which participants find a suitable response to simply 'cope' (1932), and argued that the individual is always an 'individual-in-the-laboratory', an 'individual-in-his-everyday-working-environment' or an 'individual-in-a-given-social-group' and never a pure and simple individual (1932).

Bartlett (at least the early Bartlett) never regarded social factors as what Middleton and Crook (1996) call 'another set of independent variables that can be grafted onto procedures when appropriate'. Perhaps the clearest statement about Bartlett's position on the individual/social debate is given in the following passage:

> *My own experiments on the reproduction of folk tales . . . show how the reproductions in question bring into operation various specific tendencies towards dramatisation, condensation, rationalisation and so on . . . but whether any given material does produce such an affective accompaniment depends very largely upon its relations to the customs and beliefs prevalent in the community to which the subjects belong.*

(Bartlett, 1920)

3   Discursive remembering

Middleton and Crook (1996) show how Bartlett believed that remembering is located in everyday practice and, through such activity, e.g. conversation, can be 'seen'. Over the last decade there have been many attempts (e.g. Edwards and Middleton, 1986; 1987; 1988; Hirst and Manier, 1995; Middleton and Edwards, 1990; Woofitt, 1992) to explain memory with a discursive account (via discourse analysis). The position is explained well in an influential paper thus:

> *In the study of discursive remembering, it is precisely the procedures by which versions are produced, sustained, defended, bolstered, refuted, etc. by participants that are the object of investigation. This effectively transforms the possibilities of studying remembering as an everyday activity from one restricted to the single modal, reproductive, known input studies, to one that is sensitive to the kinds of things that rememberers are ordinarily doing when they reproduce versions of events.*

(Edwards et al., 1992)

These phenomena have been studied, for example, in conversations between parents and children talking about family photographs (Edwards and Middleton, 1988); reminiscence in older people (Middleton and Buchanan, 1993) and multi-professional teams delivering neonatal intensive care (Middleton and Curnock, 1995). So how does this analysis 'work'? Edwards and Potter (1995) say:

> *. . . for discourse analysis . . . remembering is studied as action, with the report itself taken as the act of remembering, and studiable as a constructed, occasioned version of events. It is analysed directly as discourse, going on inside the reporter's mind. In examining remembering as a discursive activity, we pursue not only a real-world or everyday process . . . but also a richly symbolic and communicative activity, as Bartlett urged in criticising Ebbinghaus's pursuit of the putatively unadulterated mental faculty of memory.*

Edwards and Potter (1995), in terms of saying 'how to do it', state that 'the most economical way of introducing discourse analysis is to highlight the interrelated concepts of function, variation and construction'.

The notion of function picks up on the distinction made by Potter et al. (1990) between 'the analysis of discourses' and 'discourse analysis'. The writers argue that the former is concerned with the discursive analysis of text, in all its many forms, whereas the latter is also concerned with 'the construction of accounts, the performance of social acts through language, and the identification of the discourses and interpretive repertoires which we draw upon in our interactions' (Burr, 1995). The notion of function is located within the latter form of discourse (as opposed to the former which Potter et al. associate with the work of analysts such as Parker and Burman). Readers wishing to explore the different approaches to discourse analysis should read chapter 10 of Burr (1995) for an unusually accessible account.

Regarding the second of Edwards and Potter's concepts, they say: 'The action orientation of discourse makes for variability: what people say will differ according to what they are doing with their words'. So, for example, discourse will differ according to whether they are trying to persuade, justify or blame.

In discussing the notion of construction they say: 'The metaphor of construction highlights three things: that discourse is manufactured out of pre-existing linguistic resources; that active selection is involved; and that much of the time we understand the world in terms of specific linguistic versions'. For readers wishing to explore further the 'doing' of discourse analysis – which space constraints do not permit us to do here – we recommend Potter and Wetherell (1995) or Parker (1992).

Applications and implications

The primary consequence of what we have outlined above is that cognitive processes such as memory/remembering/forgetting can no longer be 'safely' placed in the head. Shotter (1990), in particular, exposes the implausability of the notion of an inner, scrutinising eye in the mind and demonstrates how belief in this 'cognition-in-the-head' has been constructed, and considers the purposes this notion serves.

The establishment of cross-cultural (and, indeed, inter-cultural) differences has shown that, as with almost any aspect of psychology, the notion of the Universal Man is unsustainable, and this has a number of consequences for research, one of which is the need to examine the ecological and cultural embeddedness of our methodologies. It is probably fair to say, however, that the biggest challenge to cognitivism has come from the discursive attack.

In one of the earlier of these discursive challenges, Middleton and

Edwards (1990) identify the following 'common themes' within this re-orientation:

Remembering together   When people examine photographs or other records of the past and remember together, there is more than a mere pooling of recollections.

> *What is recalled and commemorated extends beyond the sum of the participants' individual perspectives: it becomes the basis of future reminiscence. In the contest between varying accounts of shared experiences, people reinterpret and discover features of the past that become the context and content for what they will jointly recall and commemorate on future occasions.*

Social practice of commemoration   People not only remember things socially with others who have shared experiences with them, but they also share recollections about 'outsiders', such as heroes and media or political figures.

Social foundation and context of individual memory   Both of the previous two factors not only engage us in social remembering of certain events and people, they also instruct in what to remember (i.e. what to include, what is important and what is rendered insignificant and/or invisible).

Rhetorical organisation of remembering and forgetting   This refers to 'discourse analysis' as opposed to 'analysis of discourse' (mentioned above). It draws our attention to the notion that we need to attend not only to stories told and accounts given, but that the nature and style of performance are also significant. The reader will hopefully recall Bartlett's views discussed earlier concerning all that 'sits around' remembering. To concentrate purely upon material without performance is missing much.

Social institutional remembering and forgetting   Shotter (1990) shows this was a great concern of the early Bartlett (before Cambridge 'got to him'). Social institutions, such as the Church, science and the media, promote and discourage us from remembering certain things by such dynamics as emphasising, making available and making unavailable. It refers 'to the large-scale manipulation of what should or could be remembered' (Middleton and Edwards, 1990).

The forms of social practices in the continuity of our lives   This is possibly the most consequential of all of these claims. Middleton and Edwards claim that one product of our social remembering (and all of the above) is our sense of continuity (the relationship between our past and our present) of our self. They argue:

> *The integrity of individual mental life is held in place by participation in these practices. In its strongest form, this does not just refer to some form of coherence and sense of continuity in our*

social lives, but to the social construction of the 'individual' mind. The claim is that the very integrity of a person's mentality depends upon participation in an environment which owes its very shape to socio-cultural practices.

Thus, we finish where we began, with individualism and essentialism, but the sting is that, if we accept the final argument put forward by Middleton and Edwards, this belief in individualism and essentialism has been constructed by and within the very social processes it argues to be insignificant!

Psychology for women

Setting the scene

Many students who enter psychology come across the question: 'why did you choose psychology?'. The most usual answer is: 'because psychology is about people'. However, this initial promise of psychology turns out to be a let-down for many female students, who come to realise that the discipline is more about men than women. As Bohan (1992) puts it:

> Women and women's perspectives are notably absent from psychology's mainstream research and theory, from the discipline's self-presentation in curricula, from its histories, and from prominent professional and lay depictions of what psychology is and does.

However, over the last two decades, a growing number of women in psychology have organised and worked towards the production of more woman-friendly psychology. In 1987, the Psychology of Women's Section in the British Psychological Society (BPS) was formed which provided space and institutional support for the growing number of feminists in psychology. More recently, in 1991, the journal *Feminism and Psychology* was launched, allowing a platform for many women to develop their ideas and critical work of mainstream psychology. There is also an annual Women and Psychology conference serving similar ends. In addition, during the last decade there has been a boom in the publication of feminist psychology books and a considerable increase in the teaching of feminist courses and modules in a variety of higher education institutions. Despite these apparent advances, mainstream psychology continues to work primarily within the parameters of a masculinist paradigm which insists on the so-called scientific values, such as detachment, rationality, objectivity (Squire, 1989). Feminists have argued that such values characterise male forms of subjectivity and that the insistence on these leads to the exclusion of knowledge which derives from the experiences of other than middle-class, white, heterosexual males (Smith, 1988). As far back as the late 1960s, with the first wave of feminism, women in psychology began to organise and produce work which challenged almost everything psychology had ever had to say about women. Most notably, in 1969, Naomi Weisstein, presented a paper at a feminist conference at Lake Villa, Illinois, entitled provocatively: 'Psychology constructs the female; or, the fantasy life of the male psychologists (with some attention to the fantasies of his friends, the male biologist and the male anthropologist)'. In this paper, she argued that: 'psychology has nothing to say about what women are really like, what they need and what they want, essentially because psychology does not know'. Like many scholars who have followed her arguments, she drew the attention to the ways in which cultural stereotypes of women passed for 'scientific theories' about women. Often such theories were backed up ostensibly by 'biological evidence' which told more about male preoccupations (or 'fantasies', as Weisstein calls them) rather than real women. In tune with the feminist movement in general, Weisstein argued that, in order to understand women, psychology needs to understand 'the social conditions under which women live'. Biological theories, however, often did just the opposite: reduced human behaviour to instincts and hormone levels. Like society at large, psychology considered women as 'inconsistent, emotionally unstable, lacking in a strong conscience or superego, weaker, "nurturant" rather than productive, "intuitive" rather than intelligent, and, if they were at all "normal", suited to the home and the family'. In fact, such observations led some feminists to see mainstream psychology as 'a psychology against women' (Henley, 1974).

Since Weisstein's early work, the feminist movement in general has developed and endured changes. Today, there are many different kinds of feminism, so that recently Wilkinson (1996) has argued, that it is more appropriate to talk of *feminist psychologies*. Nevertheless, all start from the point of view that there are societal inequalities based on sex. For example, this is how MacKinnon (1989) defines a feminist theory. It is one which is:

> *... persuaded that women have been unjustly unequal to men because of the social meaning of their bodies. Feminist theory is critical of genders, a determinant of life chances, finding that it is women who differentially suffer from the distinction of sex. Compared with men, women lack control over their social destinies.*

Starting from the position that 'women have been unjustly unequal to men', unlike mainstream psychologists, feminists are avowed to *social and political change*.

While there are many disagreements and debates concerning the precise ways in which change should come about, in varying degrees and ways, all feminists are critical of the current social conditions under which men and women exist. In general, most but not all feminists adhere to various forms of social constructionalism, whereas mainstream psychology tends to adhere to the scientific (or positivistic) paradigm. Social constructionalism and positivism rest on different notions of what is proper knowledge and how to go about collating and formulating it, i.e. the paradigms involved different *epistemologies*. Postmodernism, which we discussed in the Introduction and in Chapter 3, is a social constructionist perspective, adopted currently by many feminists. There are three main areas of which feminists tend to be critical in relation to positivism in psychology. Bohan (1992) summarises them in the following way:

1 The inadequacy of sensory knowledge In general, positivism holds the view that, through our senses, we can observe reality objectively and acquire 'raw' data. Bohan argues that:

> *There can be no 'objective observation', no 'raw data' when human knowledge is always and inevitably filtered through multiple layers of perception and cognition, each level of which can be demonstrated to be subject to distortion.*

For example, as we shall see later in relation to the work of Schachter and Singer (1962), even our perceptions of what feelings we experience are defined by social conditions and do not reflect on some underlying reality.

2 Context stripping From its very beginning, psychology has tried to model itself on the natural sciences. In practice, this means that in order to understand human beings, psychology has treated them as if they were physical objects which have enduring characteristics (such as 'traits' or 'attitudes', for example). In order to discover these, psychology has devised experimental procedures designed to strip away the social context. However, for social constructionists, this has blinded psychology to 'the pervasive impact of contextual forces on human experience'. Moreover, this focus on the individual (outside her social environment) has led to person-blame explanations. For feminists, as we shall see later, this has important political implications in so far as psychology has tended to 'blame' rather than 'understand' women.

3 The denial of values In general, positivism claims objectivity and impartiality. However, social constructionists argue that the very methods of science reveal assumptions about human nature and reality. Moreover, interpretation and theory involves language. The arguments proposed, the terms selected, all reveal value-laden positions. For example, as we discuss later, the very conceptualisation of female menstruation involves assumptions about the female body in terms of pathology. In postmodern thinking, the question of 'true' and 'objective' theory has been replaced with questions about its usefulness.

Let's now examine what psychology has had to say about women and how feminists have responded.

The story so far

Social constructionism maintains that 'histories' are written from a particular point of view to a particular end, and they are not purely descriptive of the 'ways things were'. This awareness developed among many academics, and they began to explore the ways in which we write about the past in order to justify current ways of life and map out directions for future action. Giddens (1987) sums up this point neatly by saying that we 'use knowledge of the past to "bite into the future", thereby mobilising the present'. If knowledge of the past is needed for action in the present, for feminists who are concerned with social action and change, a history of women is essential. So, what is the 'story so far' offered by feminist psychologists?

A characteristic of feminist psychology is that it tends to *socially contextualise* whatever topic it examines. Moreover, a feminist history tends to continually underline the ways in which (in our case) psychological concepts and social practices are and were in a continuing relationship, so that often the two can be seen as mutually interdependent and supportive. For example, on critically examining Darwinian ideas and their re-interpretations in academia on the one hand, and on the other examining the social conditions at the time, Bohan (1992) makes the following observation:

> *Darwin's work reciprocally enjoyed ready acceptance precisely because of its congruence with the already prevalent respect for the human sciences and simultaneously because it could be seen as compatible with pre-existing societal beliefs regarding the sexes.*

In what follows, we shall present some examples of this 'reciprocity' between whatever 'science' had to say about women and their social conditions of existence.

At the turn of this century, following the industrial revolution, gender roles underwent a profound redefinition. Men and women were separated and assigned to the emerging public and private spheres respectively (Ehrenreich and English, 1979). New social roles emerged which were defined more and more on the basis of one's sex. While men went out to work, women's roles became progressively more confined to the family, domesticity and motherhood. Indeed, by the late 19th century, women lived, according to Welter (1966), in an era characterised by the *cult of motherhood*. This 'cult', however, did not hinder the pervading general tendency to view women as if they were 'lesser' than men. Darwin's theory of evolution was enjoying wide popularity, and in its grand scheme of evolutionary order, women, along with non-white people, were represented as if they were less 'evolved'. Allen (1889, cited in Bohan, 1992) expressed the point thus: 'All that is distinctly human is man; all that is truly woman is merely reproductive'. Many male writers at the time believed that women's energies were directed towards pregnancy which resulted in the earlier cessation of female evolution. As a result, women were seen as more childlike than men and more suited to the devalued role of child care. The public sphere was held in high esteem and was seen as an exclusive province of men. A number of academic arguments developed which functioned to consolidate and justify this state of affairs. One such argument revolved around the so-called *eminence list*. Male writers observed that Western history largely consisted of names of 'great' men and reasoned that this had something to do with men's and women's inherently different natures. The so-called *variability hypothesis* was put forward, and it sought to account for the acclaimed male superiority. According to it, men's intelligence showed more variability (Shields, 1975). This meant that somehow by nature, most women's intellectual abilities were mediocre, whereas men's abilities were more 'varied', and hence some men were extraordinarily clever, i.e. geniuses (hence the eminence list). (This also meant that there were an equal number of men at the other end of the continuum, who would have been 'duller' than most women, but that was not the point of the argument.)

Shields (1975) provides illustrations of how whatever was considered to be 'more evolved' during this period was ascribed to men. In the first instance, it was *brain size*. Evidence was presented which showed that black people and women had smaller brains than white men did. (Note the total invisibility of black women here. Like white woman, who can become submerged under whatever is considered 'human' about white man, so black woman can vanish under whatever is considered to constitute black man.) However, after a while, new 'advances' in science came, claiming that the frontal lobes of the brain were responsible for higher intellectual abilities. Very soon, research findings presented evidence claiming that, in men, the frontal lobes of the brain are, in fact, larger than those in women. But when, several years later, it was decided that the important intellectual functions were in the parietal lobes of the brain, hastily, revised evidence appeared showing that women have larger frontal lobes after all and smaller parietal ones by comparison to men!

While much of the early psychological research involved assumptions that men are 'more evolved' and 'more intellectual' than women and sought 'concrete' evidence to 'prove' this, some early female psychologists (who did not necessarily call themselves 'feminists') directed the attention to the very different ways of life which women and men led at the time. Leta S. Hollingworth was one of the first women psychologists in the United States. She worked at the turn of the century on testing the variability hypothesis. Women, according to her, lived in a 'field in which eminence is not possible' (1914, cited in Shields, 1975). She argued that there were a great number of social factors which could provide very plausible explanations for the observed differences between the sexes and that there was no need to resort to biological explanations. For a start, social life was organised around sharply differentiated sex roles. Women did not have easy access to male-dominated fields such as education, paid employment, science and politics. Their entry into such fields was continually hindered by cultural beliefs about their 'real' natures.

Moreover, science, then as now, was conceived in gendered terms, such as rationality, objectivity, emotional detachment. These were also characteristics consistent with beliefs about the psychological interior of males (Keller, 1985). While during the previous historical period, dominated by Christianity, man was believed to be made in the image of God, now he was made in the image of science. Since the female sex was conceived as the opposite to the male (and to science), with characteristics such as emotionality and irrationality, to be a woman and a scientist became a 'contradiction in terms'. Hence women's entry into the domain of science was frustrated from the start. Women did begin to gain access to education, but this process was slow. Often arguments were raised regarding the ostensibly detrimental nature of scholarly activities on the female reproductive system. Arguments were put forward saying that by forcing their brains to do academic work at puberty, girls used up blood they would need later for menstruation. Ussher (1989), for example, cites a board of a university in 1877 arguing that education of women is 'at the fearful expense of ruined health' and that it is much more preferable for 'the future mothers of the state' to be 'robust, hearty, healthy women' who do not pass onto future generations 'the germs of disease'.

However, even when women entered the educational system they were channelled into spheres separate from those of men. Jean-Jacques Rousseau captures below some of the rationalisations for this differential treatment of men and women at the time:

> *A woman's education must therefore be planned in relation to man. To be pleasing in his sight, to win his respect and love, to train him in childhood, to counsel and console, to make his life pleasant and happy; these are the duties of woman for all time, and this is what she should be taught while she is young.*

(cited in Haste, 1993)

Women's education was to prepare them for their 'feminine' role in society, which in the above extract amounts to taking care of men and their offspring. Similarly, in spheres of paid employment, women were assigned to areas which were seen to tie up with beliefs about their 'nature'. In general, women went into areas now called 'the caring professions' which were paid less and had lower social prestige than those of men. Similar fates befell those women who began work in psychology. Bohan (1993) points out that, during the First World War, psychological testing became popular within the discipline. This was considered a speciality for a 'technician', the 'secondary' status of which resonated well with the culturally allocated lower status of women. Hence, women entered the discipline in these areas. After the war, women clustered in areas of applied psychology. These specialities functioned to provide direct services to others, which once again tied up with the cultural stereotype of women, according to which they had a natural concern for others. Such fields, however, carried fewer opportunities for prestigious academic research. The emerging gendering of psychological subfields reflected wider society's organisation on the basis of sex.

Today, in a number of ways, the situation has not altered. While undergraduate students in psychology are now predominantly female, there is a seven-to-one ratio of male to female academics in psychology (Squire, 1989). In general, women hold a minority of academic positions, particularly those which are permanent or senior (Kagen and Lewis, 1989). Moreover, the BPS reflects this gender imbalance, with only 26 per cent of committee places being occupied by women (Morris et al., 1990). Similarly, there have been no major alternations in psychology's main theoretical paradigms. Biological and evolutionary perspectives are still seen to represent 'hard' science. Their application perpetuates old debates in the discipline about assumed sex differences. For example, modern psychology is still much preoccupied with 'brain' differences between women and men. Tavris (1993) says:

> *Today, just like the 19th-century researchers who kept changing their minds about which lobe of the brain accounted for male superiority, researchers keep changing their minds about which* hemisphere *of the brain accounts for male superiority.*

Tavris continues by saying that first the left hemisphere was believed to be the one which accounted for the intellect and reason, and the right which accounted for the sick, crazed, instinctual, irrational and criminal. In men, the left hemisphere turned out 'more developed' and in women, the right. By the 1960s and 1970s, genius, inspiration, creativity and mathematical brilliance were said to be specialisations of the right hemisphere, and so men were said to have 'right brain specialisation'. Today, it is believed that the left and the right hemispheres develop differently in boys and girls and that the corpus callosum also differs. During foetal development, the left hemisphere in the male foetus is believed to be attacked by testosterone, resulting in right-hemisphere dominance in men that explains why they excel in art, music and mathematics (Geschwind and Behan, 1982, cited in Tavris, 1993). Tavris goes on to illustrate how challenges to these widely accepted modern hypotheses by women working in the field are resisted by mainstream academia. Feminist neuroscientists, such as Ruth Bleier (1987; 1988), find themselves in a position similar to that of Leta S. Hollingworth and Mary Calkins, despite the fact that they are separated by over half a century. Bleier criticised the modern argument about spheres of specialisations in the brain. Her work was refused publication by *Science* on the grounds that she 'argues very strongly for the predominant role of environmental influences' (Bleier, 1988, cited in Tavris, 1993). It thus seems that, while the answer to the question 'What it is about the brain that makes men "superior" to women?' is subject to revision in every era, the question continues to persist. We may thus begin to wonder how much historical evidence it takes to consider the possibility that the question might be wrong.

Similarly, much of psychological theory and research which does not draw directly on biological evidence embodies assumptions which construct the sexes in terms of binary oppositions, oppositions which are often represented as if they were complementary. Hare-Mustin and Marecek (1990) refer to this representation of the sexes in oppositional terms as *bias alpha*. We can see this in Freud's work, for example. In his theories, the fully 'developed' woman is morally inferior to men; she is too emotional, she is deficient in her ability to make good judgements, and her mature sexuality is passive. Women appear to be not just the opposite of men, but also a negative opposite. In the work of 'more modern' psychologists, such as Erik Erikson, the binary opposition which constructs women as emotional and men as intellectual reappears:

> *. . . the affective life is more developed in proportion to the intellect in the female than in the male sex, and the influence of the reproductive organs upon the mind are more powerful.*

> (Erikson, 1964)

The assumption that the female reproductive organs somehow affect women's minds, albeit centuries old, persists in contemporary academic work. Bent on finding oppositions, Erikson argued that women have something called an 'inner space' (in contrast to male 'outer space'), a kind of psychological orientation linked to an assumed 'innate' female desire for bearing children and domesticity. The implication of this for Erikson's personality theory is that women do not really travel along the route of 'self-actualisation' (or the ultimate realisation of one's human potential):

> *Much of the young woman's identity is already defined in her kind of attractiveness and in the selectivity of her search for the man (or men) by whom she wishes to be sought.*

> (Erikson, 1964)

So, a female cannot follow the exemplary path the theory so nicely delineates, rather it seems she needs to find a suitable man (who presumably is on it) and stand by him, presumably with his children. Yet, this conceptual deviation of women from the path of 'human' development is not explicitly acknowledged in the theory. In effect, this kind of talk, whereby theorists claim to propose models for 'human' development, but end up talking about men only, is what Hare-Mustin and Marecek call *beta bias*. Hancock (1990) points out in relation to Erikson's work:

> *Erikson's contribution to adult development consists of psychobiographies of prominent men – George Bernard Shaw, William James, Martin Luther and Mahatma Gandhi . . . Many others charting the life course have followed Erikson's lead and that of Freud by limiting their studies to males . . . despite the fact that they exclude half of humankind. They seem to underscore the presumption that males equal humans and females equal something else.*

Erikson's theory is widely taught on undergraduate psychology courses, yet the majority of textbooks introducing his work rarely point out these biases embedded in it.

Beta bias can be seen also in psychological research. For example, in the popular psychology textbook *Essential Social Psychology*, Pennington (1986) cites, among others, a well-known experiment by Dutton and Aron (1974) on sexual attraction. In this experiment, male subjects are said to have been sexually aroused in the experimental condition by being asked to read a 'highly arousing' passage. In the control condition, male subjects were given a 'dull' passage. The researchers then presented the subjects with photographs of women and concluded that 'those who have read the more arousing passage rated the female depicted . . . as more attractive than those who have read the dull passage' (cited in Pennington, 1986). In another known experiment, male subjects are physiologically aroused (i.e. scared) by being asked to walk over a high suspension bridge. They are then met by a male or female researcher asking them to fill in a questionnaire measuring sexual arousal in the middle of the bridge. The conclusion of this experiment was the subjects were more likely to fall in love (with the female researcher) when 'physiologically aroused'. In both experiments, what is under scrutiny are (heterosexual) male responses, yet Pennington (1986), the editor of the book, concludes that 'these and numerous other experiments, demonstrate that *people* tend to be more attracted to another when experiencing high physiological arousal' (our italics). Beta bias here is explicit in the actual design of the studies and then in the interpretations of the results. The fact that only men have been included as subjects is not seen as a problem in making conclusions about 'people' in general.

Alpha bias and beta bias are thus male biases. At times, both biases can be present in the same theory, as for example in Erikson's. For feminists, such biases which privilege men work against women. The postmodern insight that the value of knowledge lies in relation to its usefulness led many feminists to think of ways in which they could write about psychology in ways which are more useful for women. Below we present some examples of the ways in which feminists have gone about doing that. The chosen topics (PMS and rape) are from areas of typically female experience, which in themselves are areas often excluded from social psychology courses.

Revisions and reconceptualisations

In this section, we discuss briefly female menstruation and rape in order to illustrate some of the typical issues raised by feminist psychologists. The first issue, often discussed in feminist literature involves the deconstruction of cultural myths about women and shows the ways in which these are implicated in the social oppression of women. The most widely circulated myth about women in Western culture is that the female body is problematic. This myth finds support and elaboration in academic literature. Female menstruation, pregnancy and childbirth, menopause – events which are spread throughout a woman's life cycle – are often conceived in ways that generally *pathologise* the female body (Nicolson, 1992; Burman, 1996). To take such views on board is to come to the conclusion that somehow women are ill by nature! Yet, such views are a part of everyday, common-sense discourses, and they have long historical precedents in Western cultures. Take, for example, Plato's views cited below concerning the effects of the female reproductive system:

> *The womb is an animal which longs to generate children. When it remains barren too long after puberty, it is distressed and sorely disturbed, and straying about the body and cutting off the passages of the breath, it impedes respiration and brings the sufferer into extreme anguish and provokes all manner of diseases, besides.*
>
> (Plato, cited in Tavris and Wade, 1984)

Many feminists argue that such ideas have not disappeared today, but are redressed in modern scientific language and hence appear believable to us. The negative and problematic representations of the female body, feminists argue, betray a male point of view. Gloria Steinem (1983) humorously argues this in her essay, *If men could menstruate*. Menstruation, she says, 'would become an enviable, boast-worthy, masculine event' and also:

> *Men would brag about how long and how much . . . Young boys would talk about it as the envied beginning of manhood. Gifts, religious ceremonies, family dinners and stag parties would mark the day . . . Street guys would invent slang (He's a three-pad man) . . .*

Let's now see how feminist psychologists have:

- deconstructed existing beliefs about menstruation;
- pointed out the social and political functions of discourses about menstruation;
- offered alternative explanations and reconstructions.

Menstruation and PMS

Modern Western beliefs maintain that women 'suffer' for week or so prior to menstruation (called *premenstrual syndrome* or PMS). What exactly constitutes this condition, and just how many women have to put up with it, no one seems to know exactly. Stereotypically, PMS is more than physical discomfort; it involves psychological symptoms. During this time of the month, women are believed to be unstable, bad tempered and even violent at times. Ussher (1989) has pointed out that, according to different psychology studies, there are about 150 different symptoms 'available', including increased libido, decreased libido, anger, moodiness, emotional instability, tiredness, violence, irrationality, experience of stress, being prone to accidents and so on. Some experts argue that only five per cent of women are affected by PMS, whereas others cite 95 per cent (Harrison et al., 1985). Moreover, there is no overall agreement concerning the aetiology (the cause) of the condition. Different studies cite many different hormones as the culprits that cause PMS. Hormones which are used for the treatment of PMS are as variable as the ones which are seen to be the cause. Psychologists have also offered an array of psychological theories which claim to explain PMS. Some of these are: rejection of femininity; acceptance of femininity; neuroticism; life stress; marital problems; emotional instability; psychiatric disturbance; anxious personality; negative attitude to the body and others (see Ussher, 1989, for further detail). Numerous psychological studies have set about finding answers to research questions assuming (more often than not negative) associations between PMS and, for example, academic performance, accidents at work, suicide attempts, female violence and so on. The picture which emerges from such research is as inconclusive as anything else about PMS. Ussher (1989) points out that for almost each study claiming a relationship between PMS and one other variable, there is another one which disputes the relationship.

Feminist deconstructive work begins with an analysis which throws into question scientific and psychological findings by pointing out contradictions and inconclusiveness in the study of PMS. Ussher (1989) argues that modern theories about PMS are just a transformation of traditional 'raging hormones theories' (even wandering uteruses) into contemporary scientific jargon. Moreover, particularly with postmodern developments in the discipline, other theoretical assumptions are thrown into question. One such assumption involves the widespread belief that we can separate biology from culture. Postmodernists argue that divisions such as biology/society or nature/nurture are simply imposed by researchers and that they are not very helpful to our understanding of the topics we study (Henriques et al., 1984). A useful early study which is often cited in this context was conducted by Schachter and Singer (1962). In it, subjects were artificially aroused with drugs. Afterwards, they were left in a room with stooges whom they believed to have been subjected to the same treatment. Some of the stooges labelled their experiences negatively and some positively. The study demonstrated that the subjects labelled their own experience either in a positive or a negative way depending on what the stooges reported to experience. This was an important study because it showed how experience of physical sensations is subject to interaction with cues from the environment. Ussher suggests that, during menstruation, women's physiological arousal tends to be experienced negatively due to culturally specific (negative) attributions.

Interestingly, in another study, Joan Chrisler et al. (1994) administered Menstrual Joy Questionnaire (Delaney et al., 1988). The questionnaire asked women to rate positive experiences during menstruation, such as high spirits, affection, sexual desire, intense concentration, revolutionary zeal, creativity, etc. Later, these women filled in another questionnaire which indicated that they tended to think more positively about their menstruation compared to women who had not been encouraged to think about it positively. Such studies may lead us to wonder how women would experience their menstrual cycle if it was routinely represented in the culture as a positive phenomenon.

However, we are not suggesting that whatever women experience during this period is all in their own heads or up to them as individuals. Discourses about PMS are culturally specific ways of talking about aspects of women's lives which people use to make sense of their experiences. For feminists, what is important here is not blaming individual women for using the language (or discourses) of their culture. Rather, they are interested in exploring the possible political functions of such discourses. Parlee (1981) observed that if women feel negatively prior to menstruation, they tend to make internal attributions, i.e. blame the experience on PMS. However, the argument goes on, if women are physiologically aroused and therefore find aspects of their lives less satisfactory during this time of the month (for example, demands made on them by children, husbands, living conditions, etc.), the discourse of PMS serves a function of 'hiding' such social problems and instead pathologises the woman's body. On the other hand, Parlee (1981) found that if women feel contentment or happiness during this time of the month, they tend to make external attributions (e.g. 'I am happy because it's a sunny day'). In other words, because PMS is conceptualised in negative terms, it stands in the way of constructions (and therefore experiences) of the female body as something positive which is 'healthy' or 'good' and can be celebrated, rather than feared and blamed.

In principal, feminists do *not* argue that some women do not experience discomfort during the premenstrual phase of their monthly cycles. Rather, their concern is that the way the culture talks about menstruation has real implications about women's experiences of their bodies. Such discourses make it more difficult to feel good in one's (female) body and allow 'social' problems to pass for 'women's problems'. As in the discussions of many other issues in feminism, here also the personal and the political collapse into one. However, the feminist message that the personal is political is nowhere more evident than in the study of rape. In the section below, we explore briefly how and why feminism takes women's words and their accounts of rape seriously. We use examples from the media, film, women's words, psychology, etc. in order to demonstrate the social embeddedness of the phenomenon of rape and point out some of its political dimensions. Such an approach is informed by postmodern and feminist theoretical insights. What we do not examine here is how mainstream psychology tends to research rape. Mostly, such work is experimentally based involving positivistic principles and focusing on individuals' perceptions and attitudes. Ward (1995) provides an excellent summary of the topic area. The major criticism of mainstream psychological research posed by feminists is that it tends to view rape as a discrete experience of individual women and aberrations of individual men, thus obscuring the sociopolitical nature of the problem and its pervasiveness (Kaschak, 1992).

Sexual abuse and rape

Rape, like many other things which happen predominantly to women, is under-studied in mainstream social psychology. During the 1970s, developments in the women's movement brought the topic onto feminists' theoretical agendas. Susan Brownmiller's book *Against Our Will* (1975) was one of the most influential texts produced during this era. In it, she examined the history and politics of rape and many of its psychological aspects. In addition, Brownmiller's work established a precedent for the study of cultural myths about rape operating on many different levels, such as the police, medical and law systems, the media, academia, and generally society at large. The close examination of such myths revealed, as Ward (1995) puts it, 'an unconscious rape ideology' which was 'strongly ingrained, widespread and accepted without questioning'. This focus on language, however, did not mean that feminists sat in academic ivory towers deconstructing myths about rape. Rather, the opposite was the case. Much of the early research and theory on rape grew out of grassroots work and a practical concern to help women victims. For example, in 1978 Women Against Rape (WAR), a grassroots organisation in London, began research enquiries into sexual assault. At the same time, WAR was involved in campaigning, lobbying, initiating petitions, promoting public education and so on. Research in this context had practical and political aims.

Listening to women who have experienced rape and sexual abuse and taking their words seriously fed into the development of the so-called *feminists' stand-point theories* (Griffin and Phoenix, 1994). For the moment, however, we want to begin by emphasising that feminist study of rape conveyed most clearly the message that women's views, their experiences and subjectivities are excluded from the culture at large. What do we mean by that, and why is it important? Let's take some extracts from texts in which women speak about their experiences of rape and sexual abuse as an example:

> #### Soledad
> *I was very self-destructive in terms of drugs and fighting . . . I would do drugs and I wouldn't even know what the hell it was I was using. I didn't care. That went on until I was 16.*
>
> *Fighting was an everyday occurrence on the street. As we got bigger, the toys got more dangerous. I carried knives. I got into fights with people who carried knives. And some with guns. They would be tripping, too. You would never know whether you would come out of there alive. I thought this was just the way it was, and it was fine if I died with it.*
>
> *Between what was happening to me at home with him and having to fight and live on the streets too, I always thought the only freedom would be to go to prison. Then I would be 'free'.*
>
> *I always dealt with my life on an hour-by-hour basis. For a long time, I never did want to live.*

Gizelle

The effect of the abuse manifested through my body. I sleep walked. I had high fevers that were life threatening. And they could never find a cause. I had nightmares. I had severe asthma. And I would just stop breathing . . .

I felt caught, trapped in my body. That's continued into adulthood. I never heard any messages from my body. I would be really sick and would stagger around and go to work. I made a lifetime dedication of not listening to my body, because if I had, I would have had to hear that I was raped, and I couldn't do that and survive.

Alicia Mendoza

Remembering the rape triggered the worst period of the whole healing process. It felt like I was going to die. I couldn't take a breath without thinking about incest. In fact, it was a struggle to breathe a lot of the time. I had a few days where I just sat on the kitchen floor, rocking and holding myself . . .

It felt like my body was inhabited by this thing that had happened in my childhood, that there was no cell in my body that was not involved in it. The memories felt like they were invading me, in the same way my uncle had invaded my body. I spent a lot of time feeling like I was going to throw up. I was often out of my body. I'd feel like I was floating somewhere at the other end of the room. I couldn't feel anything below the neck. My brain was working, but my legs? 'What legs?'

I had to keep reminding myself to sleep and eat. I had notes all over my house, saying, 'When did you last eat?', 'When did you last sleep?'

Mary McGrath

My greatest denial of the incest was presenting myself as a happy, bubbly kid. I did the same thing with my own family when I grew up. I presented myself to the world as a self-assured, fun, together person. 'It doesn't matter what's really going on, keep up appearances'.

I did the same thing with the alcoholism that I did with the incest: be active in church, be friendly with the neighbours . . .

I didn't feel associated with my body for many years. It was really all mental until my mid-thirties . . .

I had been totally alienated from feelings. That's how I protected myself all those years. It took me forever to feel a feeling, much less express it. People would say to me, 'How do you feel?', and I'd say, 'Well, I think . . .' It was like learning a totally different language. It was a process of getting things intellectually, then at a feeling level and finally being able to act from that position.

(Bass and Davis, 1988)

These extracts are taken from Bass and Davis' (1988) book *The Courage to Heal*, which is a guide for women survivors of sexual abuse. Such sharing of 'private' experiences grew out of the anti-rape movement during the 1970s when the first public speak-outs took place. Speaking out helped women to realise that rape was much more common than previously realised, and indeed research was carried out to illustrate this (Hall, 1985; Koss, 1992). Speaking also pointed to a great deal of human suffering carried out in silence. The women above speak of: taking 'drugs and fighting'; of 'life on an hour-by-hour basis' where life in prison means 'freedom'; of feeling 'caught' and 'trapped' in one's body; of having 'life-threatening fevers'; and flashbacks and 'nightmares'; of struggles 'to breathe'; of 'feeling invaded'; of 'wanting to throw up'; of 'being out' of their body; and of being 'alienated' from one's feelings. Put together, women were telling a story of subjective experiences *not* to be seen in the cultural representations of rape.

There were of course, *clinical models*, which attempted to categorise 'symptoms' and 'conditions' of psychological illness. In DSM-IIIR (Diagnostic and Statistical Manual), however, despite the daily occurrence of rape, there is not one model solely based on experiences of women. Instead, the condition of Post-Traumatic Stress Disorder (PTSD) mentions rape as something which can lead to the 'disorder'. PTSD, however, is based on *male* experiences of war (hence we can see beta bias again!). For feminists, in the best of cases, clinical models of rape overstress individual experience and treatment. While it is the case that individual women who have been raped need help, such a focus alone is insufficient because it does not deal with the fact that 'society' as a whole may also be in need of 'treatment' or change. Clinical and generally mainstream psychological models view the issue from the 'outside', or from the researcher's viewpoint and take this view as the one which tells the 'truth'. What remains unseen in this process is that often the women involved are telling a story of rape which is different. Instead of perspectives on rape which incorporate meaningfully women's experiences such as those cited above, what do we see?

In the popular press, glamorous, young and vulnerable women are repeatedly represented being raped by monstrous men. Brownmiller (1975) pointed out that those representations do not reflect reality much as they are 'dressed up' to fit male fantasy. Rape cases are selected and carefully worded. Take, for example, the following, all of which are taken from the same page of *The Sport* (6th December, 1996):

> *An Olympic diving hopeful told a court yesterday how a coach repeatedly raped her while she cried and begged him to stop . . . The girl, who was only 13 . . .*

> *A man who subjected three 16-year-old girls to a horrific 24-hour sex ordeal . . .*

> *A brunette told the court yesterday of her rape ordeal at the hands of a squaddie . . .*

> *A teenage au-pair was raped by a man who 'rescued' her from an amorous Italian . . .*

These, as Brownmiller has long since pointed out, are not real flesh-and-blood women, but are objectified, cardboard cut-out figures. What is, for example, the importance of a woman's hair colour in relation to her 'rape ordeal'? Such representations exclude cases of rape of black women, older women and of occasions where men are raped by other men. What is also not represented is that many rapes are not committed by monstrous strangers but by relatives and other men known to the women. In addition, while rape cases tend to be reported, attempted rapes are often left out. In all, early feminist work began to formulate the thesis that such representations do not depict some reality about rape, but construct and maintain myths about rape. Feminist research presented evidence arguing that such myths hid the facts, which were that: many more women are raped than we are led to believe; many rapists are fathers, uncles, other relatives and acquaintances, and not strangers; more women still have experienced attempted rape or some form of sexual violation; all women live in fear of rape (see Ward, 1995, for further discussion). Putting these various strands together, the issue of rape began to look as if a sex war was being waged against women, but its politics remained unacknowledged.

Instead, on various cultural platforms the issue of rape appeared in depoliticised terms. Film critics for example, observe that rape is used as part and parcel of the packaging in the making of a 'baddie' without any political dimensions involved (Rapping, 1992). The story often continues with the 'good guy' who, being benevolently inclined, usually 'saves' the woman who is about to be or was raped. Thus the audience is sent on an ego trip in the making of a male hero, rather than being presented with the thoughts, feelings, actions and the experiences of the woman involved. In other films, rape can be seen as a form of punishment for women. For example, in *She's gotta have it*, a black woman is the heroine. She is represented as a modern, sexually active woman. However, Jamie, one of her lovers, behaves throughout the film as if he wants to serve her and please her. When he rapes her in one of the final scenes of the film, he says, 'Is this what you want?' In her analysis of the film, Simmonds (1992) asks:

> *What are we meant to understand by this ending? Is it that she has made him rape her? Is it that she has really been asking for it? . . . The underlying message is that a woman who needs so much sex and, as the title suggests* has gotta have it, *deserves whatever she gets from men.*

What Simmonds' questions evoke here are a number of rape myths which circulate in our culture, namely that rape victims are responsible for the crime; that they ask for it; and that they deserve it. Other feminists have also noted that rape can be used as a form of punishment for 'being too smart, daring or liberated' (Ward, 1995). Popular modern myths that some 'women deserve it' and others 'want it' and men simply oblige are well

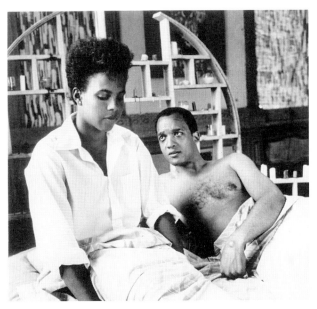

Figure 8.1 *She's gotta have it*: The heroine, Nola, with her lover, Jamie

documented (e.g. Herman, 1984).

Psychology as a discipline has often been criticised for articulating and providing such myths with ostensibly scientific credentials. Consider Freud's statement below in relation to the so-called 'normal' sexual act:

More constraint has been applied to the libido when it is pressed into the service of the feminine function . . . The accomplishment of the aim of biology has been entrusted to the aggressiveness of the men and has been, to some extent, independent of women's consent.

(Freud, 1965, cited in Nicolson, 1992)

What is suggested here is that men do a service to women; women really do want 'it', and that 'normal' (hetero)sexuality involves male aggression. It is not difficult to see the similarity between the assumptions here and the rape myths evoked in the above-mentioned film. The most damaging ideas from Freud's work about female sexuality, which were taken on by society at large, are in relation to the so-called female hysteria and masochism. In practice, this meant that if women are seen as hysterical, they are not to be believed and if they are seen as enjoying pain, then they can't be raped! Helen Deutsch (1944) expanded on such Freudian ideas and offered her own thesis on women's 'rape fantasies'.

Despite the fact that many of these initial propositions about women's warped but powerful psyches have been challenged over the years, they live on in myths that women lie about rape (LeGrand, 1973). In the courts of law, traditional cross-examining tactics suggest that female rape victims are suspected of lying, irrational behaviour and manipulation. Crawford (1995) illustrates the absurdity of the procedure with a feminist joke where the same cross-examining tactics used in rape cases are applied to a man who has been robbed:

> **The Rape of Mr Smith**
> *'Have you ever given money away?'*
> *'Yes, of course . . .'*
> *'And did you do so willingly?'*
> *'What are you getting at?'*
> *'Well, let's put it like this, Mr Smith. You've given money away in the past – in fact you have quite a reputation for philanthropy. How can we be sure that you weren't contriving to have your money taken away from you by force?'*

'Listen, if I wanted . . .'
'Never mind.'
And later:
'What were you wearing at the time, Mr Smith?'
'Let's see. A suit. Yes, a suit.'
'An expensive *suit?'*
'Well, yes.'
*'In other words, Mr Smith, you were walking round the streets late at
night in a suit that practically* advertised *the fact that you might be a
good target for some easy money, isn't that so? I mean, if we didn't
know better, Mr Smith, we might even think you were* asking *for this
to happen, mightn't we?'*

(Unknown, 1990, cited in Crawford, 1995)

However, what goes on in court is but one location where women are
subjected to such a degree of disbelief. In one, but in many ways typical,
documented case, a woman who reported being raped by a stranger was
disbelieved by almost everyone involved. The police expressed doubts that
she really had run out of petrol and therefore was unable to take herself
away from the scene of crime. The psychiatrist involved, despite seeing that
she was bleeding from being battered asked her, 'Haven't you really been
rushing toward this very thing all your life?' At home, her husband shouted
at her, 'If that's what you wanted, why didn't you come to me?' (Russell,
1975, cited in Matlin, 1987).

We have thus gone a full circle. We began by showing how women's
actual words spoke of painful personal experiences which are largely absent
from the cultural representations of rape. If rape in the first instance is
about power, where the wishes of one person override and wipe out the
wishes of another, then the police, the court procedures, psychological
theories, the media can all be seen as involved in another 'wipe out': a
second rape. Feminist work has contributed to the reconstruction of rape,
beginning with listening to women who have experienced rape and sexual
assault. Thus an alternative story is in the making. It speaks in the face of
pervading myths about rape, saying: no, women do not want to be raped;
no, women do not enjoy it; no, they are not responsible for it; no, they don't
lie about it; no, rape is not trivial and so on.

Applications and implications

Feminism in general strives to produce theories and practices which can be
applied in the service of women and have wider social and political
implications. We have seen, for example, how in relation to rape, feminist
scholarship and social activism were closely related. In this sense, one of the
implications of feminism for psychology is that it *challenges* the notion that

science is, ought to be or can be divorced from 'real life'. As we have seen, feminist scholars have constantly argued that, despite the fact that mainstream psychology claims to produce 'scientific' and objective theories, it has ended up supporting and elaborating existing patriarchal ideologies about women. In fact, many feminists have argued for a *paradigm shift* in psychology, whereby positivism is replaced by social constructionist perspectives. Such perspectives are more suitable for taking into account the social and political dimensions of human existence which are typically 'stripped away' within mainstream psychology. In addition, the postmodern perspectives, which many feminist psychologists adopted, contributed to the development of an awareness about the *politics of meaning*. Thus many argued that to develop and write a theory about women is more than simply to describe women. In such theories, certain values are inscribed, and these very values can function towards the protection of the interests of dominant social groups at the expense of those of others. Rather than seek one theory which captures the truth about all women, feminists, like many postmodernists, have focused on the ways in which dominant beliefs (or discourses) about women are reproduced in a number of social locations and are maintained in specific social practices. Thus, for example, in our discussion of rape here, we saw that feminist analyses were not interested in searching for and outlining a male or female psychology as such which could explain the phenomenon; rather, a critical examination of discourses about rape showed how these were repeatedly reproduced in many different places, the joint effect of which contributed to a social situation in which women's voices were silenced. In so far as such discourses, (or cultural myths) dictate what can be said and by whom, they regulate subjectivity (Henriques et al., 1984). Since academia (but also society at large) has been dominated by men, mainstream discourses tend to emanate from men's points of view and are implicated in the regulation of female subjectivity, or the subjection of women.

Such theoretical insights lead to the appreciation that *discursive interventions* by feminists are a political activity. Such interventions involved a two-way process. On the one hand, feminists have engaged in the *deconstruction* of mainstream theoretical views about women, and on the other they work towards producing reconstructions. Thus, for example, we saw some of the ways in which feminists have argued that PMS is not merely a real biological entity which explains aspects of female psychology. The 'deconstruction' of PMS involved historical examination of notions about the female body; critical summarative examination of 'scientific' research findings; and pointing out some of the political functions of the discourse for 'keeping women in their places'. Once 'deconstruction' has taken place, then *reconstructive* suggestions can be also made, indicating possible ways in which the female body can be viewed and experienced positively (as, for example, Chrisler's study did – see Chrisler et al., 1994).

Feminist practices also tend to differ methodologically. In this chapter, we have only indicated that, in general, feminists have found the experimental methods in psychology, which are based on positivistic principles, unfriendly to women. More specifically, we drew the attention to the ways in which allowing (female, in our case) subjectivity to direct the research, rather than attempting to control and eliminate it, may give rise to theories or understanding of women that work better for them. While we have not discussed this in much detail here, it is worth mentioning that feminists in psychology and other disciplines have made significant contributions to our understanding of the relationship between the researcher and the researched as itself implicated in the reproductions of certain types of power relations. For the moment, it suffices to say that, by adopting the view that if in the research process women researchers and their 'subjects' are more equally positioned in relation to power, then the findings of such research may speak more for women and for more women (or further reading see Banister et al., 1994).

(Ab)normality

9

To most non-psychologists, normality/abnormality is probably one of the central areas of psychology. The images of the 'shrink' and the abnormal person ('nutter', 'queer', 'loony', 'mad/bad', etc.) are ones of common evocation and usage. Every newspaper report of a murder or child abuse re-places the issue at centre stage. In addition, and perhaps of greater importance, this is an area characterised by clear and rarely contested status and power differentials. Psychologists, clinical psychologists and psychiatrists interviewed in television news reports and documentaries usually carry some 'expert' label, and unless their remarks clearly conflict with folk wisdom (e.g. Spare the rod and spoil the child) or deeply seated prejudices, they are rarely challenged by the layperson.

Consider for a moment the implications of this. The Expert is placed in a position of defining (ab)normality, frequently in terms of technical language which is inaccessible (and so unchallengable) to the layperson; explaining the causes and treatments for this 'condition'; and, because of the specialist nature of his/her expertise, being challenged only by an 'insider' (i.e. someone from the same profession).

We may be reminded here of Parker's (1992) statement that psychologists often define and explain the world in ways which suit their own purposes and then spend the rest of their professional lives researching their own fictions. This focuses our attention upon what we might call 'artefactual psychology'. Rather than our scientific endeavour 'uncovering some truth out there', our findings may merely have occurred because of the manner of our investigation. This may occur at a number of levels, from demand characteristics (participants behaving in a peculiar way because of their wish to provide what they believe the researcher wishes to see) and the Hawthorne Effect (behaviour being distorted simply because it is knowingly being observed) through to psychological reification, where psychological 'working concepts' come to take on a 'real' existence of their own. Much of what psychologists write and do about abnormality may come into this category.

As we shall see later, this is not inconsequential. History tells horrendous tales of the vilification of witches, homosexuals and the mad (amongst many others). The label of abnormal can carry with it a whole life sentence of marginalisation, powerlessness, ostracism and abuse.

The story so far

Parker et al. (1995) give three histories of abnormality:

> . . . the first is a fairly uncontentious account of the development of 'madness' as a problem in Western culture since the Middle Ages and of changes in diagnostic categories. The second is a more radical examination of the notions of mental health which lie under those categories, and the third is one which throws into question the very notions of reason and unreason which language forces into being.

We will begin here with our version of the first of these (although we will take a much earlier starting point) and return to the other two later in the Revisions and reconceptualisations at the end of the chapter.

As the opening chapter made clear, one of the main lessons to be learned from a postmodern critique of psychology is that we cannot, and certainly should not, work on the assumption that history is either singular or linear. There are a multitude of ways of viewing the past, and most of the accounts are far from a straight progression, such as A leads to B which lead to C and so on. This is rarely more clearly shown than when we consider the history of (ab)normality. As we shall see, there has been a 'toing and froing' down the centuries as different assumptions have been held and different models of the person have been dominant. Furthermore, the history we are going to explore here is one which is largely centred in Europe (and later, the USA). Indigenous psychologies have their own histories to tell.

All of this becomes even more significant if we accept that a history is not simply a re-telling of past events. The people at the times we are describing were a part of that time and place, and were embedded in it. Kvale (1992) argues that we need to see all human activity and language as 'rooted . . . in a given social and historical context'. It follows from this that we cannot view key historical figures, such as Freud for example, as 'free-standing' individuals. They both create and are shaped by their placing in time and culture.

Halgin and Whitbourne (1993) say there are three prominent themes which recur throughout the history of (ab)normality in Europe and the USA, these being belief in the mystical, the scientific and the humanitarian. Mystical explanations of abnormality view it as the result of possession by demonic or other evil spirits. So-called scientific explanations (including most of those located within psychology) offer explanations derived from the products of conventional science (for example, biological malfunctions, inappropriate learning, emotional stressors). Humanitarian explanations 'view psychological disorders as the result of cruelty, non-acceptance or poor living conditions'.

We may argue that there is considerable overlap between these three 'themes'. For example, much of the humanitarian viewpoint can be comfortably placed within the scientific viewpoint (such as humanistic psychology), and some scientists are also humanitarians! In addition, many indigenous psychologies are strongly characterised by belief in the so-called supernatural and spiritual worlds (e.g. Kim, 1990). However, the point Halgin and Whitbourne make about the recurrence of the themes and their waxing and waning in influence across the centuries is a most important one and fully supports the notion of the non-linearity of histories.

Pre-historic (ab)normalities

Most of the evidence we possess about the earliest years of human life derives from the skeletal remains of early humans and examples of the things they produced, such as their tools and art. Maher and Maher (1985) discuss trephining, where skulls dating back to the Stone Age had apparently been drilled with small holes. The regularity of placement and the ways in which the holes appeared to 'heal' would suggest that the holes were created surgically rather than by accidents. We can speculate that trephining may have been carried out to release energies or spirits from the head.

Another treatment used in prehistoric times, and recently raised in public awareness by Hollywood, was exorcism: the use of prayers, emetics (drugs which induce vomiting) and violent techniques such as flogging to cast out evil spirits. This technique was used by the early Greeks, Chinese, Hebrews and Egyptians (Sue, Sue and Sue, 1990).

The Greek and Roman periods: the beginnings of the medical model

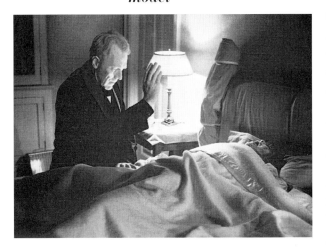

Figure 9.1 Hollywood and madness. *The Exorcist* reintroduced audiences to a view of abnormality being caused by Satanic possession

The first recorded major change in the dominant view of abnormality came with the beginning of the Greek and Roman civilisations (approximately 500BC–AD500). Hippocrates (460–370BC) is often regarded as the founder of medicine, as we understand it in our culture today. Hippocrates challenged the dominance of what he regarded as superstitious beliefs, and his ideas were later (second century AD) to form the building blocks of a new theory of abnormality expounded by Galen. The theory focused upon dysfunctioning of the brain. Three forms of mental illness – mania, melancholia and phrenitis (brain fever) – were identified', and it was argued that these were caused by imbalances in the four body fluids which were originally described by Hippocrates (black bile, yellow bile, phlegm and blood). It was argued, for example, that melancholia (closely related to what would now be called depression) was due to an excess of black bile.

Hippocrates and Galen believed that mental illnesses and personality disorders should be treated by techniques such as purgation (forced excretion), emetics and bleeding and – somewhat less dramatically – changes in diet. This constituted the first 'scientific/medical' model of abnormality, and it is interesting to note that these early ideas are still reflected in some contemporary theories. For example H. J. Eysenck's (1957) model of four temperaments – melancholic, phlegmatic, sanguine, choleric – is a clear derivative.

Other early theories concerning abnormality were forwarded by Plato, who argued that the mentally ill should not be punished, but should be the responsibility of the family (further anticipation of the UK in the 1980s and 1990s!), and Aesclepiades, who challenged the centrality of bodily fluids imbalance and argued, instead, for the importance of emotional disturbances.

The Church and abnormality

The next phase in this European history of abnormality, encompassing the Dark and Middle Ages, was attributable to the influence of the Christian Church. Sue, Sue and Sue (1990) say:

> The Church demanded uncompromising adherence to its tenets. Christian fervour brought with it the concepts of heresy and punishment: certain truths were deemed sacred and those who challenged them were denounced as heretics. Scientific thought that was in conflict with Church doctrine was not tolerated. Because of this atmosphere, rationalism and the scholarly scientific works went 'underground' for many years, preserved mainly by Arab scholars and European monks. Natural and supernatural explanations of illness became fused . . . Because illness was perceived as punishment for sin, the sick person was assumed to be guilty of wrongdoing . . . A time of trouble for everyone, the Dark Ages (AD400–900) were especially bleak for the mentally ill.

This clearly represents a reversion to the conceptualisation of abnormality being a result of evil/demonic possession, with consequential treatments, such as exorcism. Other forms of possession became prominent in the Middle Ages, such as lycanthropy (a mental disorder in which the 'afflicted' believe themselves to be wolves and act accordingly, resurrected again by Hollywood centuries later) and witchcraft. It has been estimated (Spanos, 1978) that between 1450 and 1600, well over 100,000 people were executed as witches. Feminist writers (such as Ussher, 1991) have argued that witchcraft constituted a systematic persecution of women substantially because of sexist prejudice and bigotry deriving, in the main, from a fear of erosion of male power and privilege.

One assumption common in all of the above explanations for

abnormality is that it is rooted in the individual. However, an exception to this was the peculiarly 13th-century phenomenon of so-called 'mass madness'. It began in Italy with Tarantism, which was a dance mania characterised by wild raving, jumping, dancing and convulsions (mirrored in the UK in the 1980s and 1990s at dance and rave parties?). Tarantism was most common during the height of the summer and was thought to be caused by the sting of the tarantula spider. A 'victim' would run into the street, jumping and raving, to be joined by others who believed they had also been bitten. The issue of crowd or mass hysteria has been studied and challenged by Moscovici (1985). He argues that much of the concentration of Anglo-American psychology upon the individual results from the fact that the individual is perceived (at least in our culture) as rational and intelligent, and the group as a 'lower' form of human existence. According to Foucault (1971), up until the 15th century, the greatest fear was of death, but at this point in time madness 'makes an entrance as the ghastly scourge of the Western mind' (cited Parker et al., 1995). A key difference was that whereas death was seen as something which occurred at the end of a life, madness was an ever-present possibility. It was then believed that: 'The head that will become the skull is already empty . . . Madness is the déjà-là [already there] of death' (Foucault, 1971). Parker et al. say:

> The mad filled the space that was opened up by the closure of the leprosaria at the end of the Middle Ages. Lepers ceased to be the main problem on the outskirts of life, and the new diseased of mind occupied their place.

The Asylums and Houses of Correction (such as the monastery of St Mary of Bethlehem – 'Bedlam' – which was converted to a hospital by Henry VIII in 1547 and later specialised in the incarceration of the insane) began to appear all over Europe. At first, the 'mad' were thrown in and incarcerated with all kinds of social deviants, but increasingly the specialist asylums developed. At this time, madness was not seen as being a product of illness, rather it was attributed to an inadequate inherited constitution, damaging life events or spiritual possession. Parker et al. say:

> The bridge to the medical treatment of the mad was the moral treatment of the insane in special places, treatment which was provoked by popular fears that the distressed inhabitants of the large institutions in cities were contagious . . . It was the reinterpretation of the issue as a moral one which set the way for releasing the mad from their chains.

Let us now consider how this historical shift occurred.

The period of modernity

The Renaissance saw the rise of humanism. An important influence before this was exerted by Johan Weyer (1515–1588), a German physician who resurrected the notion of mental disturbance. In many ways, he represented a return to the ideas of Hippocrates and Galen, but he was severely criticised by both the Church and the State. Reformist ideas were carried into practice by Philippe Pinel (1745–1826) and William Tuke (1732–1822). The vast majority of modern British and American textbooks of Abnormal Psychology portray these two as great liberators, reformers who freed the insane in the asylums. However, this view is severely challenged by Foucault (1961; 1977). He used the notion, forwarded originally by Jeremy Bentham, of the Panopticon, of an observer who is able to survey all at one view (for example, through a prison organised so that a central warder can observe all prisoners almost simultaneously). As Parker et al. put it:

> The fact that the observer might be unseen increases the power of this form of observation, since those observed will behave as if they are being watched, just in case; discipline thus moves from something inflicted on others to something which becomes internalised, and we move from regulation by others to self-regulation.

Foucault (1961) says:

> We must . . . re-evaluate the meanings assigned to Tuke's work: liberation of the insane, abolition of constraint, constitution of a human milieu: these are the only justifications. The real operations were different. In fact, Tuke created an asylum where he substituted for the free terror of madness the stifling anguish of responsibility; fear no longer reigned on the other side of the prison gates, it now raged under the seals of conscience. Tuke now transformed the age-old terrors in which the insane had been trapped to the very heart of madness. The asylum no longer punished the madman's guilt, it is true; but it did more, it organised that guilt.

The emergence of psychiatry

The humanism/moral conceptualisation of Renaissance madness was followed by a return to the medical view of the mad. An early indication of this occurred at the beginning of the current century with the work of Emil Kraepelin (1856–1926), the founder of psychiatry, who published the first recognised textbook of psychiatry in 1883. The mad were now re-assimilated into a medical conceptualisation.

Abnormality was individualised (located within the sick individual with little or no heed paid to social context) and pathologised (seen as an organic, i.e. physical, failure, dysfunction or abnormality).

> Kraepelin claimed that certain groups of symptoms occur together sufficiently often to be called a 'disease' or syndrome . . . He regarded each mental illness as distinct from all others, with its own origins, symptoms, course and outcome; even though cures had not been found, at least the course of the disease could be predicted. (Gross, 1996)

Kraepelin's classificatory system formed the basis for the two major diagnostic/classificatory system used in modern Western psychiatry: the Diagnostic and Statistical Manual of Mental Disorders (DSM) – the American Psychological Association's official system, first published in 1952 – and the International Classification of Diseases (ICD), published by the World Health Organisation, originally in 1948.

... and alternatives

Behaviour modification is psychology's own offering to the treatment of abnormal behaviour. Based upon learning theory, it contends that the problem is one of inappropriate or faulty learning processes and the key lies in establishing new, 'appropriate' learned associations. It concentrates upon symptoms rather than causes and upon remediation and treatments more than classification.

Some of the psychologists most closely associated with this 'psychological technology', such as B. F. Skinner and H. J. Eysenck, have written about how it can be used as a form of social engineering (e.g. Skinner, 1971). Eysenck (quoted in Heather, 1976) says:

> *The problem to be discussed is: how can we engineer a social consent which will make people behave in a socially adapted, law-abiding fashion, which will not lead to a breakdown of the intricately woven fabric of society?*

The other major model of abnormality which has dominated the 20th century has been psychoanalysis, which is sufficiently part of public as well as psychological knowledge that no exposition is necessary here.

All three of these models are based upon an appeal to a 'scientific model', in one form or another. Should this not make us rejoice in the fact that we, in our culture – unlike many others – have cast-out primitive, earlier conceptualisations? Foucault (1961), for one, believes not. He says:

> *As positivism imposes itself on medicine and psychiatry . . . the psychiatrist's [power] becomes more and more miraculous, and the doctor–patient couple sinks deeper into a strange world. In the patient's eyes, the doctor becomes a thaumaturge [a worker of miracles] . . . It is because he is a doctor that he is believed to possess these powers . . . To the doctor, Freud transferred all the structures Pinel and Tuke had set up within confinement . . . he regrouped its powers, extended them to the maximum by uniting them in the doctor's hands.*

Is it not the case that the only possible responses to such power are silence and compliance? Let us now turn our attention to some practical examples of abnormality determination and policing in practice.

(Ab)normality: some contemporary consequences

SOVIET PSYCHIATRY

Cohen (1989) writes:

> *In 1983, the Soviet Association of Neuropathologists and Psychiatrists resigned from the World Psychiatric Association. It did so to avoid an angry debate at the Association's Vienna Congress on the political abuse of psychiatry. The debate might well have demanded an inquiry into Soviet practices or even the expulsion of the Soviet Association. The Soviets denied they had too much to hide. Rather, they claimed they were resigning because they did not want grubby politics to sully the* pure science of psychiatry.

The abuses of Soviet psychiatry, in gross violation of human rights, were well known before Perestroika. Anti-psychiatrists, such as R. D. Laing and Thomas Szasz, and radical psychologists, such as Nick Heather, have, however, argued that we in the West should not be too self-congratulatory. Psychiatry and clinical psychology have been less than 'squeaky clean' right under our own noses. Films such as *One Flew Over The Cuckoo's Nest* – still regularly screened on television – have raised public consciousness about potential and possible abuses.

We are let down here by the familiar problem of psychological long-sightedness. It is frequently the case that it is most difficult to see the problems that are closest to us. Physical, cultural and historical distances help us to see malpractice 'abroad', whilst xenophobia and nationalism, for example, often blind us to the fault-lines of our own territory.

HOMOSEXUALITY

Figure 9.2   The question 'What makes a person heterosexual?' is almost never asked, whereas there is a constant effort to 'explain' homosexuality. This cartoon may suggest it is a natural condition

Let's look at homosexuality as an example of supposed 'deviant' sexuality. The term 'queer', used to derogatorily describe homosexuals, signifies abnormality. The decision to remove homosexuality from the DSM was made only as recently as 1973 (see Humphreys, 1997, for discussion). Let us consider an illustration. In England, at the time of writing, homosexual teachers are strongly discouraged from teaching in many schools, and teachers are not permitted to discuss homosexuality in the classroom. Several prominent politicians and media figures have had careers ruined in the wake of 'revelations' of their homosexuality.

Weeks (1985) argues that the point is not that we should be more liberal and accepting of sexualities other than our own, rather that sexuality should simply not be an issue. That is to say, whether a person is heterosexual, bisexual, homosexual or celibate should have implications only for their sexual relationships and behaviours, rather than being seen as a definition of their whole person. Heather (1976) supports this when he says: 'The chief contribution of psychiatry ... is that, by inviting the harassed and despised homosexual to see himself as sick, he is thereby allowed the soft option of admitting there is something wrong with him'. He continues:

> *But what are we to do with the homosexual who requests treatment? We surely cannot refuse him; our medical ethics would not allow it. The pertinent question is, why are these psychiatrists offering treatment in the first place? If homosexuality is not an illness, what have doctors to do with it? . . . Gays do not want a reformed medical attitude to homosexuality; they want no attitude at all. They do not want psychiatrists to correct their chapters on homosexuality, but to omit them.*

> (Heather, 1976)

Once again, the classification of (ab)normality can be seen to exclude certain people from many aspects of 'normal' life and exclude them from equality.

STIGMATISATION

Goffman (1963) has argued that stigma is associated with mental illness and institutionalisation, and the person is devalued and 'spoiled' because of his/her classification and label. People reject and exclude the mentally ill. Negative images and stereotypes abound, and the crude and inaccurate portrayals of 'lunatics' in old black and white films (still frequently screened) hardly help.

Miles (1988), writing about women and mental illness, gives the following examples of interview remarks showing how patients are stigmatised:

> *Life is totally changed, people just turn away.*

> *My mum has changed, she cannot accept that I am mental. She doesn't want to know.*

> *My sister-in-law doesn't want me near her children in case I hurt them or go funny, so I don't go there any more.*

> *They were very unkind, and Jack [brother-in-law] laughed at me and said I must be funny in the head if I go to the funny place. I felt humiliated. I felt that under the laughing and joking there was unkindness.*

Again, we see the label of (ab)normality leading directly to exclusion and the denial of equality.

THE (AB)NORMAL BODY

Writers such as Shakespeare (1975) and Thomas (1982) have described the 'double handicap' suffered by those who are not able-bodied. Not only do they have to live with their physical disability, but also the way in which they are treated by others (most frequently being peered and pointed at, rejected or patronised).

There is incalculable pressure upon women in most Western societies to 'look good' and 'present' themselves for the admiration of others (men, of course, or women as judges on behalf of men!) (Lott, 1994). The whole issue of fat as undesirable and abnormal ('who, in their right mind, would let themselves go like that?') has been a topic of central importance for many feminist writers over the last few decades. A person's right to their own body is being denied.

Revisions and reconceptualisations

Heather (1976) offers many examples of ideological, moral and ethical issues in both psychology and (particularly) psychiatry. Let us carry out our work towards revisions and reconceptualisations by considering a sample of these.

The worship of normality

Heather says:

> The best concrete example of this tendency in psychology is the way in which it worships the statistical norm, especially in the traditional area of personality theory and testing. The language of normal–abnormal as used in psychology carried with it the unexamined assumption that what is normal in our society is necessarily a good thing. Thus, by a subtle sleight of hand, what is really a value-judgement of immense significance is slipped into psychology's view of man, disguised as a statement of objective fact. For, when we say that someone is abnormal on some psychological scale or other, we immediately think of the personality feature in question as something undesirable that should be corrected. In this way, psychology merely adds to, and gives scientific credence for, the massive pressures society brings to bear on the individual, from birth to death, to conform and be like everybody else, to be respectable and not stray from the path.

In opposition to this Heather advocates 'a serious study of the pathology of normalcy', where we 'problematise' not the social/psychological deviant but the conformist.

The status of scientific wisdom

Heather argues that such is the power of the scientific discourse in our culture that few of us feel sufficiently confident to argue with the given wisdom. He believes that this is further endorsed by the endeavours of workers in the field to define (ab)normal psychology as a branch of medicine.

Parker et al. (1995) talk about the 'percolation' of professional knowledge into the popular domain as one dynamic in the ways in which images of abnormality are 'exchanged' between the profession and institutions of psychiatry and the lay public. They say:

> *It no longer seems sensible to talk of professional and lay concepts as separate things, since the distinction between them is not so much in the kinds of discourses used by the speakers but rather the position from which they speak . . . Madness and its contents are located within discourses of difference which serve to regulate sectors of society and . . . this concept is historically allied with a number of politically dominant institutions and their practices (medicine, the welfare state and so on).*

Johnstone (1989) has argued that not only must the power of the institution and profession of psychiatry be challenged and put under scrutiny, we also need to offer logistically and politically practical alternatives, otherwise we fall into the trap of negativity and impracticality of care provision for the distressed which lead to the demise of the Anti-Psychiatry movement.

Parker et al. (1995) end their book with a directory of 'alternative' groups and enterprises (such as the Afro-Caribbean Mental Health Project, the Alliance of Women in Psychology, Patient Power and Support Coalition International) which have 'an activist and campaigning focus around mental health (but are not) mainstream self-help organisations that deliberately reproduce medical notions or who defer to traditional scientific experts on mental distress'.

Reification

This is what Heather calls 'transforming a meaningful process into a meaningless thing'. A person is no longer depressed, they *have* depression. The condition is taken to be an out-there entity which takes over the person. Heather argues that this belief encourages patients to be passive, as the problem is not with them but with their condition.

Johnstone (1989) argues that this is one of the most powerful 'devices' for maintaining the location of power in the institutions of psychiatry and behaviour modification. She believes that those in distress should be empowered to appreciate their own role in their position and 'recovery'.

Applications and implications

Addressing ethnocentricity

You will recall from the beginning of this chapter that Parker et al. (1995) forwarded three histories of psychopathology. It is now an appropriate time to mention their second one. They say:

> *Might our suspicion that the language we use to describe 'psychopathology' is culturally specific, also be worth directing at the phenomenon itself? It is not only the terms that change, perhaps, but what we imagine to 'really' lie underneath them. Of course mainstream psychiatrists . . . will see the 'reality of mental illness' as existing at every time and place, with different cultures simply having different words for 'it'. However, different cultures have such radically different conceptions of what we call mental illness that we have to consider the possibility that not only the talk, but also what is described is radically different.*

Cochrane (1983) argues that globally psychiatry is dominated by Anglo-American conceptualisations and practices. There are a number of possible responses to this state of affairs. One, of course, is to support it; another is to ignore it. However, if we do perceive it as problematic, we could address it by systematically detailing the ways in which specific cultures and groups of people differ from the 'dominant model'. For example, Rack (1984) has written for practitioners to 'help to minimise the confusions and misinterpretations that may arise between practitioner and client when cultural differences are involved'. Rack writes:

> *When a member of an ethnic minority develops a mental illness, the manifestations may be very much the same as in the familiar British-born patient. If so, once communication problems have been overcome, treatment can be given along familiar lines. But they may be different, and then there is a danger of misdiagnosis and wrong treatment. The similarities outweigh the differences, but it is the differences that concern us. For example: a middle-aged Pakistani woman in Bradford began to behave coquettishly towards her husband, and then towards other men in the household. When rebuked, she expressed with some vehemence her right to have opinions of her own, and said that if her husband disliked her behaviour he could leave her. This forthright speech convinced all her relatives that she had gone mad, and they brought her to a psychiatrist. The doctors and nurses, who were English, found no evidence of mental illness. She appeared to them to be a rather jolly, extrovert, uninhibited person, but nothing more. It required a psychiatrist who understood the norms of Pakistani culture to point out that her lack of decorum was highly unconventional in that culture context, and probably due to hypomania [physical and/or*

mental overactivity characterised by a rapid shifting in ideas and actions] . . . Conversely, a person may behave in ways which seem odd or bizarre to the practitioner, and lead him to suppose that mental illness is present, when in fact the behaviour is culturally normal or explicable.

This example relates to diagnosis of different 'groups' *within* one culture. Another issue concerns the 'importing' of an Anglo-American model *into* a different culture. Contrast the following two views:

The manifestations of psychological disorder are culturally shaped, yet comparable. The same psychological measures can be used, albeit judiciously and cautiously, in widely different cultures.

(Draguns, 1990)

and Kleinman's rejection of the view that mental illness is:

an entity, a thing to be 'discovered' in pure form under the layers of cultural camouflage . . . There can be no stripping away of layers of cultural accretion in order to isolate a culture-free entity. Culture shapes disease, first by shaping our explanations of disease.

(Kleinman, 1977, cited in Rack, 1984)

It is this latter view of cultural determinism which is consistent with the views of Parker et al. This view would be unsympathetic to the case study of the Pakistani woman quoted above. The process, although sensitive to cultural variability, still pathologises and labels and is still saturated by the status inequality between practitioner and 'patient'.

The helper and the helped

Much has been said throughout this chapter about the damaging effects of the massive status differential between those classified as abnormal and in need of help and/or incarceration and the practitioners. Recall, for example, what was said about abuses of human rights perpetrated by Soviet psychiatry and what Heather and Johnstone said about the passivity of the patient role.

One common theme running through many of the non-mainstream activity groups given by Parker et al. in their directory is that great emphasis is placed upon status equality and co-working. It is interesting to note in passing that this co-working can be seen in many other areas of psychology (e.g. Reason and Rowan's (1981) formalisation of 'co-operative research', and the change in terminology of those studied in psychological studies from subject to participant).

Addressing sexual biases in the conceptualisation of abnormality

Writers such as Miles (1988) and Ussher (1991) have shown the biases against women which characterise much of the work in the field of abnormality and mental illness (both historically and in current practice). This is explored further in Chapters 8 and 10.

An emphasis on language

A central aspect of the postmodern critique (discussed in the Introduction) is that language does not reflect reality, but is itself reality. Thus, abnormality is seen not as some inner incapacity of a sick individual but rather as emerging out of the 'interactive dynamics' between people. Thus it can be studied as being created and existing in the linguistic space between people. Sarup (1988) considers the ways in which two postmodernists, Jacques Lacan and Jacques Derrida, have criticised Freudian psychoanalysis. Sarup calls Lacan 'Freud's greatest contemporary interpreter'. Both Lacan and Derrida have (but in different ways) emphasised the centrality of language to that which is human. Lacan believes there could not be a human subject without language, but that the subject cannot be reduced to language (it is a reciprocal relationship, the two being mutually interdependent). Lacan is highly critical of therapies such as encounter groups, which are based upon an assertion of the primacy of basic, sub-vocal experience such as intuition and feeling. We are immersed in language and cannot get out of it. And because of this, meaning is always open to negotiation. All language, like fiction or dreams, is open to interpretation.

Derrida believes that, although Lacan advanced psychoanalysis by imposing a structure of language to the unconscious which was lacking in the Freudian original, Lacan is mistaken in viewing the unconscious as a source of 'truth'. The position Derrida takes could be considered as one which views language itself as the only 'truth'.

Although there are considerable differences in the arguments of Lacan and Derrida, both emphasise that abnormal psychology is wrong to see 'truth' as some external entity which can be considered outside of a subjective, linguistic context.

The threat of the abnormal

Recall Heather's (1976) earlier cry, in the section on The Worship of Normality, for the creation of a pathology of normalcy (see page 158). It is with this subversion that we will close this chapter. This is fitting, because it means that we begin and end the chapter with a history, for this is the third and final history offered by Parker et al. (1995). Drawing upon Foucault's analysis, they argue that the development of the so-called modern world (see Introduction) was accompanied by a growth in emphasis upon the divide between 'reason and unreason'. They say, 'Modernity is held together . . . by stories of progressive rational scientific discovery of the nature of the exterior world and the interior of individual people's minds'. They argue that we should 'treat the "irrational" as it is conventionally treated, as the dustbin concept for what modernity's rationality cannot handle, but as something that signifies resistance'.

We began with the assertion that (ab)normality is one of the cornerstones of psychology; it permeates, as does sexuality, all that is around us. Perhaps our focus, however, in recent history has been misplaced. Rather than focusing upon the sick or deviant individual, perhaps we should turn the spotlight onto the relatively invisible culture, institutions and language. If distressed people do need help and care, should they not be empowered to help themselves be active in their 'treatment' (rather then taking our culture's easy fix of reifying the problem and pill-popping)? If we are talking about 'dangerous members' of society, why should psychiatry be given the power of policing?

It is argued that only in modern times – the times of reason, rationality and science – has irrationality been seen as being as problematic as it now is, presumably because it is the antithesis of what this part of human history 'stands for' and deems to be important. It is important to appreciate that what is being suggested here is not drawn from conspiracy theory. As almost all the writers in the field quoted in this chapter would agree, psychiatrists are by and large well-intentioned people, neither sick nor sinister. We need to look 'beyond' the practitioners to the institutions and culture of which they are a part. Foucault argued that power is invisible; once rendered visible, its force is challenged. Let this final point in the chapter be a call for visibility.

Therapy and clinical practice

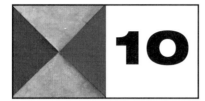

10

Introduction

The ways in which psychological abnormality is defined and conceptualised are reflected, more or less, in the ways in which society deals with and responds to it. Just as people who commit crimes are punished by being sent to prison or made to do community service in order to make good the damage and distress they have caused, so people who are judged to be suffering from a mental illness or to have a mental disorder are seen as in need of treatment or therapy, just like people who are physically ill.

While both criminal behaviour and mental illness or disorder are forms of *deviance*, there are fundamental differences in how they are judged and dealt with. As we have said, a prison sentence is a punishment (whatever else it may claim to offer the criminal, such as rehabilitation), and the underlying assumption is that the individual was responsible for his or her actions. By contrast, people who are mentally ill are the victims of something over which they have no control and are in need of professional help which will restore their mental health.

So, at least in Western cultures, crime is the province of the criminal justice system, the prison service, etc., while mental illness or disorder is the province of the medical and other caring professions, in particular psychiatry and psychology. While this might strike you as very 'sensible', obvious and uncontroversial, such 'compartmentalisation' of deviance may represent Western practices which themselves have not always been around; indeed, the *medicalisation* of mental disorder is a recent phenomenon in the history of our culture.

The story so far

Changes in the treatment of abnormality

According to Holmes (1994), it wasn't until the 16th century that it became widely recognised that disturbed people needed care, rather than exorcism or condemnation. *Demonology* – the belief that abnormal behaviour is caused by supernatural forces that take control of the mind and body – can be traced to the time before recorded history began. Early Chinese culture, the Ancient Greeks and Egyptians, Arabs and Hebrews all believed in possession by supernatural forces, such as angry gods, evil spirits and demons. The 'treatment' included incantations, prayers, potions, stoning and flogging, starvation and, of course, exorcism, all aimed at making the body uninhabitable to devils. Abnormal behaviour, understood in terms of fundamental religious beliefs, demanded a solution in terms of those same religious beliefs: belief in demons dictated that they had to be removed from the bodies of those who were possessed by them.

However, not everyone viewed things that way. Hippocrates (*c.* 460–370BC), the Greek physician who is regarded as the founding father of modern medicine, differed from his predecessors (who were as much magicians as physicians) by claiming that diseases have natural causes. He saw the brain as the organ of consciousness, intellect and emotion, and believed that the brain was responsible for mental disorders, not punishments imposed by the gods. Another Greek physician, Galen (*c.* AD129–199), maintained that illness resulted from an imbalance between the *Four Humours*, the body's main fluids, namely black bile, yellow bile, phlegm and blood. So, for example, depression (melancholia) was the result of too much black bile, and the remedy was to restore balance between all four fluids (see also Chapter 9).

Hippocrates recommended that people suffering from depression and other forms of mental illness should be cared for like other sick people. It could be said, therefore, that he was the first advocate of the *medical model* of psychological abnormality: symptoms that have their origins in something bodily (*somatogenesis*) require a bodily or physical solution. Hippocrates remained the authority among physicians throughout the classical period, i.e. up until the fall of the Roman Empire in AD476, which marked the beginning of the Dark Ages, the early part of the Middle Ages.

This period in European history (which lasted up to the Renaissance, roughly 1450) was dominated by religion, which impinged on almost every aspect of life. The Pope became an all-powerful figure in a Europe that was exclusively Roman Catholic; Christian monasticism replaced classical Greek and Roman culture. The naturalistic approach of Hippocrates was virtually abandoned; life was seen as a struggle between the forces of good and evil, the latter personified in the Devil. Belief in demonic possession took on extreme, fanatical proportions, such as brutal exorcisms and 'witch hunts', and the infamous Spanish Inquisition, which lasted until 1610.

Witch hunts spread to America and reached a peak in the 1690s with the Salem witchcraft tribunals; they were legally outlawed there in about 1700 (Holmes, 1994).

Starting in the 1500s, it began to be widely recognised that disturbed people needed care, not exorcism or condemnation. As early as 1547, the Priory of Saint Mary of Bethlehem Hospital ('Bedlam') in London was

Figure 10.1 William Norris, an inmate of 'Bedlam', in fetters, an early form of 'treatment' for mental illness

handed over by Henry VIII to the City of London exclusively for the care of the mentally ill.

The emergence of psychiatry: medicalising abnormality

However, this and other early mental hospitals were in many respects more like prisons than hospitals, and the physical conditions were appalling. It wasn't until the late 1800s that the medical specialism of psychiatry came into being, with the first recognised textbook of psychiatry appearing in 1883. Its author, Emil Kraepelin, proposed that certain groups of symptoms occur together sufficiently often for them to be called a 'disease' or 'syndrome', i.e. there is an underlying physical cause, in much the same way as a physical disease may be attributed to a physiological dysfunction (Davison and Neale, 1994).

He regarded each mental illness as distinct from all others, with its own origins, symptoms, course and outcome. Even though cures had not been found, at least the course of the disease could be predicted. He proposed two major groups of serious mental diseases: *dementia praecox* (the original term for schizophrenia) and manic-depressive psychosis, the former being due to a chemical imbalance, the latter to a faulty metabolism. His classification helped to establish the organic (bodily) nature of mental disorders as well as forming the basis for the present DSM (published by the American Psychiatric Association) and ICD (published by the World Health Organisation) classification systems. Both of these major achievements of Kraepelin's pioneering work represent essential features of the medical model.

Psychiatry, as a branch of medicine, presents a view of abnormal behaviour as reflecting physical processes and abnormalities, which might be biochemical, genetic or physical in nature (or some combination of these), and the treatments that have traditionally been used have also been physical in nature, ranging from the 'tranquillising machine' invented by Benjamin Rush (the founding father of American psychiatry) in the 1770s, along with other methods such as bleeding patients and submerging them under water in a coffin-like box with holes in it (Davison and Neale, 1994), to psychosurgery (popular during the 1930s and 1940s), electro-convulsive therapy (ECT) (first used in 1938, losing favour in the 1960s, but enjoying a recent revival; (Twombly, 1994)), and major tranquillisers or antipsychotic drugs (*neuroleptics*), which first became available in the 1950s. Despite various problems, both practical and ethical, powerful drugs remain an indispensable weapon in the psychiatrist's armoury in the 'war' against serious disorders such as schizophrenia; these 'pharmacological straightjackets' are still generally seen as preferable to the physical straitjackets previously used to restrain such patients (e.g. Davison and Neale, 1994).

Although the search for somatogenic causes dominated psychiatry well into the 1900s, other developments were taking place, both within medicine and in other disciplines, which challenged Kraepelin's fundamental assumption about the physical nature of psychological abnormality, in particular Freud's *psychoanalytic theory* and Watson's *behaviouristic* brand of psychology.

Freud and psychoanalysis

In many ways, Freud's is the more interesting of the two alternatives. Like his psychiatric predecessors and contemporaries, he was medically trained, specialising in neurology (disorders of the nervous system), was a *materialist* (believing that the universe, including the brain and nervous system, is composed of only one kind of 'stuff', namely physical matter) and a *determinist* (believing that every event, including mental events, is caused). But he was *not* a *reductionist*, i.e. he rejected the view that 'the mind' can be legitimately and adequately explained in terms of physical (brain) processes, and argued that a distinct *universe of discourse*, a separate psychological language, is needed for describing and explaining mental events. So, as a *psychologist*, he was interested in the distinctively *mental* causes of behaviour, and, in keeping with the principle that how we view normality will dictate the methods we use to remedy abnormality, as a *psychotherapist* (the first, by common agreement) he developed techniques for helping his patients to confront their unconscious memories, feelings and wishes.

While Freud is often referred to as a psychiatrist, it is much more useful (and probably accurate) to refer to him as a psychotherapist, because of the theories which underpinned his methods, which were *non-organic* and *non-physical*; indeed, 'psychotherapy' is often used to denote 'psychological' treatments *as distinct from* physical ones. For example:

> *The systematic use of a relationship between therapist and patient – as opposed to pharmacological (drugs) or social methods – to produce changes in cognition, feelings and behaviour.*
>
> (Holmes and Lindley, 1989, cited in Clarkson, 1994)

Alternatively, Freedman et al. (1975, cited in Clarkson, 1994) distinguish psychotherapy from 'such other forms of psychiatric treatment as the use of drugs, surgery, electric shock treatment and insulin coma treatment' (the last of these being introduced in the 1930s as a treatment for schizophrenic patients, which often cured them of their schizophrenia, but killed them in the process!). This implies that psychotherapy is a part of psychiatry, and in the USA, psychoanalysts are required to be psychiatrists first, while this is not true in the UK. A more generic, all-embracing term is 'mental health professional', which covers psychiatrists, psychotherapists and clinical psychologists, as well as counsellors, psychiatric nurses, psychiatric social workers and others.

Watson and behaviourism

When Watson delivered his 'behaviourist manifesto' in 1913, he claimed to be putting the young discipline of psychology on a scientific footing for the first time. In its attempt to emulate the natural sciences, psychology should confine itself to investigating the only aspect of human activity that could be studied *objectively*, namely overt behaviour, and the theory of learning that was to underpin this objective approach was *conditioning*.

Like Freud, Watson was a determinist and a materialist, but unlike Freud, he was also a reductionist, seeing human thought as nothing more than the tiny, silent movements of the vocal chords. He rejected the mind, both its existence and its validity as part of the subject matter of a scientific psychology, and Freud's concept of the unconscious mind would have been a meaningless one for him.

However, once again, as we have now seen several times, the behaviourist account of normal behaviour implied, more or less directly, ways in which abnormal behaviour could be changed. According to Eysenck (1992), who was responsible for setting up clinical psychology as a profession in the UK, *behaviour therapy* (based largely on the principles of classical conditioning) was 'sketched' in two very famous studies involving Watson: the Little Albert experiment, in which Watson and Rayner (1920) deliberately induced a fear of a white rat in an 11-month-old baby; and the Little Peter study, in which Mary Cover Jones (1924), supervised by Watson, removed a young child's fear of rabbits by using what is generally regarded as the first example of *systematic desensitisation* (although the term was first used by Wolpe in 1958).

The ethics of therapeutic change

While it may seem obvious to you that the Little Albert experiment is unethical – and for what reasons – it may not seem at all obvious in what ways, if at all, the Little Peter study in particular, and behaviour therapy in general, might be considered unethical. Indeed, should we be looking at psychotherapy as a whole (both *psychodynamic* approaches, based on Freud's psychoanalysis, and *behavioural* approaches, based on Watson's and, later on, Skinner's theories of operant conditioning) in terms of its ethical status? For what all health professionals have in common is their role as *agents of change*, and whenever one person attempts to change the behaviour, thoughts and feelings of another, questions arise about power and influence; these are essentially ethical questions.

Where someone is voluntarily seeking help from a psychologist or psychotherapist (as opposed to the position of an involuntary, sectioned patient in a psychiatric hospital, a situation that raises ethical questions of its own), it might seem that there would not be an issue regarding *informed consent*, which is such an important ethical principle in the context of psychological research. But according to Holmes (1994), this is a problem throughout the caring professions.

While the law in the UK and USA differs as to the extent to which doctors are expected to explain in advance every detail of the possible adverse consequences of a procedure or treatment, in the case of psychotherapy this is particularly problematic. Why?

Firstly, the patient may well be in a vulnerable and emotionally aroused state, which will reduce his or her ability to make a balanced judgement regarding the suitability of the particular form of therapy being offered and/or the 'suitability' of the therapist.

Secondly, unlike medical procedures, the range of different forms of psychotherapy that are available tend to be poorly understood by the general public and the media.

Thirdly, the lack of any generally agreed standards of training, practice or regulatory procedures, within psychotherapy as a whole, means that there are no external criteria against which a particular therapy can be assessed. (This issue will be discussed further in the Applications and Implications section below.)

Fourthly, there are special problems of informed consent associated with particular therapies. For example, in psychoanalysis, some degree of 'opacity' is necessary if certain techniques, such as transference, are to be effective, i.e. the analyst must remain partially 'obscure' if the patient is to be able to project onto him or her unconscious feelings (for parents and/or other close relatives) which are then discussed and interpreted. Clearly, it is very difficult to fully inform a patient in advance about transference, which must occur spontaneously within the therapeutic relationship that gradually develops over time. As Holmes (1994) says, when assessing patients for treatment, the analyst must strike a balance between providing legitimate information on the one hand, and maintaining a 'professional distance' on the other.

Differences in power and the ability to control one's situation are most apparent within the context of a psychiatric hospital, where staff can exercise subtle coercion, even when the patient is a voluntary patient. The in-patient is subjected to strong persuasion to accept the treatment recommended by the professional staff; 'even a "voluntary" and informed decision to take psychotropic medication or to participate in any other regimen is often (maybe usually) less than free' (Davison and Neale, 1994).

The issue of the influence of the therapist on the patient has been central to a long-standing debate between traditional (psychodynamic) psychotherapists and behaviour therapists. Many psychotherapists believe that behaviour therapy is unacceptable (even if it works) because it is manipulative and demeaning of human dignity. By contrast, they see their own methods as helping patients to realise their potential, to express their true self and so on. Instead of influencers, they see themselves as a kind of psychological midwife, present during the birth, possessing useful skills, but there primarily to make sure that a natural process goes smoothly (Wachtel, 1977).

This, according to Wachtel, himself a psychodynamic therapist, is an exaggeration and misrepresentation of both approaches; for many patients, the 'birth' would probably not happen at all without the intervention of the therapist who undoubtedly influences the patient's behaviour. Conversely, behaviour therapists are successful at least partly because they establish an active, co-operative relationship with the patient who plays a much more active role than psychotherapists believe.

Wachtel argues that *all* therapists, whatever their approach, if they are at all effective, influence their patients; therapy involves:

> ... *a situation in which one human being (the therapist) tries to act in such a way as to enable another human being to act and feel differently than he has, and this is as true of psychoanalysis as it is of behaviour therapy.*

(Wachtel, 1977)

The crucial issue, for Wachtel, is not *whether* influence takes place, but rather the *nature* of the influence and to what extent, and in what ways, it is the *patient* who benefits from the therapist's influence. The neutrality of the therapist is a myth:

> *Unlike a technician, a psychiatrist cannot avoid communicating and at times imposing his own values upon his patients. The patient usually has considerable difficulty in finding the way in which he would wish to change his behaviour, but as he talks to the psychiatrist, his wants and needs become clearer. In the very process of defining his needs in the presence of a figure who is viewed as wise and authoritarian, the patient is profoundly influenced. He ends up wanting some of the things the psychiatrist thinks he should want.*

(Davison and Neale, 1994)

What are 'some of the things the psychiatrist thinks he should want'? In general terms, the answer concerns some of the psychiatrist's (or psychotherapist's) basic values and beliefs about what is normal, desirable, acceptable, etc., which may reflect the particular approach to therapy that he or she subscribes to (i.e. what he or she believes officially and consciously *in the role of psychiatrist or psychotherapist*) and/or what he or she believes *as a person*, which may not be (fully) conscious and may not necessarily be compatible with the former. In many ways, it is the latter that is more important, because it is likely to be a greater source of influence on the therapeutic relationship; it is more likely to remain unrecognised and unverbalised, by both parties.

The heterosexual therapist and the homosexual patient

One example is the therapist's attitudes towards homosexuals and homosexuality. According to Stein (1988), the strong tradition within psychotherapy of an association between homosexuality and mental illness has proved very resistant to change, including overwhelming scientific evidence to the contrary; this resistance is reinforced by society's *homophobia*, which refers not only to an unjustified fear of gays and lesbians (the literal meaning), but also to hatred, loathing, as well as fear, of homosexual desires (Cabaj, 1988). It is very closely tied to *heterosexism*, which refers to discrimination against gays and lesbians because of their homosexuality (see Chapter 4).

The lack of relevant theoretical frameworks for thinking about homosexuality except within a context of pathology leaves many therapists with a void in their understanding as to how to treat gay men and lesbians. Each therapist wishing to work with gays and lesbians will have to struggle to overcome a lack of formal training and experience in this area, such as attitudes about homosexuality in general, and about specific sexual acts in particular, awareness of the effects of stigmatisation, familiarity with gay lifestyles, knowledge about patterns and stages of 'coming out', and the meaning of a homosexual identity (Stein, 1988).

Stein argues that lack of knowledge about any of the above may restrict a therapist's ability to understand and conceptualise about a gay person's experience and, more importantly, it may limit the therapist's ability to establish an empathic attitude towards the gay or lesbian patient. How the therapist 'stands' on homosexuality, both consciously and unconsciously, will represent a crucial feature of the whole therapeutic relationship, and, hence, a crucial influence on the likely benefits of therapy for the patient. Clearly, it is impossible for the therapist to be neutral in this situation.

Similarly, issues of race and gender inevitably enter into, and influence the course of, the therapeutic relationship. Just as homophobia and heterosexism are influences on therapy because they impinge on the lives of everyone living in a homophobic and heterosexist society, so will racism and sexism.

Revisions and reconceptualisations

Psychiatry and racism

According to Fernando (1991), the importance of racial bias in the practice of psychiatry in multiracial settings is often ignored except when it is very obvious (as in South Africa, for instance). In countries such as the USA and Britain, racism in psychiatry is not usually a matter of prejudiced behaviour by individual practitioners or of an organised movement to deprive black people of their rightful access to mental health services:

Racism within psychiatry derives from the traditions of the discipline, its history, its ways of assessing and diagnosing, the criteria it uses for designating treatment, its organisation, its involvement with the powers of the state . . . and its struggle to be accepted as a scientific discipline.

(Fernando, 1991)

Based on Kendell (1975), Fernando argues that the diagnostic interview consists primarily of taking the patient's history and assessing the patient's current 'mental state'.

TAKING THE PATIENT'S HISTORY

The patient's history if often thought of as comprising objective facts, but, in reality, it is a highly selected account of whatever information has been obtained from the patient and others, and it is the psychiatrist who does the crucial sorting out. The psychiatrist also influences the content of the history, in two interrelated ways:

- the type and extent of information given by the patient and others reflect the way that he or she perceives the people who provide it. For example, if a black Asian patient says little about an arranged marriage (because he or she thinks it will be disapproved of by the white psychiatrist), this may well be interpreted by the psychiatrist as a negative quality of the patient (e.g. secretiveness or deviousness);
- the selection of information during the history-taking depends on the beliefs, value judgements, understanding and knowledge of the psychiatrist. White, middle-class psychiatrists are unlikely to have personal experience of predominantly black areas (such as Harlem in New York, Tower Hamlets in London and St Paul's in Bristol), and so will be unaware of the pressures faced by black people who live there. This is likely to result in a misinterpretation of their lifestyles and behaviour, which may well reinforce their racist attitudes.

ASSESSING THE PATIENT'S MENTAL STATE

Assessment of the patient's 'mental state' is probably the major determinant of the final diagnosis. What the patient reports of his or her experiences is taken as evidence of an inner state of mind, i.e. it is taken quite literally as indicating mental states that exist in some objective way. However, the validity of such an inference is dubious at the best of times (even when there is excellent rapport and full understanding between patient and psychiatrist); in a multicultural/multiracial setting, it is highly unlikely that such rapport exists:

The meanings attached to experiences and perceptions, the concept of illness, and the overall significance of the interview situation . . . are but some of the parameters along which variation must occur when cultural differences are present between the participants of an interaction.

(Fernando, 1991)

Deductions that are made from an 'examination' of the mental state cannot be thought of as equivalent to a medical description of the state of a bodily organ, which has at least some degree of objective validity:

> *What a doctor 'finds' in a 'mental state' is as much a reflection of the observers as the so-called patient. It is a result of an interaction rather than a one-sided observation.*

(Fernando, 1991)

What Fernando is saying, in essence, is that the assessment and diagnosis that takes place within the context of psychiatry are fundamentally social processes, in which the prejudices, expectations, beliefs, values and personal experience of both patient and psychiatrist play a major role and which render the situation far less objective than it is often taken to be (especially by psychiatrists).

All of these factors also contribute to any therapeutic situation involving a patient and therapist from different cultural or racial backgrounds. If *self-disclosure* is important in relation to assessment and diagnosis, it is, arguably, even more important in the context of psychotherapy.

According to Sue and Sue (1990, cited in Grant, 1994), black clients, because of their past experience of racism and racial prejudice, often find it difficult to trust a white therapist and so find self-disclosure difficult. For example, Grant (1994) refers to cases of black clients who have deliberately sought a black therapist because of their fear that, to disclose certain family issues to a white therapist might lead the therapist to make a negative judgement of black people. (This is, of course, directly equivalent to Fernando's example of the Asian patient who fails to tell the white psychiatrist of the arranged marriage for fear of disapproval.)

Relationships with authority figures are often influenced by one's racial heritage: a black client who is subservient in relation to the dominant white culture will relate to the therapist in basically the same way, seeing him or her as essentially an authority figure, expecting to be directed and instructed by the therapist. Some clients may even begin to doubt the therapist's competence if these expectations are not met (Grant, 1994).

Other black clients are very anti-white, very angry with whites and distrustful of them, and so are likely to seek a black therapist. However, such black clients may also *resist* having a black therapist whom they see as 'selling out', adopting white, middle-class values, and abandoning their own people ('white man in black clothing'). Alternatively, if they do decide to see a white therapist, they may look for ways to sabotage the relationship. What is certain is that there are very few black therapists (Grant, 1994).

On the therapist's part, someone from a white, middle-class, British background may see the nuclear family as the norm, so that the black West Indian who was brought up by a family friend in a different home, a few streets away from the mother's home, will be considered to have had an abnormal upbringing, which then becomes an 'issue' for the therapy. (In fact, the modified extended family involves ties that are as important as blood ties, and such family friends are chosen to be part of the family (Grant, 1994).)

> *One of the important factors in the client-psychotherapist relationship is the power-authority dimension . . . This hierarchical dimension takes on an added significance when one of the participants in the relationship is a 'majority person' (in this case, the white psychotherapist) and the other is a 'minority person' (in this case, the black client) primarily because it is a microcosm of the larger social context.*

(Grant, 1994)

Psychotherapy and sexism

Another 'microcosm of the larger social context' is represented by the situation in which a male therapist treats a female client. More generally, if gender is such an integral part of a person's identity, we would expect to find that when someone is in distress and seeking therapy, gender and gender-related problems are often experienced as key issues (Ernst and Gowling, 1994).

According to Ernst and Gowling (1994), while Freud posed some fundamental questions about gender, he failed to question the division between men and women in his society, which he assumed to be natural.

Some of the subsequent development of psychoanalytic theory has laid a foundation for feminist theorists and practitioners to look at new ways of working with clients which challenges this conservative aspect of Freud's work.

For example, since 1980 or so, much work has been done in relation to how the social reality of gender relations is incorporated into the psychological make-up of each individual man and woman; this has then to be incorporated into the therapeutic relationship:

> *What feminism brings to psychoanalysis is the understanding that we can only grasp the different development of men and women if we understand that femininity and therefore mothering have been devalued in our society . . .*

(Ernst and Gowling, 1994)

Addressing the issue of gender in psychoanalytic and humanistic psychotherapy means helping the patient to find the repressed masculine and feminine parts of themselves. To do this, the psychotherapist must be aware of the ways in which social forces influence the psychological development of boys and girls:

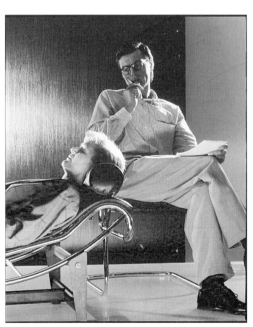

Figure 10.2 The fact that this therapist is male and his patient is female will influence the therapeutic relationship in ways that will remain unconscious for both

> *Psychotherapists themselves are also part of this society and will need to work on their own, often unconscious, adaptation to gender stereotypes; this needs to be as much a part of any psychotherapist's training as uncovering the other aspects of the life of the unconscious.*
>
> (Ernst and Gowling, 1994)

Applications and implications

Feminist approaches within psychotherapy

Some of the most radical feminist therapists are lesbian feminist therapists, and the more radical amongst these (e.g. Perkins, 1991; Kitzinger and Perkins, 1993) have been very critical of much of what goes on in the name of 'lesbian therapy' in particular, and 'feminist therapy' in general.

The central criticism is that the oppression of lesbians, in the form of homophobia and heterosexism, becomes 'transformed' into the psychopathology of individuals, i.e. since it is individual women who seek therapeutic help, the social and political roots of their problems are largely ignored, and therapy focuses on helping her to achieve a higher self-esteem, better psychological adjustment, and a more integrated self-identity. Although her psychological difficulties are often seen in terms of 'internalised homophobia', i.e. the application to oneself of society's fear and hatred of homosexuals, the process of change is performed by individual therapists working with individual clients; *social* oppression, prejudice and discrimination becomes *individual* pathology.

However, the concept of 'feminist therapy' is a very fuzzy one: often women therapists who support the general ideals of reformist feminism will describe themselves as feminist therapists although they lack an integration of feminist theory into their work:

> *. . . feminist therapy is not women therapists working with women on 'women's issues' (i.e. sexual abuse, body and eating) unless that practice is accompanied by explicit feminist analysis which ties individual distress to collective political struggles toward societal change.*
>
> (Brown, 1992)

At the same time:

> *A feminist process of therapy respects the woman who walks in the door of the therapy office by meeting her at the point where she stands; rarely, in my experience, is this a place in which she is ready or willing to share her shamed inner self with a large community. Feminist therapy offers the lesbian client a safe base from which to make decisions about how to move her healing process into a broader sphere, while never losing sight of the relationship of the client and therapist both to that context.*
>
> (Brown, 1992)

While Perkins and Kitzinger seem to regard all individual therapy for lesbians as 'selling out' to a homophobic, heterosexist, male-dominated society, Brown is arguing that individual therapy and political action (the latter, by definition, being a collective, 'community'-based process) are complementary and equally necessary aspects of change.

Agreeing with Brown, Sender (1992) maintains that the ultimate question is: does therapy work?

> *If, through therapy, we improve our self-concepts and have more open, rewarding relationships with friends, lovers and children, who can say that it is a bad thing, a selling-out to mainstream culture?*
>
> (Sender, 1992)

Similarly, instead of asking whether women should or shouldn't be doing therapy, Sender believes that we should be asking why the vast majority of those who are doing it are white and middle class: why do other race and class groups see it as irrelevant or feel excluded from it?

Protecting clients from therapist abuse

Unless you adopt the extreme position represented by Perkins and Kitzinger (and even then you might still accept the principle), you will certainly accept the argument that clients, regardless of race, gender or sexual orientation, need protection from all possible forms of abuse on the part of therapists. Even in theory, it may only be possible to protect clients from the more tangible forms of abuse, such as sexual and financial, along with basic ethical rights which apply throughout the caring (and other) professions, such as confidentiality. More 'abstract' forms of abuse, such as the imposition of the therapist's values, prejudices and so on, are very difficult to legislate against, if only because these are often unconscious and, therefore, unrecognised by both the therapist him or herself and the client.

However, as we have seen above, it may be through professional training that such values and prejudices are confronted and explored, so that they are prevented from 'getting in the way' of the therapeutic relationship to the detriment of the client. As things stand, clients, at the very least, have the right to expect that any therapist whom they consult has been properly trained (even if that training is not ideal in terms of these issues regarding values and prejudices).

Until quite recently, anybody could set themselves up as a psychotherapist. In 1989, the United Kingdom Standing Conference for Psychotherapy (UKSCP) was founded, with the aim of creating a professional register to enable members of the general public to identify appropriately trained practitioners who are subject to an enforceable Code of Ethics. It changed its name in 1993 to the United Kingdom Council for Psychotherapy (UKCP) when a Voluntary Register was created.

The UKCP is an organisation of organisations, i.e. instead of individual therapists being members, individual therapy associations/bodies belong to a particular Section. For example, the British Association of Psychotherapists (BAP) and the Women's Therapy Centre belong to the Psychoanalytic and Psychodynamic Psychotherapy Section, while the British Association for Behavioural and Cognitive Psychotherapy belongs to the Behavioural Psychotherapy Section. In 1994, membership consisted of 73 organisations grouped into eight Sections (Pokorny, 1994).

The Voluntary Register formed the basis for a Statutory Register of psychotherapists (*National Register of Psychotherapists*), which is individual rather than organisational (Clarkson, 1994), and which came into existence in 1995. The 1997 edition includes the names, addresses and telephone numbers of over 3,600 psychotherapists with recognised training qualifications (i.e. who have met the training requirements of organisations recognised by and affiliated to the UKCP), indicating the therapeutic orientation of each practitioner. It also includes ethical guidelines and the aims of member organisations. The Register is updated annually.

References

Adams, N. M. & Caldwell, W. (1963) The children's somatic apperception test. *Journal of General Psychology*, 68, 43–57.

Adorno, T. W., Frenkel-Brunswick, E., Levinson, D. J. & Sanford, R. N. (1950) *The Authoritarian Personality*. New York: Harper & Row.

Allen, G. (1889) Woman's place in nature. *Forum*, 7, 258–63.

Allport, G. W. (1954) *The Nature of Prejudice*. Reading, MA: Addison-Wesley.

Allport, G. W. (1955) *Becoming*. New Haven, CT: Yale University Press.

American Psychiatric Association (1994) *Diagnostic and Statistical Manual of Mental Disorders* (4th ed.). Washington, DC: American Psychiatric Association.

Appel, W. (1983) *Cults in America: Programme for paradise*. New York: Henry Holt.

Archer, J. (1994) Introduction: Male violence in perspective. In J. Archer (Ed.) *Male Violence*. London: Routledge.

Archer, J. & Lloyd, B. (1985) *Sex and Gender*. New York: Cambridge University Press.

Argyle, M. (1992) *The Social Psychology of Everyday Life*. London: Routledge.

Argyle, M. (1994) *The Psychology of Interpersonal Behaviour* (5th ed.). Harmondsworth: Penguin.

Argyle, M. & Henderson, M. (1985) *The Anatomy of Relationships*. Harmondsworth: Penguin.

Argyle, M., Henderson, M. & Furnham, A. (1985) The rules of social relationships. *British Journal of Social Psychology*, 24, 125–39.

Atkinson, R. C. & Shiffrin, R. M. (1968) Human memory: a proposed system and its control processes. In K. W. Spence & J. T. Spence (Eds) *The Psychology of Learning and Motivation* (Vol. 2). London: Academic Press.

Atkinson, R. C. & Shiffrin, R. M. (1971) The control of short-term memory. *Scientific American*, 224, 82–90.

Baddeley, A. D. & Hitch, G. (1974) Working memory. In G. A. Bower (Ed.) *Recent Advances in Learning and Motivation* (Vol. 8). New York: Academic Press.

Baddeley, A. D. (1981) The concept of working memory: A view of its current state and probable future development. *Cognition*, 10, 17–23.

Baddeley, A. D. (1986) *Working Memory*. Oxford: Oxford University Press.

Bakan, D. (1966) *The Duality of Human Existence*. Boston, MA: Beacon.

Baldwin, J. A. (1992) The role of black psychologists in black liberation. In A. K. H. Burlew, W. C. Banks, H. P. McAdoo & D. A. ya Azibo (Eds) *African American Psychology: Theory, research and practice*. Newbury Park, CA: Sage Publications.

Bandura, A. (1973) *Aggression: A social learning analysis.* London: Prentice Hall.

Bandura, A. (1986) *Social Foundations of Thought and Action: A social cognitive theory.* Englewood Cliffs, NJ: Prentice Hall.

Bandura, A. (1989) Perceived self-efficacy in the exercise of personal agency. *Psychologist*, 2, 411–24.

Banister, P., Burman, E., Parker, I., Taylor, M. & Tindall, C. (1994) *Qualitative Methods in Psychology: A research guide.* Oxford: Oxford University Press.

Baron, R. A. & Byrne, D. (1994) *Social Psychology: Understanding human interaction* (7th ed.). Boston, MA: Allyn & Bacon.

Barstow, A. L. (1994) *Witchraze. A New History in European Witch Hunts.* London: Pandora.

Bartlett, F. C. (1916) An experimental study of some problems of perceiving and imaging. *British Journal of Psychology*, 8, 222–66.

Bartlett, F. C. (1923) *Psychology and Primitive Culture.* Cambridge: Cambridge University Press.

Bartlett, F. C. (1932) *Remembering: A study in experimental and social psychology.* Cambridge: Cambridge University Press.

Bartlett, F. C. (1937) Cambridge, England: 1887–1937. *American Journal of Psychology*, 50, 97–110.

Bass, E. & Davis, L. (1988) *The Courage to Heal: A guide for women survivors of child sexual abuse.* London: Cedar.

Berger, J. (1972) *Ways of Seeing.* London: BBC.

Berkowitz, L. (1966) On not being able to aggress. *British Journal of Clinical and Social Psychology*, 5, 130–9.

Berkowitz, L. (1972) Social norms, feelings, and other factors affecting helping and altruism. In L. Berkowitz (Ed.) *Advances in Experimental Social Psychology* (Vol. 6). New York: Academic Press.

Berkowitz, L. (1993) *Aggression: Its causes, consequences and control.* New York: McGraw Hill.

Bidney, D. (1953) *Theoretical Anthropology.* New York: Columbia University Press.

Billig, M. (1976) *Social Psychology and Intergroup Relations.* London: Academic Press.

Billig, M. (1987) *Arguing and Thinking: A rhetorical approach to social psychology.* Cambridge: Cambridge University Press.

Bleier, R. (1987) Sex difference research in neurosciences. Paper presented at the annual meeting of the American Association for Advancement of Science, Chicago.

Bleier, R. (1988) Sex difference research: Science or belief? In R. Bleier (Ed.) *Feminist Approaches to Science*, New York: Pergamon.

Bohan, J. S. (Ed.) (1992) *Women in Psychology: Seldom Seen, Rarely Heard.* Oxford: Westview Press.

Bowlby, J. (1969) *Attachment and Loss* (Vol. 1). Harmondsworth: Penguin.

Brewer, M. B. (1968) Determinants of social distance among East African tribal groups. *Journal of Personality and Social Psychology*, 10, 279–89.

Brown, H. (1985) *People, Groups and Society.* Milton Keynes: Open University Press.

Brown, L. S. (1992) While waiting for the revolution: The case for a lesbian feminist psychotherapy. *Feminism and Psychology*, 2 (2), 239–53.

Brownmiller, S. (1975) *Against Our Will: Men, women and rape.* New York: Simon & Schuster.

Bruner, J. S. (1990) *Acts of Meaning*. Cambridge, MA: Harvard University Press.

Burkitt, I. (1991) *Social Selves. Theories of the social formation of personality*. London: Sage.

Burlew, A. K. H., Banks, W. C., McAdoo, H. P. & ya Azibo, D. A. (1992) Preface. In A. K. H. Burlew, W. C. Banks, H. P. McAdoo & D. A. ya Azibo (Eds) *African American Psychology: Theory, research and practice*. Newbury Park, CA: Sage Publications.

Burman, E. (1996) Introduction: Contexts, contests and intervention. In E. Burman, P. Alldred, C. Goldberg, C. Heenan, D. Marks, J. Marshall, K. Taylor, R. Ullah & S. Warner (Eds) *Challenging Women: Psychology's exclusions, feminist possibilities*. Milton Keynes: Open University Press.

Burns, R. B. (1979) *The Self Concept*. London: Longman.

Burr, V. (1995) *An Introduction to Social Constructionism*. London: Routledge.

Buss, D. M. (1991) Evolutionary personality psychology. *Annual Review of Psychology*, 42, 459–91.

Butler, J. M. & Haigh, G. V. (1954) Changes in the relation between self-concept and ideal concepts consequent upon client-centred counselling. In C. R. Rogers & R. F. Dymonds (Eds) *Psychotherapy and Personality Change*. Chicago: University of Chicago Press.

Cabaj, R. P. (1988) Homosexuality and neurosis: Considerations for psychotherapy. *Journal of Gay and Lesbian Psychotherapy*, 15 (1/2), 13–24.

Campbell, A. & Muncer, S. (1994) Men and the meanings of violence. In J. Archer (Ed.) *Male Violence*. London: Routledge.

Cardwell, M. C. (1996) *The Complete A-Z Psychology Handbook*. London: Hodder & Stoughton.

Cardwell, M. C., Clark, L. & Meldrum, C. (Eds) (1996) *Psychology for A Level*. London: Collins Educational.

Carver, C. S. & Scheier, M. F. (1996) *Perspectives on Personality* (3rd ed.). Needham Heights, MA: Allyn & Bacon.

Cash, T. F., Kehr, J. A., Polyson, J. & Freeman, V. (1977) Role of physical attractiveness in peer attribution of psychological disturbance. *Journal of Counselling and Clinical Psychology*, 45, 987–93.

Cherry, F. (1995) *The 'Stubborn Particulars' of Social Psychology: Essays on the research process*. London: Routledge.

Chodorow, N. (1987) *The Reproduction of Mothering*. Berkeley, CA: University of California Press.

Chrisler, J. C., Johnston, I. K., Champagne, N. M., Preston, K. E. (1994) Menstrual joy: The construct and its consequences. *Psychology of Women Quarterly*, 18, 375–85.

Clarkson, P. (1994) The nature and range of psychotherapy. In P. Clarkson & M. Pokorny (Eds) *The Handbook of Psychotherapy*. London: Routledge.

Clore, G. L. & Byrne, D. (1974) A reinforcement-affect model of attraction. In T. L. Huston (Ed.) *Foundations of Interpersonal Attraction*. New York: Academic Press.

Cochrane, R. (1983) *The Social Creation of Mental Illness*. London: Longman.

Cohen, D. (1989) *Soviet Psychiatry: Politics and mental health in the USSR today*. London: Paladin.

Cohen, G. (1986) Everyday memory. In G. Cohen, M. W. Eysenck & M. E. LeVoi (Eds) *Memory: A cognitive approach*. Milton Keynes: Open University Press.

Cohen, G. (1990) Memory. In I. Roth (Ed.) *Introduction to Psychology*. Hove: Erlbaum, in association with the Open University.

Cole, M. (1990) Cultural psychology: A once and future discipline? In J. J. Berman (Ed.) *Nebraska Symposium on Motivation: Cross-cultural perspectives*. Lincoln, NA: University of Nebraska Press.

Cooley, C. H. (1902) *Human Nature and Social Order*. New York: Shocken.

Coolican, H. (1994) *Research Methods and Statistics in Psychology* (2nd ed.). London: Hodder & Stoughton.

Cosslett, T. (1994) *Women Writing Childbirth: Modern discourses of motherhood*. Manchester: Manchester University Press.

Coupland, N. & Nussbaum, J. F. (1993) Introduction: discourse, selfhood and the lifespan. In N. Coupland and J. F. Nussbaum, *Discourse and Lifespan Identity*. London: Sage.

Cousins, C. D. (1989) Culture and self-perception in Japan and the United States. *Journal of Personality and Social Psychology*, 56, 124–31.

Coward, R. (1984) *Female Desire: Women's sexuality today*. London: Paladin.

Craik, F. & Lockhart, R. (1972) Levels of processing. *Journal of Verbal Learning and Verbal Behaviour*, 11, 671–84.

Crawford, M. (1995) *Talking Difference: On gender and language*. London: Sage.

Cross, W. E. (1971) The negro of black conversion experience: towards a psychology of black liberation. *Black World*, 20, 13–37.

Cunningham, M. R. (1986) Measuring the physical in physical attraction: quasi-experiments on the sociobiology of female beauty. *Journal of Personality and Social Psychology*, 50, 925–35.

Daly, M. & Wilson, M. (1981) Abuse and neglect of children in evolutionary perspective. In R. D. Alexander & D. W. Tinkle (Eds) *Natural Selection and Social Behavior*. New York: Chiron.

Daly, M. & Wilson, M. (1982) Homicide and kinship. *American Anthropologist*, 84, 372–78.

Daly, M. & Wilson, M. (1984) A sociobiological analysis of human infanticide. In G. Hausfater & S. B. Hrdy (Eds) *Infanticide: Comparative and evolutionary perspectives*. New York: Aldine de Gruyter.

Daly, M. & Wilson, M. (1985) Child abuse and other risks of not living with both parents. *Ethology and Sociobiology*, 6, 197–210.

Daly, M. & Wilson, M. (1987) The Darwinian psychology of discriminative parental solicitude. *Nebraska Symposium on Motivation*. 35, 91–144.

Daly, M. & Wilson, M. (1988a) *Homicide*. Hawthorne, NY: Aldine de Gruyter.

Daly, M. & Wilson, M. (1988b) Evolutionary social psychology and family homicide. *Science*, 242, 519–24.

Daly, M. & Wilson, M. (1900) Killing the competition: Female/female and male/male homicide. *Human Nature*, 1, 8, 81–107.

Daly, M. & Wilson, M. (1993) Stepparenthood and the evolved psychology of discriminative parental solicitude. In S. Parmigiani & F. S. vom Saal (Eds) *Infanticide and Parental Care*. London: Harwood Academic Publishers.

Daly, M. & Wilson, M. (1994) Evolutionary psychology of male violence. In J. Archer (Ed.) *Male Violence*. London: Routledge.

Darwin, C. R. (1859) *The Origin of the Species by Natural Selection*. London: John Murray.

Darwin, C. R. (1871) *Descent of Man*. London: John Murray.

Davison, G. C. & Neale, J. M. (1994) *Abnormal Psychology* (6th ed.). New York: John Wiley & Sons.

Delaney, J., Lupton, M. J. & Toth, E. (1988) *The Curse: A cultural history of menstruation* (2nd ed.). Urbana: University of Illinois Press.

Deutsch, H. (1944) *Psychology of Women.* New York: Grune & Stratton.

Dion, K. K. (1972) Physical attractiveness and evaluation of children's transgressions. *Journal of Personality and Social Psychology,* 24, 207–13.

Dipboye, R. L., Arvey, R. D. & Terpstra, D. E. (1977) Sex and physical attractiveness of raters and applicants as determinants of resumé evaluations. *Journal of Applied Psychology,* 61, 288–94.

Dixon, J. A. (1966) Discourse, Self and Race. *Psychology Review,* 3.1, 28–31.

Dobson, C. B., Hardy, M., Heyes, S., Humphreys, A. & Humphreys, P. W. (1981) *Understanding Psychology.* Oxford: Oxford University Press.

Dollard, J., Doob, L. W., Miller, N. E., Mowrer, O. H. & Sears, R. R. (1939) *Frustration and Aggression.* New Haven, CT: Harvard University Press.

Doob, L. W. (1964) Eidetic images among the Ibo. *Ethnology,* 3, 357–63.

Doob, L. W. (1966) Eidetic imagery: A cross-cultural will-o'-the-wisp? *Journal of Psychology,* 63, 13–34.

Doob, L. W. (1970) Correlates of eidetic imagery in Africa. *Journal of Psychology,* 76, 223–30.

Douglas, M. (1980) *Evans-Pritchard.* London: Fontana.

Doyle, J. A. (1983) *The Male Experience.* Dubuque, IA: Wm. C. Brown.

Draguns, J. (1990) Applications of cross-cultural psychology in the field of mental health. In R. Brislin (Ed.) *Applied Cross-cultural Psychology.* Newbury Park, CA: Sage.

Durkin, K. (1995) *Developmental Social Psychology: From infancy to old age.* Oxford: Blackwell.

Dutton, D. C. & Aron, A. P. (1974) Some evidence for a heightened sexual attraction under conditions of high anxiety. *Journal of Personality and Social Psychology,* 30, 510–17.

Eagley, A. H. (1987) *Sex Differences in Social Behavior: A social role interpretation.* Hillsdale, NJ: Erlbaum.

Ebbinghaus, H. (1885) *Über das Gedächtnis.* Leipzig: Dunber, H. Ryer and C. E. Bussenius. Published in translation (1913) as *Memory: A contribution to experimental psychology.* New York: Teachers' College Press.

Edley, N. & Wetherell, M. (1995) *Men in Perspective: Practice, power and identity.* Hemel Hempstead: Prentice Hall/Harvester Wheatsheaf.

Edwards, D. & Middleton, D. (1986) Joint remembering: Constructing an account of shared experience through conversational discourse. *Discourse Processes,* 9, 423–59.

Edwards, D. & Middleton, D. (1987) Conversation and remembering: Bartlett revisited. *Applied Cognitive Psychology,* 1 (2), 77–92.

Edwards, D. & Middleton, D. (1988) Conversational remembering and family relationships: How children learn to remember. *Journal of Social and Personal Relationships.* 5, 3–25.

Edwards, D., Middleton, D. & Potter, J. (1992) Towards a discursive psychology of remembering. *The Psychologist,* October, 441–55.

Edwards, D. & Potter, J. (1992) *Discursive Psychology.* London: Sage.

Edwards, D. & Potter, J. (1995) Remembering. In R. Harré & P. Stearns (Eds) *Discursive Psychology in Practice.* London: Sage.

Ehrenreich, B. & English, D. (1979) *For Her Own Good: 150 years of the experts' advice to women.* London: Pluto.

Erikson, E. (1964) Inner and outer space: Reflections on womanhood. *Daedalus,* 93, 582–606.

Ernst, S. & Gowling, D. (1994) Psychotherapy and gender. In P. Clarkson & M. Pokorny (Eds) *The Handbook of Psychotherapy.* London: Routledge.

Eysenck, H. J. (1957) *Dynamics of Anxiety and Hysteria.* London: Routledge & Kegan Paul.

Eysenck, H. J. (1992) The outcome problem in psychotherapy. In W. Dryden & C. Feltham (Eds) *Psychotherapy and its Discontents.* Milton Keynes: Open University Press.

Fanon, F. (1965) *The Wretched of the Earth.* London: MacGibbon & Kee.

Feeney, J. A. & Noller, P. (1990) Attachment style as a predictor of adult romantic relationships. *Journal of Personality and Social Psychology,* 58, 281–91.

Feingold, A. (1992) Gender differences in mate selection preferences: A test of the parental investment model. *Psychological Bulletin,* 112 (1), 125–39.

Fernando, S. (1991) *Mental Health, Race and Culture.* London: Macmillan, in association with MIND Publications.

Festinger, L., Schachter, S. & Back, K. (1950) *Social Pressures in Informal Groups: A study of human factors in housing.* Stanford, CA: Stanford University Press.

Fine, M. & Addelston, J. (1996) Containing questions of gender and power: The discursive limits of 'sameness' and 'difference'. In S. Wilkinson (Ed.) *Feminist Social Psychology.* Milton Keynes: Open University Press.

Foucault, M. (1961) *Madness and Civilization: A history of insanity in the age of reason.* London: Routledge.

Foucault, M. (1970) *The Order of Things.* New York: Vintage Books.

Foucault, M. (1977) *Discipline and Punish: The birth of the prison.* London: Allen Lane.

Fox, N. J. (1993) *Postmodernism, Sociology and Health.* Milton Keynes, Open University Press.

Franklin II, C. W. (1992) 'Hey, home – Yo, Brother': Friendships among black men. In P. M. Nardi (Ed.) *Men's Friendships.* London: Sage.

Freeman, M. (1993) *Rewriting the Self: History, memory, narrative.* London: Routledge.

Freud, S. (1965), J. Strachey (Ed. & Trans.) *New Introductory Lectures in Psychoanalysis.* New York: Norton. (Originally published 1933.)

Freud, S. (1984) *Beyond the Pleasure Principle.* Pelican Freud Library (11), Harmondsworth: Penguin. (Original work published 1920.)

Freud, S. (1984) *The Ego and the Id.* Pelican Freud Library (11), Harmondsworth: Penguin. (Original work published 1923.)

Geertz, C. (1984) 'From the native's point of view': On the nature of anthropological understanding. In R. A. Shweder & R. A. LaVine (Eds) *Culture Theory: Essays on mind, self and emotion.* Cambridge: Cambridge University Press.

Gergen, K. J. (1973) Social psychology as history. *Journal of Personality and Social Psychology,* 26, 309–20.

Gergen, K. J. (1985) The social constructionist movement in modern psychology. *American Psychologist,* 40, 266–75.

Gergen, K. J. (1991) *The Saturated Self: Dilemmas of identity in contemporary life.* New York: Basic Books.

Geschwind, N. & Behan, P. (1982) Left-handedness: Association with immune disease, migraine, developmental learning disorder. *Proceedings of the National Academy of Sciences*, 79, 5097: 100.

Giddens, A. (1979) *Central Problems in Social Theory*. Basingstoke: Macmillan.

Giddens, A. (1987) *Social Theory and Modern Sociology*. Cambridge: Polity Press.

Giddens, A. (1991) *Modernity and Self-Identity*. Cambridge: Polity.

Gilbert, P. (1994) Male violence: Towards an integration. In J. Archer (Ed.) *Male Violence*. London: Routledge.

Gilligan, C. (1982) *In a Different Voice*. Cambridge, MA: Harvard University Press.

Goffman, E. (1959) *The Presentation of Self in Everyday Life*. Harmondsworth: Penguin.

Goffman, E. (1963) *Stigma: Notes on the management of spoiled identity*. Englewood Cliffs, USA: Prentice Hall.

Goodwin, R. (1994) Putting relationship violence in its place: Contextualising some recent research. In J. Archer (Ed.) *Male Violence*. London: Routledge.

Gould, S. J. (1981) *The Mismeasure of Man*. New York: Norton.

Grant, P. (1994) Psychotherapy and race. In P. Clarkson & M. Pokorny (Eds) *The Handbook of Psychotherapy*. London: Routledge.

Griffin, C. & Phoenix, A. (1994) The relationship between qualitative and quantitative research: Lessons from feminist psychology. *Journal of Community and Applied Social Psychology*, 4, 287–98.

Gross, R. D. (1996) *Psychology: The science of mind and behaviour* (3rd ed.). London: Hodder & Stoughton.

Gulerce, A. (1995a) An interview with K. J. Gergen (Part 1). Culture and self in postmodern psychology: Dialogue in trouble? *Culture and Psychology*, 1 (1), 147–59.

Gulerce, A. (1995b) An interview with K. J. Gergen (Part 2). Culture and psychology in postmodernism: A necessary dialogue. *Culture and Psychology*, 1 (2), 299–308.

Halgin, R. P. & Whitbourne, S. K. (1993) *Abnormal Psychology: The human experience of psychological disorders*. Fort Worth, USA: Harcourt Brace Jovanovich.

Hall, R. E. (1985) *Ask Any Woman: A London inquiry into rape and sexual assault*. Bristol: Falling Wall Press.

Hancock, E. (1990) *The Girl Within. A radical new approach to female identity*. London: Pandora.

Hare-Mustin, R. T. & Marecek, J. (Eds) (1990) *Making a Difference: Psychology and the construction of gender*. New Haven & London: Yale University Press.

Harlow, H. F. & Harlow, M. K. (1962) Social deprivation in monkeys. *Scientific American*, 207 (5), 136.

Harré, R. (1983) *Personal Being: A theory of individual psychology*. Oxford: Blackwell.

Harré, R. (1985) Situational rhetoric and self-presentation. In J. P. Forgas (Ed.) *Language and Social Situations*. New York: Springer Verlag.

Harré, R. (1989) Language games and the texts of identity. In J. Shotter & K. J. Gergen (Eds) *Texts of Identity*. London: Sage.

Harré, R. (1991) *Physical Being*. Oxford: Blackwell.

Harré, R. (1995) Discursive psychology. In J. A. Smith, R. Harré & L. Van Langenhove (Eds) *Rethinking Psychology*. London: Sage.

Harré, R. & Secord, P. F. (1972) *The Explanation of Social Behaviour*. Oxford: Blackwell.

Harrison, W., Sharpe, L. & Endicott, J. (1985) Treatment of the premenstrual syndromes. *General Hospital Psychiatry*, 17 (1), 54–65.

Haste, H. (1993) *The Sexual Metaphor*. Hemel Hempstead: Harvester Wheatsheaf.

Hayes, N. (1994) *Foundations of Psychology*. London: Routledge.

Hayes, N. (1995) *Psychology in Perspective*. London: Macmillan.

Hayes, P. (1996) Memory. In M. C. Cardwell, L. Clark & C. Meldrum (Eds) *Psychology for A Level*. London: Collins Educational.

Heather, N. (1976) *Radical Perspectives in Psychology*. London: Methuen.

Henley, N. (1974) Resources for the study of psychology and women. *RT: Journal of Radical Therapy*, 4, 26–43.

Henriques, J., Hollway, W., Urwin, C., Venn, C. & Walkerdine, V. (1984) *Changing the Subject: Psychology, social regulation and subjectivity*. London & New York: Methuen.

Herman, D. (1984) The rape culture. In J. Freeman (Ed.) *Women: A feminist perspective* (3rd ed.). Palo Alto, CA: Mayfield.

Hilliard III, Asa G. (1992) IQ and the courts: *Larry P. V. Wilson Riles & PASE v. Hannon*. In A. K. H. Burlew, W. C. Banks, H. P. McAdoo & D. A. ya Azibo (Eds) *African American Psychology: Theory, research and practice*. Newbury Park, CA: Sage Publications.

Hirst, W. & Manier, D. (1995) Opening vista for cognitive psychology. In L. M. Martin, K. Nelson & E. Tolbach (Eds) *Sociocultural Psychology: Theory and practice of doing and knowing*. Cambridge: Cambridge University Press.

Hogg, M. A. & Vaughan, G. M. (1995) *Social Psychology: An introduction*. Hemel Hempstead: Prentice Hall/Harvester Wheatsheaf.

Hollingworth, L. S. (1914) Variability as related to sex differences in achievement. *American Journal of Sociology*, 19, 510–30.

Hollway, W. (1989) *Subjectivity and Method in Psychology: Gender, meaning and science*. London: Sage.

Holmes, D. S. (1994) *Abnormal Psychology* (2nd ed.). New York: HarperCollins.

Holstein, J. A. & Gubrium, J. F. (1990) *What is a Family?* Mountain View, CA: Mayfield.

Holstein, J. A. & Gubrium, J. F. (1994) Constructing family: Descriptive practice and domestic order. In T. R. Sabrin & J. I. Kitsuse (Eds) *Constructing the Social*. London: Sage.

Horgan, J. (1995) The new social Darwinists. *Scientific American*, October, 150–7.

Howitt, D., Billig, M., Cramer, D., Edwards, D., Kniveton, B., Potter, J. & Radley, A. (1989) *Social Psychology: Conflicts and continuities*. Milton Keynes: Open University Press.

Howitt, D. & Owusu-Bempah, J. (1994) *The Racism of Psychology: Time for change*. Hemel Hempstead: Harvester Wheatsheaf.

Humphreys, P. W. (1996) Social relationships. In M. C. Cardwell, L. Clark & C. Meldrum (Eds) *Psychology for A Level*. London: Collins Educational.

Humphreys, P. W. (1997) Societal, cultural and subcultural determinants of (ab)normality. *Psychology Review*, 3.4, 10–15.

Huston, T. L. (1973) Ambiguity of acceptance, social desirability and dating choice. *Journal of Experimental Psychology*, 9, 32–42.

James, W. (1890) *The Principles of Psychology*. New York: Henry Holt.

James, W. (1892) *Psychology: The briefer course*. New York: Harper Torch Books.

Johnstone, L. (1989) *Users and Abusers of Psychiatry: A critical look at traditional psychiatric practice*. London: Routledge.

Jones, M. C. (1924) The elimination of children's fears. *Journal of Experimental Psychology*, 7, 382–90.

Josselson, R. & Leiblich, A. (1995) *Interpreting Experience. The narrative study of lives.* London: Sage.

Josselson, R. (1995) Imagining the real: Empathy, narrative and the dialogic self. In R. Josselson & A. Leiblich *Interpreting Experience. The narrative study of lives.* London: Sage.

Kagen, C. & Lewis, S. (1989) Transforming psychological practice. Paper presented at the annual conference of the British Psychological Society, St Andrews, April.

Kaschak, E. (1992) *Engendered Lives: A new psychology of women's experience.* New York: Basic Books.

Keller, E. F. (1985) *Reflections on Gender and Science.* London: Yale University Press.

Kelly, L. (1988) *Surviving Sexual Violence.* Cambridge: Polity Press.

Kemp, A. (1996) Black writer who lived a white lie. *The Observer*, 16 June, 24.

Kendell, R. (1975) *The Role of Diagnosis in Psychiatry.* Oxford: Blackwell.

Kim, U. (1990) Indigenous Psychology: Science and applications. In R. Brislin (Ed.) *Applied Cross-Cultural Psychology.* Newbury Park, USA: Sage.

Kitzinger, C. (1990) The rhetoric of pseudoscience. In I. Parker & J. Shotter (Eds) *Deconstructing Social Psychology.* London & New York: Routledge.

Kitzinger, C. & Perkins, R. (1993) *Changing our Minds: Lesbian feminism and psychology.* London: Onlywomen Press Ltd.

Klein, V. (1971) *The Feminine Character. A history of ideology.* London: Routledge & Kegan Paul.

Kleinman, A. M. (1977) Depression, somatisation, and the new cross-cultural psychiatry. *Social Science and Medicine*, 11, 3–10.

Koss, M. P. (1992) The underdetection of rape: Methodological choices influence incident estimates. *Journal of Social Issues*, 48, 61–75.

Kvale, S. (Ed.) (1992) *Psychology and Postmodernism.* London: Sage.

Landy, D. & Sigall, H. (1974) Beauty is talent: task evaluation as a function of the performer's physical attractiveness. *Journal of Personality and Social Psychology*, 29, 299–304.

LeGrand, C. (1973) Rape and rape laws: Sexism in society and law. *California Law Review*, 63, 919–41.

Lerner, G. (1979) *The Majority Finds its Past: Placing women in history.* New York: Oxford University Press.

Lerner, M. J. (1965) The effect of responsibility and choice on a partner's attractiveness following failure. *Journal of Personality*, 33, 178–87.

Lerner, M. J. (1980) *The Belief in a Just World: A fundamental delusion.* New York: Plenum.

Littlewood, R. & Lipsedge, M. (1989) *Aliens and Alienists: Ethnic minorities and psychiatry* (2nd ed.). London: Routledge.

Lorenz, K. Z. (1966) *On Aggression.* London: Methuen.

Lott, B. (1994) *Women's Lives: Themes and variations in gender learning.* Pacific Grove, USA: Brooks/Cole.

MacKinnon, C. A. (1989) *Toward a Feminist Theory of the State.* Cambridge, MA: Harvard University Press.

Macpherson, C. B. (1962) *The Political Theory of Possessive Individualism.* Oxford: Oxford University Press.

Madhubuti, H. R. (1990) *Black Men: Obsolete, single, dangerous?* Chicago: Third World Press.

Maher, W. B. & Maher, B. A. (1985) Psychopathology 1: From ancient times to the 18th century. In G. A. Kimble & K. Schlesinger (Eds) *Topics in the History of Psychology* (Vol. 2). Hillsdale, NJ: Erlbaum.

Mama, A. (1995) *Beyond the Mask: Race, gender and subjectivity.* London: Routledge.

Marsh, P., Rosser, E. & Harré, R. (1978) *The Rules of Disorder.* London: RKP.

Matlin, M. W. (1987) *The Psychology of Women* (3rd ed.). London: Harcourt Brace.

McDougall, W. (1908) *An Introduction to Social Psychology.* London: Methuen.

Mead, G. H. (1934) *Mind, Self and Society.* Chicago: University of Chicago Press.

Messner, M. A. (1992) Like a family: Power, intimacy and sexuality in male athletes' friendships. In P. M. Nardi (Ed.) *Men's Friendships.* London: Sage.

Middleton, D. & Buchanan, K. (1993) Is reminiscence working? Accounting for the therapeutic benefits of reminiscence work with older people. *Journal of Ageing Studies,* 7 (3), 321–33.

Middleton, D. & Crook, C. (1996) Bartlett and socially ordered consciousness: a discursive perspective. *Culture and Psychology,* 2.4, 379–96.

Middleton, D. & Curnock, D. (1995) Talk of uncertainty: Doubt as an organizational resource in neonatal intensive care. In *Risk in organizational settings.* London: ESRC.

Middleton, D. & Edwards, D. (Eds) (1990) *Collective Remembering.* London: Sage.

Miles, A. (1988) *Women and Mental Illness: The social context of female neurosis.* Hemel Hempstead: Harvester Wheatsheaf.

Miller, J. (1984) Culture and the development of everyday explanation. *Journal of Personality and Social Psychology,* 46, 961–78.

Miller, J. (1986) *Toward a New Psychology of Women* (2nd ed.) Boston, MA: Beacon.

Miller, N. E. (1941) The frustration-aggression hypothesis. *Psychology Review,* 48, 337–42.

Moghaddam, F. M.; Taylor, D. M. & Wright, S. C. (1993) *Social Psychology in Cross-Cultural Perspective.* New York: W. H. Freeman.

Morris, P., Holloway, J., & Noble, J. (1990) Gender representation within British psychology. *The Psychologist: Bulletin of the British Psychological Society,* 3, 408–11.

Moscovici, S. (1985a) Comment on Potter and Litton. *British Journal of Social Psychology,* 24, 91–3.

Moscovici, S. (1985b) *The Age of the Crowd: A historical treatise on mass psychology.* Cambridge: Cambridge University Press.

Moyer, K. E. (1976) *The Psychobiology of Aggression.* New York: Harper & Row.

Much, N. (1995) Cultural psychology. In J. A. Smith, R. Harré & L. Van Langenhove (Eds) *Rethinking Psychology.* London: Sage.

Murstein, B. I. (1973): Physical attractiveness and marital choice. *Journal of Personality and Social Psychology,* 22 (1), 8–12.

Neisser, U. (1967) *Cognitive Psychology.* New York: Appleton Century Crofts.

Neisser, U. (1976) *Cognition and Reality: Principles and implications of cognitive psychology.* San Francisco, CA: W. H. Freeman.

Neisser, U. (1979) The Concept of Intelligence. In R. J. Sternberg & D. K.

Detterman (Eds) *Human Intelligence: Perspectives on its theory and measurement.* New Jersey, USA: Norwood.

Neisser, U. (1981) John Dean's memory: A case study. *Cognition,* 9, 1–22.

Neisser, U. (1982) *Memory Observed: Remembering in natural contexts.* San Francisco, CA: W. H. Freeman.

Newcombe, T. (1943) *Personality and Social Change.* New York: Holt, Rinehart & Winston.

Newcombe, T. (1961) *The Acquaintanceship Process.* New York: Holt, Rinehart & Winston.

Nicholson, L. (1988) The age of the family. Paper presented at the Symposium on Literature and Family, 15 April. Milwaukee, WI: Marquette University.

Nicolson, P. (1992) Feminism and academic psychology: Towards a psychology of women? In K. Campbell (Ed.) *Critical Feminism. Argument in the disciplines.* Milton Keynes: Open University Press.

Nicolson, P. (1995) Feminism and psychology. In J. A. Smith, R. Harré & L. Van Langenhove (Eds) *Rethinking Psychology.* London: Sage.

Nobles, W. W. (1976) Extended self: Rethinking the so-called Negro self-concept. *Journal of Black Psychology,* 2 (2), 15–24.

O'Connor, P. (1992) *Friendships between Women: A critical review.* Hemel Hempstead: Harvester Wheatsheaf.

O'Neil, W. M. (1968) *The Beginning of Modern Psychology.* Harmondsworth: Penguin.

Paludi, M. A. (1992) *The Psychology of Women.* Dubuque, IA: Wm. C. Brown.

Parker, I. (1992) *Discourse Dynamics: Critical analysis for social and individual psychology.* London: Routledge.

Parker, I., Georgaca, E., Harper, D., McLaughlin, T. & Stowell-Smith, M. (1995) *Deconstructing Psychopathology.* London: Sage.

Parlee, M. (1981) Gaps in the behavioural research on the menstruation cycle. In K. Komneich, M. McSweeny, J. Noack & N. Elder (Eds) *The Menstrual Cycle II.* New York: Springer.

Pennington, D. C. (1986) *Essential Social Psychology.* London: Edward Arnold.

Peplau, L. A. & Gordon, S. L. (1985) Women and men in love: Gender differences in close heterosexual relations. In V. E. O'Leary, R. K. Unger & B. Wallston (Eds) *Women, Gender and Social Psychology.* Hillside, NJ: Lawrence Erlbaum.

Perkins, R. (1991) Therapy for lesbians? The case against. *Feminism and Psychology,* 1 (3), 325–38.

Petkova, B. (1995) New Views on the Self: Evil women – witchcraft or PMS? *Psychology Review,* 2.1, 16–19.

Petkova, B. (1996) Cultural discourses and 'womanhood' in Bulgaria before and after perestroika. Unpublished PhD thesis, Birmingham University.

Pokorny, M. (1994) Appendix A: Structure of the United Kingdom Council for Psychotherapy and list of its member organisations. In P. Clarkson & M. Pokorny (Eds) *The Handbook of Psychotherapy.* London: Routledge.

Potter, J. (1996) Attitudes, social representations and discursive psychology. In M. Wetherell (Ed.) *Identities, Groups and Social Issues.* London: Sage, in association with the Open University.

Potter, J. & Wetherell, M. (1987) *Discourse and Social Psychology: Beyond attitudes and behaviour.* London: Sage.

Potter, J., & Wetherell, M. (1995) Discourse analysis. In J. A. Smith, R. Harré & L. Van Langenhove (Eds) *Rethinking Psychology.* London: Sage.

Potter, J., Wetherell, M., Gill, R. & Edwards, D. (1990) Discourse: Noun, verb or social practice? *Philosophical Psychology*, 3 (2), 205–17.

Rack, P. (1984) *Race, Culture and Mental Disorder*. London: Tavistock.

Rapping, E. (1992) *Movie of the Week: Private stories, Public Events*. Minneapolis: University of Minnesota Press.

Rattansi, A. (1992) Changing the subject? Racism, culture and education. In J. Donald and A. Rattansi (Eds) *'Race', Culture and Difference*. London: Sage, in association with the Open University.

Reason, P. & Rowan, J. (Eds) (1981) *Human Inquiry: A sourcebook of new paradigm research*. Chichester: John Wiley.

Richards, G. (1996) Arsenic and old race. *Observer Review*, 5 May, 4.

Rogers, C. R. (1942) *Counselling and Psychotherapy: Newer concepts in practice*. Boston: Houghton Mifflin.

Rosa, A. (1996) Bartlett's psycho-anthropological project. *Culture and Psychology*, 2.4, 355–78.

Rosch, E. H. (1973) Natural categories. *Cognitive Psychology*, 4, 328–50.

Ross, B. M. & Millsom, C. (1970) Repeated memory of oral prose in Ghana and New York. *International Journal of Psychology*, 5, 173–81.

Ross, L. (1977) The intuitive psychologist and his shortcomings. In L. Berkowitz (Ed.) *Advances in Experimental Social Psychology, 10*. New York: Academic Press.

Rubin, Z. (1973) *Liking and Loving*. New York: Holt, Rinehart & Winston.

Russell, D. E. H. (1975) *The Politics of Rape*. New York: Stein and Day.

Sacks, O. (1995) *An Anthropologist on Mars*. London: Picador.

Sampson, E. (1990) Social psychology and social control. In I. Parker & J. Shotter (Eds) *Deconstructing Social Psychology*. London & New York: Routledge.

Sampson, E. (1993) *Celebrating the Other: A dialogic account of human nature*. Hemel Hempstead: Harvester Wheatsheaf.

Sarup, M. (1988) *An Introductory Guide to Poststructuralism and Postmodernism*. Hemel Hempstead: Harvester Wheatsheaf.

Schachter, S. (1959) *The Psychology of Affiliation*. Stanford, CA: Stanford University Press.

Schachter, S. & Singer, J. (1962) Cognitive, social and physiological determinants of emotional states. *Psychological Review*, 69, 379–99.

Searles, P. & Berger, R. J. (Eds) (1985) *Rape and Society: Readings on the problem of sexual assault*. Oxford: Westview Press.

Secord, P. F. & Backman, C. W. (1964) *Social Psychology*. New York: McGraw Hill.

Segall, M. H., Dasen, P. R., Berry, J. W. & Poortinga, Y. H. (1990): *Human Behaviour in Global Perspective*. Oxford: Pergamon Press.

Seid, R. P. (1988) *Never Too Thin: A history of American women's obsession with weight loss*. New York: Prentice Hall.

Sender, K. (1992) Lesbians, therapy and politics: Inclusion and diversity. *Feminism and Psychology*, 2 (2), 255–57.

Shakespeare, R. (1975) *The Psychology of Handicap*. London: Methuen.

Sheehan, P. W. & Stewart, S. J. (1972) A cross-cultural study of eidetic imagery among Australian Aboriginal children. *Journal of Psychology*, 87, 179–88.

Shields, S. A. (1975) Functionalism, Darwinism and the psychology of women: A study in social myth. *American Psychologist*, 30, 739–54.

Shotter, J. (1990) Social construction of remembering/forgetting. In D. Middleton & D. Edwards (Eds) *Collective Remembering*. London: Sage.

Shotter, J. (1993) Becoming someone: identity and belonging. In N. Coupland & J. F. Nussbaum (Eds) *Discourse and the Lifespan Identity*. London: Sage.

Shotter, J. (1996) *Cultural Politics of Everyday Life*. Milton Keynes: Open University Press.

Shweder, R. A. (1990) Cultural psychology – what is it? In J. W. Stigler, R. A. Shweder & G. Hardt (Eds) *Cultural Psychology: Essays on comparative human development*. New York: Cambridge University Press.

Sigall, H. & Ostrove, N. (1975) Beautiful but dangerous: effects of offender attractiveness and the nature of the crime on juristic judgement. *Journal of Personality and Social Psychology*, 31, 410–14.

Simmonds, F. N. (1992) She's Gotta Have It: The representation of black female sexuality on film. In F. Bonner, L. Goodman, R. Allen, L. Janes & C. King *Imagining Women: Cultural representations and gender*. London: Polity Press, in association with Open University Press.

Skinner, B. F. (1971) *Beyond Freedom and Dignity*. Harmondsworth: Penguin.

Smith, D. (1988) *The Everyday World is Problematic: A feminist sociology*. Milton Keynes: Open University Press.

Smith, J. A., Harré, R. & Van Langenhove, L. (1995) Introduction. In J. A. Smith, R. Harré & L. Van Langenhove (Eds) *Rethinking Psychology*. London: Sage.

Spanos, N. P. (1978) Witchcraft in histories of psychiatry: A critical analysis and an alternative conceptualization. *Psychological Bulletin*, 85, 417–39.

Squire, C. (1989) *Significant Differences: Feminism in psychology*. London & New York: Routledge.

Stainton Rogers, R., Stenner, P., Gleeson, K. & Stainton Rogers, W. (1995) *Social Psychology: A critical agenda*. Cambridge: Polity Press.

Stein, T. S. (1988) Theoretical considerations in psychotherapy with gay men and lesbians. *Journal of Gay and Lesbian Psychotherapy*, 15 (1/2), 75–93.

Steinem, G. (1983) *Outrageous Acts and Everyday Rebellions*. New York: New American Library.

Stevens, R. (Ed.) et al. (1996) *Understanding the Self*. London: Sage & Oxford University Press.

Storr, A. (1968) *Human Aggression*. Harmondsworth: Penguin.

Strauss, A. S. (1973) Northern Cheyenne ethnosociology. *Ethos*, 1, 32–357.

Sue, D. & Sue, D. W. (1990) *Counselling the Culturally Different*. New York: John Wiley.

Sue, D., Sue, D. W. & Sue, S. (1990) *Understanding Abnormal Behaviour*. Boston, MA: Houghton Mifflin.

Tajfel, H. (1969) Social and cultural factors in perception. In G. Lindzey & E. Aronson (Eds) *Handbook of Social Psychology* (Vol. 3). Reading, MA: Addison-Wesley.

Tajfel, H., Billig, M. G. & Bundy, R. P. (1971) Social categorization and intergroup behaviour. *European Journal of Social Psychology*, 1 (2), 149–78.

Tajfel, H. & Turner, J. (1979) An integrative theory of intergroup conflict. In G. W. Austin & S. Worchel (Eds) *The Social Psychology of Intergroup Relations*. Monterey, CA: Brooks & Cole.

Tavris, C. (1993) The mismeasure of woman. *Feminism and Psychology*, 3 (2), 149–68.

Tavris, C. & Wade, C. (1984) *The Longest War: Sex differences in perspective* (2nd ed.). New York: Harcourt Brace Jovanovich.

Thomas, D. (1982) *The Experience of Handicap.* London: Methuen.

Trevarthen, C. (1980) The foundations of intersubjectivity: development of interpersonal and co-operative understanding in infants. In D. R. Olson (ed.) *The Social Foundations of Language and Thought.* New York: Norton.

Trivers, R. (1985) *Social Evolution.* Menlo Park, CA: Benjamin/Cummings.

Tseëlon, E. (1995) *The Masque of Femininity.* London: Sage.

Tulving, E. (1972) Episodic and semantic memory. In E. Tulving & W. Donaldson (Eds) *Organization of Memory.* London: Academic Press.

Twombly, R. (1994) Shock therapy returns. *New Scientist,* 5 March, 21–3.

Unger, R. K. (1979) *Female and Male: Psychological perspectives.* New York: Harper & Row.

United Kingdom Council for Psychotherapy (1996) *National Register of Psychotherapists 1997.* London: Routledge, in conjunction with the UKCP.

Ussher, J. M. (1989) *The Psychology of the Female Body.* London & New York: Routledge.

Ussher, J. M. (1991) *Women's Madness: Misogyny or mental illness?* Hemel Hempstead: Harvester Wheatsheaf.

Ussher, J. M. (1992) Gender issues in clinical research. In J. M. Ussher and R. Nicolson (Eds) *Gender Issues in Clinical Psychology.* London: Routledge.

Van Langenhove, L. (1995) The theoretical foundations of experimental psychology and its alternatives. In J. A. Smith, R. Harré & L. Van Langenhove (Eds) *Rethinking Psychology.* London: Sage.

Wachtel, P. L. (1977) *Psychoanalysis and Behavior Therapy: Toward an integration.* New York: Basic Books.

Walster, E. & Walster, G. W. (1969) The matching hypothesis. *Journal of Personality and Social Psychology,* 6, 248–53.

Walster, E., Aronson, E., Abrahams, D. & Rottman, L. (1966) Importance of physical attractiveness in dating behaviour. *Journal of Personality and Social Psychology,* 4, 508–16.

Ward, C. A. (1995) *Attitudes toward Rape: Feminist and social psychological perspectives.* London: Sage.

Watson, J. B. (1913) Psychology as the behaviourist views it. *Psychological Review,* 20, 158–77.

Watson, J. B. & Rayner, R. (1920) Conditioned emotional reactions. *Journal of Experimental Psychology,* 3, 1–14.

Weeks, J. (1985) *Sexuality and its Discontents: Meanings, myths and modern sexualities.* London: Routledge.

Weininger, O. (1903) *Sex and Character.* London: Heinemann (1906). (First published in Vienna, 1903.)

Weisstein, N. (1971) Psychology constructs the female, or the fantasy of the male psychologist (with some attention to the fantasies of his friends, the male biologist and the male anthropologist). *Social Education,* 35, 362–73.

Welter, B. (1966) The cult of true womanhood. *American Quarterly,* 18, 151–74.

Wetherell, M. (1996) Group conflict and the social psychology of racism. In M. Wetherell (Ed.) *Identities, Groups and Social Issues.* London: Sage, in association with the Open University.

Wetherell, M. & Potter, J. (1988) Discourse analysis and the identification of interpretative repertoires. In C. Antaki (Ed.) *Analysing Everyday Explanation: A casebook of methods.* London: Sage.

Wetherell, M. & Potter, J. (1992) *Mapping the Language of Racism: Discourse and the legitimation of exploitation.* Hemel Hempstead: Harvester Wheatsheaf.

Wilkinson, S. (Ed.) (1996) *Feminist Social Psychology: International perspectives.* Buckingham: Open University Press.

Wilson, E. O. (1975) *Sociobiology – The New Synthesis.* Cambridge, MA: Harvard University Press.

Wilson, G. T., O'Leary, K. D., Nathan, P. E. & Clark, L. A. (1996) *Abnormal Psychology: Integrating perspectives.* Needham Heights, MA: Allyn & Bacon.

Wilson, M. & Daly, M. (1985) Competitiveness, risk-taking and violence: the young male syndrome. *Ethology and Sociobiology,* 6, 59–73.

Wilson, M. & Daly, M. (1993a) The psychology of parenting in evolutionary perspective and the case of human filicide. In S. Parmigiani & F. S. vom Saal (Eds) *Infanticide and Parental Care.* London: Harwood Academic Publishers.

Wilson, M. & Daly, M. (1993b) Lethal confrontational violence among young men. In N. J. Bell & R. W. Bell (Eds) *Adolescent Risk-Taking.* Newbury Park, CA: Sage.

Winch, R. F. (1958) *Mate Selections: A study of complementary needs.* New York: Harper & Row.

Witkin, H. A. (1978) *Cognitive Style in Personal and Cultural Perspective.* Worcester, MA: Clark University Press.

Wolf, N. (1990) *The Beauty Myth.* London: Chatto & Windus.

Wolpe, J. (1958) *Psychotherapy by Reciprocal Inhibition.* Stanford, CA: Stanford University Press.

Wood, J. T. & Duck, S. (1995) *Understudied Relationships: Off the beaten track.* London: Sage.

Wooffitt, R. (1992) *Telling Tales of the Unexpected: The organization of factual discourse.* Hemel Hempstead: Harvester Wheatsheaf.

World Health Organisation (1992) *The ICD-10 Classification of Mental and Behavioural Disorders: Clinical descriptions and diagnostic guidelines.* Geneva: WHO.

Wright, P. H. (1982) Men's friendships, women's friendships, and the alleged inferiority of the latter. *Sex Roles,* 8, 1–20.

Index